Low Wage in High Tech

ISSUES OF GLOBALIZATION

Case Studies in Contemporary Anthropology

Series Editors: Carla Freeman and Li Zhang

Low Wage in High Tech

An Ethnography of Service Workers in Global India

KIRAN MIRCHANDANI
SANJUKTA MUKHERJEE
SHRUTI TAMBE

New York   Oxford
OXFORD UNIVERSITY PRESS

Oxford University Press is a department of the University of Oxford.
It furthers the University's objective of excellence in research, scholarship,
and education by publishing worldwide. Oxford is a registered trade mark of
Oxford University Press in the UK and certain other countries.

Published in the United States of America by Oxford University Press
198 Madison Avenue, New York, NY 10016, United States of America.

© 2020 by Oxford University Press

Library of Congress Cataloging-in-Publication Data

CIP data is on file at the Library of Congress
978-0-19-086886-4

9 8 7 6 5 4 3 2 1
Printed by LSC Communications, Inc., United States of America

CONTENTS

....

LIST OF ILLUSTRATIONS

....

ACKNOWLEDGEMENTS
....

This project would not have been possible without the generous funding of the Social Sciences and Humanities Research Council of Canada (Grant #410-2011-1901 held at the University of Toronto) and the enthusiastic participation of the respondents who shared their time and life histories with us. We came together because of our common intellectual interests in exploring globalization from the vantage point of those rarely represented in its discourses. We found remarkable overlaps in our approaches despite the fact that we worked in different countries and taught in different disciplines. Our engagement with a team of scholars and students in India and Canada enriched our collaboration.

We would like to thank the University of Pune (now called Savitribai Phule Pune University) and in particular the Department of Sociology, which provided the intellectual space for imagining this project and starting the pilot work in 2009–2010. The department also facilitated the involvement of students in the research, while the university provided access to many individuals and firms during fieldwork.

Throughout the past eight years, we benefited from the generous intellectual contributions and hard work of a number of scholars, including Prashant Apte, Rahul Dalvi, Chintamani Dhengale, Nilima Gavade, Olivia Hauck, Anjali Helferty, Vandana Kulkarni, Anjali Ashish Limaye, Rahul Paithankar, Vandana Palsane, Gouri Patwardhan, Meaghan Smith-Brugha, Dulani Suraweera, Nitin Thorat, Shruti Vispute, and Swaroop Ashok Waghmare.

It has been an absolute pleasure to work with the editors and editorial staff at Oxford University Press including Jill Crosson, Meredith Keffer, Jana MacIsaac, and Sherith Pankratz. We also benefited immensely from the insightful comments of the manuscript reviewers commissioned by Oxford including Kiran Jayaram, York College of The City University of New York; Heather Levi, Temple University; Winifred Poster, Washington University in St. Louis; Rashmi Sadana, George Mason University; Laura Zeeman, Red Rocks Community College; and two anonymous reviewers.

Finally, we are grateful to each of our local communities, our friends, and our families for providing the bedrock that is foundational to the success of all our projects. Kiran would like to thank Enakshi Dua; Yasmin Gopal; Ashwin, Suvan, and Syona Joshi; Audrey Macklin; Ajit, Sheeley, Sandeep, Ria, and Kai Mirchandani; Shahrzad Mojab; Winifred Poster; Pushkala Prasad; Alissa Trotz; Leah Vosko; and Jingjing Xu. Sanjukta would like to acknowledge and thank the College of Liberal Arts and Social Sciences at DePaul University for providing financial support for this project through a faculty summer research grant in 2016. She also thanks Beth Catlett, Ann Russo, Laila Farah, Sandra Jackson, Maureen Sioh, Kalyani Mennon, Shailja Sharma, Rocio Ferreira, Virginia Keller, Diane Swords, Poonam Srivastava, Vidura Jang Bahadur, Geeta Banerjee, Amita Chatterjee, Sumita Mukherjee, Ratan Kumar Mukherjee, and Surodeep Mukherjee. Shruti would like to thank Richa Nagar for helping the team reimagine its research strategies in light of methodological challenges inherent in transnational research. Ganesh sustained Shruti through the difficult stages of this research project both intellectually and emotionally. Ashwini Tambe brought back the energy when it was lacking. Finally, Shruti thanks Aai, Baba, Rahee, and Sajal for bearing with all her absences and standing by her.

The tall, gleaming glass and steel office towers that pepper the landscapes of many Indian cities symbolize an anticipated future of wealth and prosperity. Over the past three decades the multinational technology companies that occupy these towers and their middle-class employees have received enormous attention. Yet very little is known about the less visible workers who labor within these spaces. Only a few may notice that the areas surrounding India's high-tech corporations house contractors whose employees provide housekeeping, transportation, and security for these firms.

At one such location, we met Sada, the owner of a housekeeping company that he had established a little over a decade ago in order to provide cleaning services to nearby software companies. Sada invited us to his office, a small, clean, air-conditioned space where all who entered were required to leave their footwear outside as though they were entering a temple. While serving us tea, Sada was effusive in his enthusiasm for the growing mechanization and professionalization of the cleaning sector. Although he spoke to us in Marathi and his English was clearly limited, he shared with us booklets in English from multinational cleaning supplies companies. Partway through our interview, there was a power failure, but Sada seemed unaffected by this, as it was likely a regular occurrence. He continued to tell us about the better standards of foreign companies compared to more home-grown operations and declared that adherence to these standards would make India better by leading to greater professionalization and improved training. After inviting us to tour a software company during nonworking hours, Sada, who had full-keyed access to multiple corporate offices, introduced us to many of the women and men he hired as housekeepers. He characterized his company as "a family" and said that he knew and cared about each of the housekeepers he hired, giving them loans when needed and eating with them on occasion. Like a benevolent patriarch, he described the regular inspections he conducted to ensure that their hair was properly cut, their uniforms ironed, and their fingernails clean. His effusive pride in the growing professionalization of cleaning work was entangled with civilizing discourses that he evoked in reference to the working poor who comprised his labor force.

We were struck by how closely these sentiments were mirrored by Naresh, the owner and facilities manager of a software company that contracted with Sada for his cleaning services. Naresh told us that he liked dealing with contractors who provided documentation to confirm that they were not hiring "slave labor." While both Naresh and Sada lamented the high cost of living in the city, they did not emphasize the inadequacy of the state-established minimum wage that their workers were paid to meet basic costs. Instead, Naresh stressed that his company, like other multinational technology firms, demanded documentary records that showed that workers were being paid minimum wages and benefits. Given this strong emphasis on the rhetoric of compliance, we were somewhat surprised to learn from workers employed by Sada and working at Naresh's firm that there was considerable flexibility in the practices in which companies actually engaged. Workers Aditya and Raj reported earning slightly more than Neeta and Devika, but all received wages that were lower than even the legislatively stipulated minimum wage—a figure widely regarded as itself significantly lower than the amount needed to meet basic expenses. Only Aditya mentioned receiving benefits. Raj said he was given no benefits and in fact was working under his cousin's name because he could not provide proof of identity himself. Neeta expressed confusion when asked about her pension benefits, saying, "They say that we have it. But I haven't got any." Devika reported that since she had recently joined the company, she did not feel she could ask about benefits and had not been informed about them either. All four workers were paid in cash, and none of them had bank accounts.

Such disjunctures characterized many of the stories we heard in the course of this project. Our respondents included facilities managers of technology firms; contractors providing transportation, housekeeping, and security services to these firms; and drivers, cleaners, and guards in Pune, India. Our interviews were respondent-driven, open-ended conversations with women and men about work, identities, livelihoods, families, and futures. While labor informality is conventionally associated with temporary, short-term, or street-based work, we found that large numbers of workers serving wealthy global firms were informally employed and did not have direct employment relationships with the companies for which they worked. Despite working in the formal sector and being required to wear uniforms, carry identity cards, and display an organizationally sanctioned form of "professionalism," workers were hired through contractors, and many did not have written contracts, could be fired without cause, and did not receive legislatively established minimum levels of pay and benefits, let alone salaries that constituted a living wage. Workers' accounts provided a clear illustration of the ways in which labor informality supports worker precarity. As a result, we found that many low-wage service workers employed in India's architecturally glamorous multinational technology sector were ambivalent about their social and economic prospects. Many were proud to be associated with clean, modern organizations where they were surrounded by foreigners and members of the Indian elite who did not require them to demonstrate the daily subservience expected in other settings. Yet many were also ashamed to inform friends and family members about their work and talked about feeling disposable, peripheral, and stagnant. Despite being required to embody the standards of these clean, modern organizations, they did not earn enough to either maintain home spaces where they could properly engage in the bodily work that these standards require or amass the savings that would allow them or their children to gain more permanent access to the wealth that surrounded them in their places of work.

Indeed, the narratives of immobility and exclusion we encountered represent an important addition to the now numerous studies that have been conducted of software and call center workers who are employed at India's multinational technology firms. Our study contributes to the emerging body of research that gives voice to those who work extremely long hours within wealthy global corporations but nevertheless perceive few prospects for social or economic mobility.

New Service Workers
in the Global Economy

Virtual flows characterize so much of contemporary global capitalism that it is sometimes easy to forget that multinational firms also require local infrastructures in cities around the world. Buildings within which global corporations are housed are often sprawling, imposing, and immovable—a significant counterpoint to the fluidity of ownership, employment, and work that characterizes these firms. Many global cities are known as such because of the presence within them of lavish corporate architectural projects that are both reminders of modernity and spaces within which modern citizens are constructed and recognized. Technology and technology services firms, focused on service provision rather than manufacturing, are prototypical symbols of clean and ultramodern development. Services are exchanged through encounters via computers and telephones and are often consumed at the point of exchange, as in the case of call center interactions, or distributed through electronic means, such as software code. At the same time, many employees carrying out this work are housed in large fixed sites. Just as these sites are part of neoliberal globalization, so too are the workers who maintain them. This book focuses on service workers tasked with maintaining and navigating the fixed assets of global high-tech firms. We explore the lives of three sets of workers who are deeply implicated in multinational capital even though they are rarely seen as part of the global workforce. These include the housekeepers who clean the premises and buildings of multinational firms, creating their sanitized ultramodern ambience; the security guards who maintain these corporations' physical borders and enforce their internal access norms; and the drivers who facilitate the movement of company employees into and out of corporate spaces. We focus on India, although parallel processes can be recognized in global cities around the world.

India's gross domestic product (GDP) has experienced a spectacular rise since the 1990s. GDP in 2010 exceeded 10 percent, and even with the subsequent dip, it has remained above the world average for emerging economies. The expansion of the country's services sector, based on foreign direct investments, has been an important contributor to this economic growth. Based on an analysis of United Nations (UN) national accounts statistics, economists reveal that the services sector in India has far outpaced global averages: global growth rates have been between–1 and 4 percent since 1998, while the annual growth of the services sector within India has been between 6 and 11 percent (Verma & Karinje, 2014). Reports indicate that the services sector in India accounts for 51 percent of the nation's foreign direct investment and 28 percent of its employment, a significant proportion of which is linked to information technology (IT) firms (Chakraborty, 2016). The Ministry of Electronics and Information Technology estimates that 4 million people held IT and IT services sector jobs in 2018 (http://meity.gov.in/content/employment). Despite recent reports that India's policy on special economic zones may not have lived up to expectations in terms of facilitating economic growth and employment (Salve, 2015; Barnes, 2015), the IT sector in particular continues to be promoted as a symbol of bright future prospects.

Up to a fourth of the population of India, which comprises millionaires as well as educated "ordinary" Indians (Drèze & Sen, 2013), have witnessed dramatic changes in their lives in the past three decades. Pune, the city where the research for this book was conducted, has experienced some of the highest rates of proliferation of multinational technology firms, which are also collectively referred to as the IT/ITES (information technology and information technology–enabled services), or "hi-tech," sector (Platz, 2012). Pune projects itself as a "global city," with technical educational institutions and corporate head offices. City leaders envision the region as an IT hub competing with Hyderabad and Bangalore. Its proximity to Mumbai and relatively secure supplies of water (due to its proximity to the Sahyadri ranges and four water reservoirs) and electricity (thanks to initiatives by the Maratha Chamber of Commerce) make it a preferred destination for many investors (*Forbes*, 2006). The results are visually inescapable—architecturally imposing free trade zones that house large corporate "campuses" now cover large fenced sections of the landscape (see figure 0.1).

Pune's geographical landscape epitomizes the concept of "two Indias"—a metaphor that has captivated both local and global media because of its succinct description of the vast social and economic disparity on display in the nation. Mass abject poverty on a scale that is not seen in many other countries exists alongside displays of wealth that are lavish even by the standards of the most affluent global cities (Ramesh, 2006). Indeed, Bhatt et al. (2010) characterize the "two India" discourse as the story of the nation itself—one that is split not only economically but also aspirationally between those who are forward looking and those who are said to "resist" progress (see also Gooptu, 2013a).

This book, however, is on neither of these two Indias; rather, it is about those who are situated in between. It points to the fluidity and

FIGURE 0.1 **The imposing architecture of technology firms.**
Source: Photo by the authors

overlaps between the two Indias and the limited explanatory power of this metaphor to capture the experiences of those who both aspire for better lives and are skeptical of current development trajectories. Among such in-between groups are the drivers, housekeepers, and security guards who service India's multinational technology firms. They are significant for several reasons. They work in organizational sites that are distinctively associated with wealth, progress, and promise. Despite their backgrounds, they have the desire and imagined possibility of entering the ranks of those included in India's economic miracle. But they also experience social and economic barriers that continually threaten to perpetuate long-established cycles of poverty, and in this sense they remain outside the "new India" that their places of work represent. They are not part of India's "modern" service industry—which includes "skilled" computer-related, banking, and financial service jobs and has been the primary driver of growth—but they are not quite "traditional" service workers either, even though they are officially classified as such and command a low minimum wage under the law. Despite their legal classification as unskilled workers, they are required to be educated, literate, and "trained" in modern comportment, dress, attitudes, and orientation to work. They are an often-cited group whose jobs exist because of foreign investors who have supported or set up multinational information technology firms and transnational call centers in India. They work within the organizational spaces of these foreign multinational firms and in fact create the environments that make these firms foreign—that is, clean, timely, and secure. Often it is this group to which advocates of neoliberal globalization refer in making links between development and employment in response to critics who challenge the limited potential of "jobless growth" to achieve enhanced livelihoods and better quality of life for a broad range of people (Gupta, 2012). Researchers note that for every job created by transnational corporations in India, four additional indirect jobs are created (Das, 2010). The workers who are the focus of this book occupy the "indirect" jobs that India's openness to foreign investors and global firms is said to have created. Not only are these workers in this sense ideologically in the middle of the development trajectory, but they also literally occupy an economic middle space. Some earn just over and others just under the median per capita income for India of 5,999 Indian rupees (INR) (Drèze & Sen, 2013, p. 75).[1] They are part of neither the 30 percent of Indians who live below the poverty line (Drèze & Sen, 2013, p. 190) nor the upwardly mobile skilled "new Indian middle class" (Lakha, 1999; Fernandes, 2006; Bhatt, Murty, & Ramamurthy, 2010; Baviskar & Ray, 2011; Radhakrishnan, 2011) who have seen dramatic improvements in their standards of living since India opened up its economy to global capital in the mid-1980s. Rather, they are the large, heterogeneous group in between.

The Missing Economic Trickle Down

We got a vivid sense of this "in-betweenness" when we met Kaveri on one of her days off in her home, which was a small room where she lived with her husband and two young children. Her mother-in-law owned the room, and the couple spent their income on school fees, transportation, and groceries. There was a single bed and fan in the room, as well as a television and fridge. Kaveri was multilingual and spoke a significant amount of English. She reported, "My English is very good. I know how to talk with the employees. Actually how you speak is very important in security line. I know how to give respect, how to maintain voice tone. No one believes that I have studied only till eighth standard." Kaveri had wanted to join the army or police force, but with only an eighth-grade education she had been unable to do so. She preferred working as a security guard at a multinational technology firm because she said the employees there were educated and treated guards with respect, rather than like "watchmen," as they were often called elsewhere. She gave us detailed descriptions of the training she received in fire safety, data protection, use of computers for data entry, and comportment. With pride she reported that she had been identified as a model employee during a fire drill when she had been among the only workers who had managed to follow the protocols. However, she told us, her fortunes had now changed.

Partway through our conversation, Kaveri's husband returned and sat with us. He was also a security guard, and although he contributed to the conversation, Kaveri did most of the talking. In his presence, Kaveri told us that the reason the family was financially so precarious was because her husband's job was intermittent and irregular. Three years ago both had come to the agreement that her earning potential was higher than his, and so she had begun her job as a security guard. She had initially been posted at hotels, but given her language abilities, she had been shifted to a transnational call center. However, eight months earlier, the firm's contract at the call center where Kaveri was a guard had not been renewed. She had been offered only night-shift work, which she could not accept because of her young child, and so she was still waiting to be redeployed. She had also approached another contractor, who had given her a few hours of work over the past month. But with no income, she told us that the family was now in dire financial need, and that she and her husband worried about how they would pay their children's school fees for the upcoming year. They now survived on loans from friends and family. Her "one big dream" that she would "get a stable job where I will get a good salary which will help me to improve the future of my children" remained elusive.

Service workers like Kaveri employed in India's multinational technology firms provide a unique opportunity to explore notions of "trickle-down" globalization. More involved in the newly emerging sectors fueled by multinational corporations than service workers generally, they are close to the epicenter of global economic development and should be among the first in India to receive its benefits. Knowing the impact of India's development trajectory on this group of workers in the middle (i.e., those who do not experience abject poverty but also do not have access to the lavish lifestyles of the domestic elite) is particularly significant in light of growing skepticism about how development in India has affected the poor. Scholars note that since the early 1990s, the number of India's poor has barely declined, and while the introduction of global firms has resulted in more salaried, highly paid jobs, precarious work has also proliferated (Jhabvala & Standing, 2010). Many note that global firms have had a limited widespread positive impact on local livelihoods. Drèze and Sen (2013, p. 29), for example, argue that for poor Indians, "it is not that their lives have not improved at all, but the pace of change has been excruciatingly slow and has barely altered their abysmal living conditions." Not only have wages remained stagnant, but social welfare provision has come to resemble "a sprawling and hugely expensive 'clogged pipes' system" (Jhabvala & Standing, 2010, p. 239). Similar findings are reported by Cross (2009, 2014) in his study of educated young men employed as diamond cutters in India's free trade zones, who experience stagnation rather than mobility as a result of their jobs. Based on their analysis of the National Sample Survey, Sarkar and Mehta (2010) conclude that the lower half of wage earners in India have seen negative growth in their wages while high wage earners have seen dramatic growth in their wages since the introduction of liberalization initiatives in the early 1990s. This is particularly so for regular rather than casual or contract employees; the latter have experienced a much slower growth in their wages. Among all sectors, the multinational technology sector has had the highest wage growth and has created a significant number of full-time, relatively well-paid jobs. Yet there is little evidence that these benefits have had a positive impact on those not part of the elite.

Among the 92 drivers, housekeepers, and security guards and 46 contractors, supervisors, managers, and labor officials we interviewed in Pune, there was significant skepticism about the economic benefits of the proliferation of multinational tech firms for service workers. We were surprised to find this skepticism even among the managers we met at large service firms, such as Shridhar, who had retired from the Indian air force and then joined a large security contractor as a manager. His security company was set up much like a technology firm, with a reception area, corporate directory, and well-labeled offices. As we were led to Shridhar's office, we noticed computer-laden desks lined up against large, clean glass windows. We were therefore not surprised to hear that the company saw itself as being at the forefront of the effort to "professionalize" the security sector by promoting standardized training. Yet when we asked Shridhar about the 1,500 guards his company employed, he was much more circumspect and told us in English that as a result of the emergence of multinational technology firms,

> people get employment opportunities and salaries. Overall industry also grows with other support services like cabs, canteen, AC maintenance, electronics, communication, gardening, everything is growing. But the other part is that [with] the coming [of] IT companies in Pune, the cost of living has gone so high. Surviving for these people just became very difficult. Earlier people used to stay in a room where the room rent was around 500 or 700. The same security person is paying now 3,000 where his salary is 5,000 or 7,000. It is an adverse effect actually. So on one side they get job opportunity, supposedly "good" salary, and at the same time living cost have gone so high [that] it is difficult for them to survive. Also this is with raised aspirations about quality of life.

Despite the fact that service jobs barely allow workers to meet their basic economic needs, Shridhar explained that with over 500 security contractors in competition, it is difficult to increase wages beyond the minimum levels established by the state. With little collaboration between vendors, foreign firms set up competitive bidding processes, which favor vendors who cut costs. Despite the limited economic mobility, jobs are demanding, as Shridhar told us in a mocking tone:

> In IT companies now ... the expectation from a security guard is more.... They want a Superman.... He should know everything, managing computers, CCTV [closed-circuit television], manage government officials also and foreigners also, everything he should know.

Bringing this type of people in this industry is really challenging and retaining also. The attrition rate is very high, as there are no career prospects. So this is a big challenge. . . . There is a huge gap between demand and supply.

Indeed, contractors and facilities managers uniformly informed us that they experienced high attrition rates and labor shortages among service workers. Many recognized the reasons for these trends—poor wages, long hours, shift work, and job instability. Yet, there seemed to be no attempt to address these less than ideal working conditions; instead, contractors engaged in continuous cycles of attrition, hiring, and training. Labor in this way was seen as both scarce and expendable.

Aside from the system of contract employment, which depresses wages, economic "trickle down" is also hindered by a paradox that arises from the coming together of neoliberalism and globalization.[2] The Indian state plays an active role in promoting foreign direct investment in India by establishing free trade zones, providing legal exemptions from labor laws, and giving tax incentives. Global firms set up companies in India with the explicit and widely stated goal of lowering their labor costs, yet, for reputational reasons, especially in light of the negative publicity associated with global sweatshops, they are simultaneously keen to be seen as being in compliance with labor standards. They therefore endeavor to both maximize labour savings and be seen to be providing decent jobs. Indeed, the most striking feature of our interviews with managers and contractors was the universal importance placed on maintaining records that showed that these individuals were not promoting, as one manager told us, "slave labor." While large formal technology firms cannot fully ensure that contractors pay their workers more than slave labor–level wages, they can ensure that documentation is produced that certifies this.

The Indian state plays an important role in helping companies remain compliant with labor standards while keeping their costs down. It does this by setting low and confusing minimum wage standards. Rather than a national minimum wage, minimum wage rates in India depend on region and industry, making both calculation and enforcement significant tasks. There are 1,171 different minimum wage rates in India (Belser & Rani, 2011). As Srija (2014, p. 4) summarizes, "The calculation of minimum wages is a cumbersome exercise often beyond the capacity of the small scale unorganized sector employer and most often beyond the awareness level of the employee." Not only does the minimum wage law have limited coverage, and not only is it ripe for evasion, but rates themselves are not in line with the costs of living. Despite the existence of alternatives—such as rates set in line with the "decent work" agenda developed by the International Labour Organization (ILO) or living wage calculations—multinational corporations choose to use more restrictive minimum wage levels as benchmarks (Lerche, Guérin, & Srivastava, 2012; Sampath, 2016). As a recent ILO report (Anker, 2011) reveals, multinational corporations often support the principle of a living wage but set their wage levels in line with state minimum wages, which tend to be lower.

The setting of wage standards by multinational companies using local legislative minimums is both ideologically and discursively significant. Local social scientists have thoroughly established how unreasonably low the minimum wage standard is in India. Jhabvala (1998), for example, shows that workers require almost four times the amount that the minimum wage rate provides to meet basic consumption needs. Sampath (2016) similarly observes that minimum wage rates remain under INR 10,000 per month despite a state-appointed task force that noted that a living wage of INR 26,000 would be more appropriate. The state has little interest in either raising or enforcing minimum wage standards, given that the national branding of the "Make in India" campaign is based on low labor costs.

As a result, despite widespread acknowledgement of the insufficiency of the minimum wage, we found that compliance with this standard was widely promoted by multinational corporations. This compliance not only allowed multinational corporations to occupy an ideological high ground as beacons of progress and transparency, but also allowed corporate work to occur at low organizational cost. The workers we interviewed echoed the challenges already noted of being employed in the lavish multinational technology sector at less than subsistence-level wages. When we met Vasant after one of his shifts, he was enthusiastic about participating in research associated with the university. His brothers were both well educated and held government jobs, but his opportunities were more constrained. As a housekeeping supervisor, he had climbed the career ladder and had been working through a contractor at a large call center for the past five years, although he referred to his job as one with no prospects. He was responsible for training, managing a team of housekeepers, diluting chemicals, and completing cleaning logs. Despite his relatively long tenure, he blamed the contract system for his poor wages and noted that the company constantly tried to underpay senior staff in order to save on costs. After deductions, he reported that he received INR 7,200 per month, which was barely enough, even though he lived with extended family in a house owned by the family. He estimated that every month he spent INR 3,000 on groceries, INR 2,000 on house-related expenses, and INR 2,000 for van transport and fees for his two sons, who attended an English-medium school.[3] He had a loan of INR 20,000 on which he was paying interest. He lamented that he could not "fulfil everyone's needs so the atmosphere in the home is always tense.... The neighboring children go to the malls. Naturally my children also want to go visit these malls.... I can't afford to take them."

Indeed, almost all the workers we interviewed told us that despite their long hours of wage work, they had trouble meeting their basic living costs, let alone fulfilling their desires for new consumer goods. Atul, a 29-year-old single male security guard informed us that even though he had no addictions and no dependents, his rent, food, and transportation costs exceeded his salary. Akhil, another male driver with a wife and young child, earned INR 6,500 every month and worked a twelve-hour shift. He listed his monthly expenses as INR 1,600 for rent, INR 150 for electricity, INR 2,000 for groceries, and INR 1,200 for remittance to his village. With no benefits, Akhil paid for medical costs and other unanticipated expenses out of pocket and thus had no savings. He lamented having to send his son to a Marathi-medium school, as access to English-medium schools required donations that he could not afford to make. When we asked about her dreams and plans for the future, Gauri, a 30-year-old female housekeeper, smiled hopelessly and simply said, "I can't even reach the level needed to have any dreams for the future." Such narratives of economic constraint, despite long hours of work in lavish settings, were a prominent theme among the workers we interviewed.

If Not Economic Prosperity, Then What is Trickling Down?

While the trickling down of economic prosperity arising from the proliferation of multinational technology firms in India has been limited, the trickling down of numerous labor practices through these global firms has been unambiguous. First among these are outsourcing regimes, which took hold in the United States in the 1960s with the relocation of work from large urban centers to regions with lower labor costs (Dossani & Kenney, 2004). Such regimes involve a "triangular employment relationship" in which a worker's employer is not the same as the organization for which he or she works (Barrientos, 2013). Weil (2014) notes that there was a "seismic shift" toward the fissured workplace in organizations in the United States between 1980 and 2000, which led to an erosion of workers' wages and a widening of wage gaps. Despite productivity gains of 80 percent during these two decades in the United States, there was only a 7 percent increase in wages (p. 280). As a result of the new focus on "core competencies," organizations hired many of their workers through third-party contractors rather than as direct employees. Apple Computers, for example, employed 63,000 workers directly but had 750,000 people working on its products (Weil, 2014). Indeed, a large part of the growth of the Indian technology sector has been based on organizational fissuring in the United States, United Kingdom, and Europe. Its emergence has been based on the offshoring and outsourcing of software programming, medical transcription, and customer service work to countries where labor costs are lower. This trend toward the use of subcontracted labor is a key feature of global capitalism today.

While many Indian software companies and call centers are contractors to large multinational companies, they in turn subcontract out work to labor service organizations to meet their housekeeping, security, and transportation needs. This fissuring of service provision seems to be a common trend globally. Barrientos's (2013) study of transnational horticulture firms in South Africa reveals the widespread use of labor intermediaries who meet seasonal demands for fruit and flowers by using a "cascade" system of multiple networks of contractors. Workers with different levels of remuneration and benefits work alongside each other. As a result, as Barrientos notes, "some workers have access to jobs with relatively better working conditions and security. Working alongside them, however, there are often workers who have been hired through third-party contracts" (p. 1058). In a similar manner, Zlolniski (2006) traces the role of subcontracting in Silicon Valley, which is widely regarded as the epicenter of technological growth in the United States. There, technology companies benefit from subcontracting regimes through which they contract cleaning work out to other companies that have access to large pools of low-wage immigrant workers. Zlolniski traces the decline in janitors' wages from the late 1970s to the 1990s to the proliferation of flexible contract employment.

As a result of the influence of U.S. firms, researchers have documented a significant shift within Indian organizations toward hiring contract workers whose jobs are extremely unstable. Niteesh, a manager at a software company whom we interviewed, declared, "Everybody can get fired at any time. That's U.S. culture in my office." Contract workers may be hired by small firms that are not required to maintain the same levels of benefits and are much more difficult to monitor (Das, 2010). Based on an analysis of wage rate surveys since the pre-reform period, Sarkar and Mehta (2010) show how, compared to the wages of regular employees, the wages of self-employed, casual, and contract workers have experienced little growth as a result of liberalization and the influx of multinational companies. Bhowmik's (2004) study of Unilever, which dominates the market for shampoos and creams in India, is telling. In 2003, Unilever's factory in Mumbai employed about a quarter of the workers that it had in 1985. Work had been shifted to labor contractors, each with fewer than a hundred employees. These small contract companies could shut down without government approval, which they did every five years in order to establish new companies and make use of government incentives. Needless to say, worker wages paid by subcontractors were much lower than those paid within the Unilever factory.

Despite the fact that multinational technology firms distinguish themselves within the Indian organizational landscape on the basis of their clean, air-conditioned, secure, "modern" facilities, the service labor required to maintain these organizations are described as "noncore." There is nothing transient about dirt in India, yet the requirement of cleaning is constructed as peripheral through the contracting out of this work by many large organizations. Similarly, security and transportation are required year-round, and often on a twenty-four-hour basis, yet they are cast as peripheral to key organizational work. Inder, a manager at a large security firm, explained to us that the company outsourced security "because they want to pay attention to their core business. Their core business is IT; they don't want to get in to this. . . . They are ready to pay, but they don't want to waste their time. These things are time-consuming, you know, managing the facilities and all, so what people feel, instead of utilizing that time for this noncore activity, it is better they outsource it." Such a discursive characterization of cleanliness, security, and transportation as "noncore" yet essential allows firms to legally hire contract labor under the Contract Labour Act, which permits the use of contract labor only for work deemed peripheral to the organization or seasonal. Not only do service workers not have the protections that accompany direct employment relationships with formal firms, but they also feel peripheral. Atul, a security guard whom we met, summarized this sentiment: "Who bothers about us at all? If something happens to us while we are not on duty, they don't take any responsibility. If something happens to a company employee, the administration will respond promptly. Nobody takes care of the contract boys in the same way."

In order to make a claim of compliance with the Contract Labour Act, transnational corporations require housekeeping, security, and transportation vendors to present them with documents that prove this compliance. Significant managerial resources are devoted to identifying loopholes in the law and producing documentary evidence, often to the detriment of workers. Despite this assertion of security work as noncore, Inder, who is trained in labor law and as part of his job ensures compliance with the law, told us that since security requirements are constant, the security contractor was "required" to constantly shift guards from location to location in order to maintain compliance under the law: "As far as the Contract Labour Act, companies cannot keep a guard for more than six months," he said. "If they are on contract more than six months, then it becomes a requirement to make that guard permanent."

Despite this construction of service work as "noncore," however, organizations are extremely active in defining the nature, embodied traits, tasks, and even gender of the workers they require. This leads to a second set of practices that are trickling down as a result of the presence of global firms. The requirements for particular kinds of aesthetic and embodied labor are systematically being transmitted from transnational firms to Indian service workers. Despite the fact that it is widely recognized that the service sector has been the source of a significant percentage of India's GDP growth since the 1990s, not all service sector jobs in India have experienced dramatic growth. Computer-related, financial, and communication services, all of which are broadly seen as part of the "modern" service industry, have provided much of the employment growth within the new economy services sector. Other occupations typically classified as part of traditional services, such as transportation, defense, and corporate services, have also created employment (Eichengreen & Gupta, 2011). Many researchers note that the growth of the services sector has limited potential to lift large masses of Indians out of poverty because many of these seemingly "modern" sectors demand skills and training that are inaccessible to the rural masses.[4]

These corporations have increasingly required service workers to develop skills related to what one worker whom we interviewed cogently termed "body personality"—that is, the transmission of a particular work ethic, professionalism, or "culture" through the way one's body looks and sounds. This body personality is deemed uniquely necessary for service jobs within multinational technology firms. Vikram, a housekeeping contractor who met us at his difficult-to-find office one afternoon, succinctly explained this expectation to us. Vikram's office was on the top floor of a low-rise building that had shops on the ground floor, and its walls were stained and unpainted. The office was a tiny room, no more than 40 square feet in area, with a desk that occupied almost the whole room. As we spoke, Vikram referred to his space as India's "domestic climate" and contrasted this with the "foreign climate" at IT firms, which he defined as an environment of constant scrutiny and negative repercussions for the presence of any dust or grime. He explained that workers had to look "formal," with uniforms, proper shoes, haircuts, clean nails, no beards, and no rings. Vikram reported that meeting these expectations was challenging for workers, because they were poor and from rural areas and were used to living in "huts"; consequently, they had to be trained to produce foreign climates. Our conversation with Vikram made us acutely aware that while there may have been little economic trickling down to low-wage service workers, development narratives of progress and modernization were widely used by both corporate managers and contractors, who frequently referred to their "civilizing" mission of transforming rural, backward, traditional, and parochial women and men into appropriate service workers for the multinational technology industry. Managers and contractors uniformly used the word "grooming" (which in other contexts is associated with the pet industry) to refer to the training provided to workers. The considerable efforts directed toward training Indians to become correctly embodied service workers for high-tech firms should be contextualized within discussions of the distinctively higher "standards" that these firms uphold compared to their Indian counterparts.

It was not difficult to get a sense of the distinctiveness of the standards in place in the technology sector in India during our visits to special economic zones. On one occasion, we made an appointment to meet Nidhi, and when we arrived it took 40 minutes to complete the security formalities at her company, which was a large call center. The company was in a multistory building in a busy urban area of the city and had numerous checkpoints that visitors were required to pass. Once the security guard at the entrance of the building confirmed our appointment, we were asked to complete forms listing our names and addresses, after which name tags with photographs were produced, and our bags were checked. Our name tags identified us as "Visitor VIPs." We were then escorted to the floor where the company was located. In our conversations with the guards we realized that they assumed we were there for job interviews. When Nidhi finally arrived she was suspicious of our interest in the experiences of facilities personnel and made it clear that she had only a brief window of time to speak to us. She asked us not to use our voice recorder. One of Nidhi's main responsibilities was meeting foreign clients during their site visits, during which they set the standards for housekeeping, security, and transportation services. Her job involved not only ensuring the compliance of various vendors, but also making sure that service staff met the aesthetic expectations required by the company. She said that if a driver was being sent to pick up a foreign client at the airport, his clothes had to be well ironed. She also demanded that catering staff employed by vendors undergo skin and medical tests, set standards for cleanliness for housekeepers, and gave vendors phrases in English to teach security personnel. Nidhi was proud that her company was able to help the poor by giving them jobs and cultivating ideas about proper cleanliness. She described her organization's strategy vis-à-vis contractors as one of "de-risking," a process in which multiple vendors were hired so that the company could minimize its dependence on any one contractor. Indeed, the comparison of backward, chaotic, and unorganized India and the organized, clean, and orderly foreign climate of multinational technology firms was a persistent theme in the narratives of both managers at technology firms and contractors; both groups celebrated the potential for moral development that foreign firms engender even if the economic prospects of service workers have not improved much as a result of the flow of global capital into India.

Alongside the emphasis on aesthetic and embodied labor, a third set of practices also trickles down to workers, focusing on the fostering of neoliberal identities, specifically orientations toward entrepreneurialism, and the related attempt to develop aspirational capital. Cross (2014) notes that special economic zones that house both high-tech and manufacturing export-oriented firms are "arenas of imagination, hope, aspiration and desire" (p. 9). The high-tech services sector in India is an example of such a "dream zone" (Cross, 2014), not only because of its assumed potential for high and continuous employment growth, but also because it gives rise to new identities and ideologies (Nayyar, 2012a). The multinational technology industry in India provides a vivid illustration of the ways in which neoliberalism operates as a "mobile technology" (Ong, 2006), with a unique genealogy and configuration within India. Capital flows have followed the migration trajectories of highly educated Indians who moved to the United States, Canada, and Europe in the 1960s and 1970s. These professionals were well poised within large U.S. corporations to facilitate the establishment of companies in India, and some even relocated to India to head Indian divisions or establish new local companies (Mann, 2007). Multinational technology companies are thus "Western,"[5] but in a far from straightforward sense. They may be Indian, European, Japanese, or U.S. owned, and in many cases, their executives may be Indian citizens, dual citizens, or citizens of a host of other countries. They may comprise higher-end software and IT consulting firms as well as call centers and business processing outsourcing (BPO) companies that function as back-office operations. For example, IBM and Microsoft have their software development outfits and back-office operations in India. But the Indian multinational business landscape also involves numerous Indian-owned and -operated companies that have adopted a U.S.-style corporate culture and mode of operation. Many of these Indian entrepreneurs are part of a transnational network of elite engineers and businessmen linked to Silicon Valley who returned to India after years of education and training to set up their own multinational technology firms. Stories of these return migrants are often accompanied by rags-to-riches narratives that are circulated with vigor by local and national media. Such narratives promote the idea that class aspirations are attainable through hard work and ensure that "middle class membership becomes a powerful, life-altering goal for many of those poised on its margins" (Heiman, Freeman, & Liechty, 2012, p. 18). The low-wage service workers we interviewed uniformly noted the importance of English-medium education for their children, although for many the high fees of such education or inadequate social networks made this an elusive goal. Workers talked about their aspirations that their children would gain access to technology firms, but as software and customer service workers, rather than as cleaners, drivers, or guards. Heiman and colleagues observe that "to aspire to middle classness is to live for the future" (p. 18). Indeed, many workers' narratives were both hopeful about possibilities for their children and pessimistic about the reality of those aspirations.

Work processes within multinational high-tech firms also demand employee entrepreneurialism through processes such as performance-based incentives and heavy monitoring of outputs. Such expectations of entrepreneurialism are also upheld for service staff. The very emergence and proliferation of the technology sector in India has been an exercise in neoliberal entrepreneurialism, according to which individual self-initiative is valorized and benefits are assumed to accrue to those who provide the best service at the lowest cost. Indian service workers are required to simultaneously embody these ideals of neoliberal entrepreneurialism and be the source of the low-cost labor that allows firms to acquire and secure India's competitive advantage. This focus on the theoretical possibilities and benefits of entrepreneurialism for poorly paid workers resonates with the "poverty pornography" that Roy (2011) writes about in relation to the characterization of the slum as a site of small business development. This glamorization of a place of desperation as a site of agency masks the impact of such rhetoric on those unable to convert their marginalization to strength. Our interview with Gulab captured this disconnect between effort and aspiration. A housekeeper employed full-time as a supervisor at a large call center, Gulab also held a second job as an event manager. He told us that after paying rent, grocery bills, school fees, donations to schools, and medical bills, his expenses were regularly higher than his income. This was despite the fact that he maximized his overtime shifts. It was in this context that when we asked about his future plans, he stated flatly, "Dreams are many, but it is impossible to fulfill these dreams on this income." Notwithstanding the strategic and active negotiation that poverty necessitates, our analysis reveals that both neoliberalism and entrepreneurialism have deeply diverse impacts on workers depending on their class, caste, and gender positions.

Finally, gendered workers are being produced through the practices at play within multinational technology firms. Out of the 92 workers interviewed for this study, 16 were women, all employed as housekeepers and security guards. In contrast to the gender-neutral construction of software and customer service jobs within these companies, and despite the rhetoric of Westernization, progress, and high-tech modernity that underpins the aesthetic architecture of these organizations, service work provides limited opportunities for women, who are viewed as less suitable for service jobs based on gender, caste, and class-based stereotypes. Only a narrow set of housekeeping and guarding tasks are defined as suitable for women, and they are rejected wholesale as inappropriate transportation providers. When women workers are hired, their employment is justified on gendered grounds. For example, many facility managers informed us that they hired women because there were female employees in the call center and software companies who used the toilets, which thus needed to be cleaned by women. By and large, service jobs are feminized and poorly paid and yet defined as most appropriate for male workers. Our research shows that poor women, especially those from lower-caste communities, may not face wholesale exclusion from service jobs in the technology sector, but their opportunities are certainly not as great as those of men, and often they are stuck in jobs that are considered low skilled, poorly paid, and temporary. Nevertheless, when poor, rural, lower-caste women are hired, they are trained rigorously so that they can become sufficiently "modern" and acquire the necessary embodied characteristics valued in the industry.

Data Gathering

Despite many studies on India's IT professionals (Carrillo Rowe, 2013; Mirchandani, 2012; Mukherjee, 2008b; Nadeem, 2011; Norhona & D'Cruz, 2009; Patel, 2010; Poster, 2007; Radhakrishnan, 2011; Russell, 2009; Upadhya, 2016), there have been comparatively few ethnographies of the low-wage employees who work alongside these employees within the same organizational spaces (for examples, see Cross, 2014; Ferus Comelo 2014; Kumar, 2016, Kumar and Beerepoot 2017; Gooptu, 2013b; Upadhyay, 2011). We argue that not only are low-wage service workers part of globalization, but they create the infrastructure that makes global firms in India possible. The methodological approach we followed was based on our interest not just in connections between global firms and the workers who service them but also in the *relations* through which globalization occurred (Feldman, 2011). We drew on institutional ethnography (Smith, 2005), using the experiences of low-wage service workers as a point of entry to understand the social organization of service work that supported multinational technology firms. Interviews allowed for "personal narrative analysis" (Maynes, Pierce, & Laslett, 2008; DeVault & Gross, 2012) to understand the socially contextualized experiences of service workers. We found that workers were almost uniformly hired through contractors, who comprise an often-precarious elite deeply influenced by policies and practices established within transnational firms. In addition to interviewing contractors, we spoke to managers responsible for facilities services at multinational technology firms (Mirchandani et al., 2018). We were influenced by feminist, postcolonial, and critical international development scholarship that uses a multiscalar approach to link local and global processes and spaces of production with those of social reproduction (Mohanty, 2003; Freeman, 2001; Nagar et al., 2002). Scholars such as Carla Freeman (2001) alert us to the importance of multiscalar perspectives and gender, race, and class analysis in examining globalization and macroeconomic processes. Such an approach allows for analysis not just of how "global" processes impact the "local" (e.g., microanalysis of how Third World women in different regions are inserted into the global economy) but also of how local regimes influence the global, thus highlighting the relations between the two. Feminist geographers like Nagar and colleagues (2002) provide similar insights (p. 260). They argue for a more inclusive account of globalization that foregrounds informal sites like the household, communities, cooperatives, and transnational networks instead of formal sectors like corporations, markets, and financial and development institutions. These scholars note that without tracing the "interdependencies between the formal and informal circuits" and "how people experience globalization processes in their communities and homes," we are left with an incomplete understanding of globalization (Nagar et al., 2002, p. 262). Others similarly argue that approaches that only focus on the experiences of those directly involved in the work of producing internationally exchanged goods and services also provide a partial understanding of globalization. As Sassen (2002) observes, "Insufficient attention has been paid to the actual array of jobs, from high paying to low paying. . . . Services need to be produced, and the buildings that hold the workers need to be built and cleaned" (pp. 5–6). Fernandez (2004) terms this omission a "politics of forgetting" (p. 2415) whereby the middle class is considered the sanitized, purified visual embodiment of globalization and the impact of economic restructuring on marginalized groups is masked. In this context, despite their daily presence in global multinational firms, many of the workers we interviewed told us that their participation in our study constituted their first opportunity for sustained interaction and knowledge sharing in an activity that involved a global team.

We quickly encountered numerous methodological challenges during the process of doing this research. Figure 0.2 is an example of the architecture of IT firms, many of which are located in gated, securitized communities. All visitors, including researchers, require permission to enter these spaces, and such permission is not always granted, particularly to those interested in functions emphatically defined as peripheral to the organization's central functions. Therefore, rather than assuming the traditional ethnographic focus on empirical immersion and participant observation, most of our research occurred on the borders of organizational spaces of work. High attrition rates, frequent "shift changes," and insecurity of tenure made it very difficult to contact, recruit, and conduct interviews with workers. Contractors were sometimes hesitant to share information on their businesses, especially given the highly competitive nature of the bidding process for contracts. Managers at multinational technology firms were busy executives with limited time or desire to share organizational protocols related to issues overtly defined as noncore, that is, housekeeping, security, and transportation services.

There are significant differences between the various special economic zones within the city of Pune, and these impacted our methodological

FIGURE 0.2 **Gated and securitized corporate spaces.**
Source: Photo by Mitwa Abhay Vandana

approach. These zones included Magarpatta and Hinjewadi, gated townships containing apartments, company offices, and markets on the outskirts of the city, as well as large buildings within the city that were often surrounded by already established developments such as hospitals, homes, and universities. Special economic zones also differ in terms of their security setups and access policies. Magarpatta, for example, had a gate where security personnel questioned all entrants and searched cars. Each set of buildings also had a security "booth" where guards issued or checked company-specific passes. Individuals with passes could enter the appropriate company building, where their bags would be scanned, while visitors would be met by company officials at yet another security desk. In many companies we found security desks at each floor of the building. Magarpatta is densely populated, and guards reported that they were monitored on camera as well as by a supervisor who made continuous "rounds." At this location we distributed information about the research project to guards, housekeepers, and drivers both verbally and through a flyer and exchanged phone numbers, but interviews themselves occurred at bus stops, tea shops, homes, or public benches, usually after the end of the worker's shift. In other special economic zones within the city it was less difficult to have conversations with drivers or guards because they worked independently and were not themselves monitored by camera. Since housekeepers in these settings did not wait outside organizational sites, most were contacted by phone or approached at bus stops. Guards and drivers at geographically remote firms were often interviewed on weekends, when there were few corporate employees present. In two cases, both in smaller companies, contractors invited us into corporate offices and arranged for us to interview service workers in the canteen or a meeting room. Most often, though, except for our interviews with facilities managers working at technology companies, we did not access organizational sites where cleaning and security work occurred. We limited our access to these sites because we did not want guards, housekeepers, or drivers who may have participated or been planning to participate in the study to witness us interacting with their bosses.

Language politics infused not only the technology firms, which were our site of research, but also our research endeavor itself. English was valorized and used by all software programmers, call center workers, and managers as their primary means of communication. Facilities managers were fluent English-language speakers, as were many of the contractors who provided transportation, housekeeping, and security services. Service workers were encouraged to develop basic communication skills in English but used Marathi as their primary medium of communication. Within our research team, two faculty researchers were fluent in English and Hindi, while one was fluent in Marathi as well, and students were most comfortable with Marathi and Hindi. Because it was a common language among the research team, Hindi was often the language of group meetings, which required continuous translations, as different interviews were conducted in English (with contractors and managers), Hindi (with some contractors), or Marathi (with service workers and some contractors). Hindi and Marathi interviews were translated for analysis. Interviews in English were transcribed verbatim, and quotes in this book reflect the varied ways in which the English language was spoken among the sample.

The status of English as the language of mobility was evident not only in the prominence of English-language signs within special economic zones, but also during our interviews. Reena, a housekeeping vendor whom we interviewed, for example, struggled to express herself in English and so switched to Hindi. After a few sentences in Hindi, however, she switched back to English and told us that part of her motivation for participating in the research project was to give herself an opportunity to practice her English. She said she would be more successful in obtaining contracts from transnational companies if her English-language skills were stronger. Language mixing was common. For example, one worker used the word "body personality" to describe the embodied requirements that recruiters sought. Although he spoke in Hindi, he coined this term in English.

We developed several strategies for meeting workers. First, in a few cases, some contractors offered to introduce us to workers they employed. In one case, when we went to meet workers we found that supervisors had been instructed by the contractor to set up tables for us to interview workers selected by them. It was fortuitous in this case that we were offered fans, as they were noisy and made it difficult for supervisors to overhear our conversations. In other cases, we met workers through students at the university who had friends or relatives employed at technology firms as housekeepers, drivers, or security guards. The largest number of interviews, however, were conducted through team visits to technology parks and firms, where we approached guards at security desks, housekeepers as they waited at bus stops or benches, and drivers as they waited in their vehicles at company gates (see figures 0.3–0.5). We told workers about the research and made appointments for interviews if they expressed interest in participating or asked them to pass on contact information to friends or relatives. In many cases, workers were intrigued by and interested in the research project, particularly when they discovered that they would not require employer permission to participate and that employers would not be informed about their involvement. Some expressed interest in being interviewed on the spot if they had time, and others gave us telephone numbers so we could make appointments. Overall, we discovered that there was much more privacy for workers when we conducted interviews in public places such as bus stops, coffee shops, or roadside benches compared to when we met them at organizational sites or homes. When others were present during interviews, we attempted to create more privacy by suggesting a change in place, but in some cases workers said that they were more comfortable with their peers present.

Not all of our initial contacts led to interviews. On one occasion, for example, we approached four housekeepers in uniform walking together within a special economic zone. One was very interested in participating, but she said that her shift was from 8 a.m. to 8 p.m., and she was required to return straight home afterward. Although we offered

FIGURE 0.3 **Tea shops where some workers were interviewed.**
Source: Photo by Mitwa Abhay Vandana

FIGURE **0.4 Bus stop where some workers were interviewed.**
Source: Photo by the authors

FIGURE **0.5 Parking lot where some workers were interviewed.**
Source: Photo by the authors

to meet her at her home, she said that her in-laws would not approve. In other cases, some workers did not keep appointments, or the phone numbers they provided were not in service. We had partial conversations with many people. On one of our field visits to a large special economic zone, for example, we approached several security guards clustered at the gate of a large international call center. We told them about the project and asked them to distribute the information. One guard immediately said he would like to share his experiences and invited us into a nearby cabin where there was space to sit. We started telling him about the project, but a few minutes later he suddenly received a text message about an appointment and said he had to leave. However, another guard was present at the time, and since he had listened to our explanations about the project, he said he would like to be interviewed.

At times our interviews were based on chance encounters. In one special economic zone we saw a uniformed guard sitting in a relaxed posture in a chair just outside a restaurant. Curious, we asked about his work, and he told us that his job was to guard a visible "cable" that was the technological link for one of the large international call centers in the zone. Prathamesh's job with the call center was to ensure that no one tampered with the cable, and since he worked alone, he was free to talk to us while he was on duty. He reported that despite his employment with a large security subcontractor, he received neither a pay slip nor any official benefits. An ex-army man and a migrant from Kashmir, a conflict-ridden region far away in the northernmost tip of the country, he told us he had been lured to Pune on the false promise of a recruiter who had claimed he would receive a high-paying job. Instead, he earned only INR 8,000 and referred to his job as "slavery." Prathamesh's plan was to save some money and then return to his native town and start a small shop.

On a few occasions we were invited to workers' homes. About a year after we first interviewed Rakesh, for example, we bumped into him again during one of our visits to a special economic zone. He greeted us warmly and said he would introduce us to other housekeepers. As we were in a taxi and he had just completed his shift, he asked for a lift to his home. He lived with nine roommates in a small two-bedroom apartment. Although it was the middle of the day, mattresses had been laid out on the floor, and several men were asleep. The room was dark and had no windows or ventilation. A man was washing clothes in the washroom. We exchanged telephone numbers and arranged to meet some of the workers at their convenience.

Like Rakesh, Narendra not only was enthusiastic about being interviewed but also called a few days later to ask whether all the researchers on the team liked listening to the audio recording of his interview. Born into a landowning family, he had left his village because he had become involved in an intercaste relationship that was not accepted within his community. After attending a recruitment "camp" held in his village by the contractor who now employed him, he and his partner decided that he should move to the city and she would later follow. He became a security guard, although with his savings he also purchased a vehicle that he contracted to a company that provided driving services. His family in the village was told nothing of his job; given their relatively high status, Narendra said that they would be offended that he had chosen to work as a security guard. Instead, he told them that he was helping his cousin set up a domestic call center. He was clearly proud to be included in research by university scholars.

We provided respondents with an honorarium of INR 500 for participation in the interview. As per ethics protocols, this was to ensure that prospective participants were compensated for costs they may have incurred through their participation, such as lost hours of pay, travel costs, or childcare expenses. We tried to set an amount that was high enough to properly compensate respondents for any out-of-pocket expenses but not so high that they would feel coerced into participating if they did not want to. Local team members also noted that too low an honorarium would have been perceived as a "slap in the face" by respondents, who felt that a project with "foreign" funding should be able to compensate them fairly. We also did not want respondents to view their involvement as an unfair extraction of their labor—which is how many workers characterized the behavior of the foreign companies that employed them. Contractors and managers were not paid an honorarium. Responses to the honorarium were extremely varied. Some respondents did not want to accept it, as they had established friendships with the researchers during interviews that they felt would be sullied by the monetary exchange. One worker told us he would donate the honorarium to his church. Many were surprised to receive compensation, as they did not perceive their participation in the interview as "work." Others were appreciative of the honorarium, as they had immediate monetary needs.

Over the course of four years (2011–2014), we interviewed a total of 138 respondents. Of these, 92 were workers (31 drivers, 33 housekeepers, and 28 security guards), and 46 were subcontractors/vendors, supervisors, company facilities managers, or labor officials connected to the multinational technology industry. The participants represented 59 different companies that provided services to the multinational technology industry in Pune.

The research team included the three academic collaborators of this project and authors of this book, along with eight graduate students based in India and Canada and two local scholars. The particular composition of this team was essential for the field research. Some of the student researchers from India shared some gender, class, and caste backgrounds with workers, which allowed respondents to more comfortably share their life stories. Local scholars were able to share contextual knowledge. All academic researchers could access government officials. Those working outside India may have been able to access key company officials and documents with greater ease because of their foreign affiliations. Over the years, we had opportunities to hold many group analysis meetings, and we worked together for weeks at a time each year. Interviews were conducted in English, Hindi, Marathi, or a combination of these languages. Interviews with workers were transcribed in the language in which they were conducted (most often Marathi) and then translated into English. Local and conversational modes of speech were retained even if they came across as somewhat awkward when reproduced in written form. Most interviews with key informants occurred in either English or Hindi in their workplaces, giving us an opportunity to engage in participant observation. A handful of workers were also interviewed at their workplace, but in most cases worker interviews occurred in homes or at bus stops, tea shops, and other public places. Respondent-driven conversations that focused on participants' analyses of their life and organizational histories, career trajectories, challenges, and aspirations provided rich and vivid insight into at least some of the experiences of low-wage service workers in India's high-tech firms.

Demographic Characteristics of Respondents

As figure 0.6 illustrates, the average individual income of workers we interviewed was INR 6,230 for housekeepers, INR 9,310 for security guards, and INR 13,879 for drivers. The minimum wage rate for unskilled workers in Maharashtra was INR 6,830 in 2012.[6] This means that on average, a housekeeper's monthly salary was slightly lower than the minimum

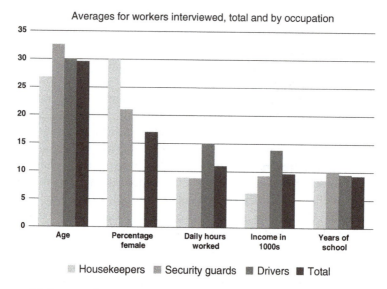

Averages for workers interviewed, total and by occupation

FIGURE 0.6 Demographic characteristics of workers interviewed.

wage and a driver's or security guard's income was above it. However, a large proportion of the workers we interviewed were engaged in paid work for more than the stipulated eight-hour workday. When hours of work were taken into account, drivers earned the lowest hourly rate among the three occupational groups, far below minimum wage, followed by housekeepers and then security guards, some of whom also earned incomes below the minimum wage. Compared to other casual and informal workers like sweepers, domestic workers, street vendors, and daily wage earners, however, workers in our sample were in a relatively higher income bracket. Some had acquired the means to send their children to school and support their extended family networks. However, many of the participants we interviewed noted that with the city's rising standards of living and increasing prices of basic food and services, they did not have any savings. Our sample of workers was neither part of the urban poor nor part of the urban middle classes. Throughout the analysis, we have chosen not to convert local currency amounts mentioned by respondents into U.S. dollar equivalents, since this comparison does not necessarily provide much insight into local living costs. A more useful approach to understanding the significance of the amounts mentioned is to examine the data on the local cost of living shown in figure 0.7.[6]

PRODUCT	COST IN INR
Milk (regular), (1 liter)	47
Loaf of Fresh White Bread (500 g)	29
Rice (white), (1 kg)	52
Eggs (12)	58
Apples (1 kg)	157
Domestic Beer (0.5 liter draught)	109
Meal, Inexpensive Restaurant	170
One-way Ticket (Local Transport)	20
Monthly Pass (Regular Price)	1,000
Basic (Electricity, Heating, Water, Garbage) for 85m² Apartment	1,450
Apartment Rent (1 bedroom) in City Centre	13,770
Apartment Rent (1 bedroom) Outside of Centre	8,896

FIGURE 0.7 Pune cost of living index.

The workers we interviewed were stratified along the lines of caste, tribe, and religion.[7] The stratified caste system continues to significantly structure the lives of Indians. Caste positions are inherited and, unlike class, do not change in the course of a person's life. Under this system there are four categories. At the top of the hierarchy are the Brahmins, who historically were priests and scholars. They are followed by the Kshatriya, who were historically warriors, and then the Vaishyas, petty traders and artisans. The lowest is the Shudra, who are considered impure and defiling and are condemned to do menial labor. The lowest among these are termed Atishudras, or Untouchables. Within each category there are a number of caste groups with specific names and regionally defined taboos on food and marriage.

In India today, caste continues to define and control access to formal education, respectable social status, and general standing. As the Sengupta Commission report states, many of the 93 percent of Indians who still work in the unorganized sector of the economy continue to follow hereditary occupations. Since independence, caste-based discrimination in occupational, civil, and religious life has been challenged and numerous state- and national-level initiatives have aimed at combating unequal access to educational resources and work opportunities; nevertheless, these efforts have had mixed results. Even today the taboo on marriage between castes influences individual choices through community control. Food exchange among castes is now more permissible, especially in urban areas and in ultramodern industries like IT or ITES.

Hindu workers in our sample belonged to three categories of caste groups—upper castes, other backward classes [OBCs], and scheduled castes [SCs]. Several respondents whom we refer to as "upper caste" were Marathas, part of the Kshatriya group. There were also many respondents drawn from the "other backward classes" [OBCs] who hailed from the Vaishya category. Those termed as members of the "scheduled castes"[SCs] in our sample belonged to either the Shudra or Atishudra categories. Other respondents were from scheduled, denotified, or nomadic tribes, while a few identified as Muslims and Christians.

More than half of the workers we interviewed (55 percent, or 51 out of 92) belonged to the lower castes. As shown in figure 0.8, almost half (49 percent, or 25 out of 51) of the lower-caste workers worked as housekeepers and were members of the scheduled castes. Thirty percent of the workers in our sample (28 out of 92) identified as upper caste and were

Caste		Security Guards	Housekeepers	Drivers
	Upper Castes	14	3	11
	Other Backward Castes	3	0	0
	Scheduled Caste	4	21	12
Tribe				
	Denotified Tribe	0	2	1
	Nomadic Tribe	1	1	2
	Scheduled Tribe	3	1	0
Minority Religions				
	Muslims	0	0	1
	Christians	0	0	2
Unspecified		3	5	2
TOTAL		28	33	31

FIGURE 0.8 Castes, tribes, and religions represented in the sample of workers interviewed.

poor rural migrants. The security sector in our sample was dominated by upper-caste Marathas (42 percent, or 12 out of 28 security workers), although members of scheduled castes and especially neo-Buddhists worked alongside them. Within the driving sector, the scheduled castes (12 out of 31 drivers, or 38 percent) and upper-caste Marathas (10 out of 31 drivers, or 32 percent) were significantly represented.

Tribal members in India are considered outside the fold of Hindu caste-based society. Maharashtra has a large population of scheduled tribes, and members in our sample belonged to various tribal communities. Members of the denotified and nomadic tribes are mostly landless, precariously situated migrants in the urban job market. The denotified tribes are communities that were stigmatized by the British as criminal and hence are also termed "ex-criminal" tribes. They still face stigma and humiliation in both rural and urban society.

Indian society also includes members of all religious communities. The majority are Hindus, followed by Muslims. Smaller communities like Christians and Sikhs, Parsis, Jains, and Jews also exist. Neo-Buddhists are those who converted to Buddhism under the leadership of Dr. B. R. Ambedkar to free themselves from the shackles of Untouchability and the stigma of the caste hierarchy.

Amongst the three occupational groups in our sample, the drivers worked the longest hours and also had higher incomes. They are also exclusively male. Many drivers' higher salary is linked to their long hours, which includes night duty and overtime, as explained in chapter 3. Housekeepers not only had the lowest figures for postsecondary education, they were also the youngest workers in the group.

A large proportion of the workers were migrants from rural areas and owned small plots of land (between 2 and 10 acres). Most of them had moved to Pune from the surrounding districts of Maharashtra, but a few were migrants from out of state. Based on the interviews, it is clear that the reasons for their migration included the ongoing agrarian crisis, environmental problems like chronic drought, and perceptions of better economic opportunities in Pune. As Purandara (2013) and Narayanamoorthy (2013) note, Maharashtra has been suffering from droughts as a result of the transfer of water from irrigation uses to non-irrigation (industrial and domestic) uses in cities. Many respondents whose families owned small plots said that they had migrated to the city because their farms had been unable to produce enough crops and there had been few job opportunities in their villages. Indeed, several workers told us that they regularly sent money home from Pune to support their family in the village. Contractors, well aware of the poor economic situation in rural areas, targeted these regions to recruit workers. Many workers' initial source of contact in the city was a friend or family member from their village working there. A number of workers reported that they had gained access to multinational technology sector through these contacts.

In addition to workers, we also interviewed contractors who owned or managed transportation, security, or housekeeping firms, as well as facilities managers at multinational technology firms, workers' or union advocates, and state officials connected to the Ministry of Labour (see figure 0.9). Although spread more or less equally among the sectors, all but 5 of these 46 respondents were male. While multinational technology firms hire many women as programmers or call center workers, it is clear that facilities management and labor contracting remain heavily male dominated. Despite our efforts, we were able to identify very few women working as facilities managers and contractors.

Our interviews with various groups (e.g., workers, contractors, facilities managers) were extremely instructive, especially since in several cases we interviewed participants employed at the same organization who had no knowledge of one another. In many cases, our interviews

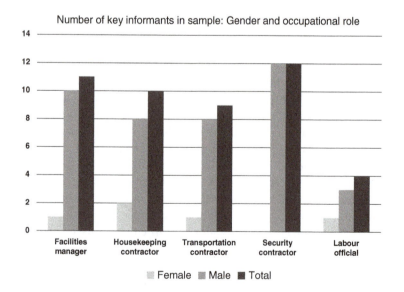

FIGURE 0.9 Characteristics of officials, managers, and contractors interviewed.

with particular contractors were followed up with visits to technology firms with which they held contracts. Independent of contractors, we requested interviews with facilities managers at these companies and also shared recruitment information with workers wearing uniforms with contractor or company logos. In other cases, workers told us about their employers, and we then called companies or contractors to request interviews without revealing the information provided by the workers. In these ways, we were able to trace connections and divergences between narratives of differently located respondents. Weaving together these multiple narratives allowed us to trace the larger structural forces of neoliberal globalization, industry operations, and local regimes of class-, caste-, and gender-based difference that affect workers' experiences. We were able to document, for example, the ways in which those occupying different roles discussed the issues of minimum wage, compliance, or training differently.

Outline of the Book

In the chapters that follow, we explore the lives and livelihoods of workers who provide services to multinational technology firms in Pune, India. These are not workers who are part of India's new middle class (Fernandes, 2006), yet they do possess some assets. These assets include levels of education, which are higher than the Indian average but not high enough to allow these individuals to access professional or managerial-level jobs. In chapter 1, we situate these workers within the context of informality in the Indian labor market and reflect upon the different manifestations of informality within the housekeeping, transportation, and security sectors. We explore the paradox within the multinational technology sector of a glut of wealth and infrastructural assets on the one hand and persistent informality on the other. We trace the ways informality is "hidden" by its situation within lavish, formal firms and the use by contractors and managers of discourses of compliance.

Chapters 2, 3, and 4 focus on worker experiences within each of three service sectors that serve multinational technology firms—housekeeping, transportation, and security. Housekeepers (chapter 2) occupy a key role in maintaining the lavish campuses on which multinational firms are housed, since part of the aura of the sector is based on the cleanliness of its architectural spaces of work. Such companies tend to launch prominent building projects that serve to distinguish them as key players in the global economy. The dirty work of cleaning in India has traditionally been delegated to those labeled as "contaminated" within caste structures. In stark contrast, cleaning within the multinational technology sector requires "mechanized housekeepers" who are embodiments of cleanliness, which through training is connected to moral virtues such as honesty, discipline, self-control, and good manners. Unlike cleaning in domestic households, corporate cleaning involves the unfettered use of water, chemicals, and equipment. Yet housekeepers continue to experience social stigma associated with cleaning work. Despite the professionalization of their work, they do not earn salaries that allow them to challenge these stereotypes or upgrade their own residences. Instead, even though they both maintain and embody the modernity associated with the multinational technology sector, they can access this modernity only through the exploitative employment relations within which they are situated.

In chapter 3, we trace the ways in which drivers are tasked with managing the transitions between the gated organizational communities of multinational technology firms and the India outside these spaces. These workers are key to the modernity project in that they ensure that Western standards of timeliness, cleanliness, and order are extended into the assumed spaces of chaos outside the free trade zones where most corporate employees reside. They are also themselves ideal neoliberal subjects because they are or aspire to become entrepreneurial owners of their vehicles. Drivers assume the risks of ownership, which include a lack of protection under labor laws, extremely long workdays, and exposure to the financial risks of accidents. In undertaking these risks, however, they are part of the growing tide of Indians who are valorized for taking control of their economic destinies through self-employment. Yet this construction of drivers as model entrepreneurs has been interrupted by a number of highly publicized incidents of violent rape of female call center employees by drivers over the years. This violence has cast all drivers as suspect. As a result, drivers experience continuous technological surveillance and are required to wait for their passengers outside the physical boundaries of organizations. In these ways drivers are simultaneously constructed as model entrepreneurs and prospective criminals—a tension that is exacerbated by their social location as migrant men who are enmeshed in the system of contract labor within which they are employed.

In chapter 4 we discuss the different consequences of contract employment for those security guards who are responsible for providing "soft security" for India's multinational technology firms. Despite the unstable and peripheral nature of these jobs, the guards are required to be reliable, trustworthy, and committed to protecting the organization and its members from external threats. Much of the work of security guards involves scrutinizing visitors and employees and their possessions as they enter and exit the organizational site. They are responsible for excluding those who may pose a threat to the organization's assets, reputation, or employees. At the same time, the soft skills required of security guards involve looking clean and professional and doing one's job in a way that does not offend visitors or employees. Given guards' temporary contract status, complaints made against them by company personnel often result in negative consequences. They face the constant risk of being fired if they are unable to negotiate the complex emotional requirements of their work. At the same time, because most guards are poor migrants, they are themselves assumed to be carriers of risk and experience significant surveillance in their work lives. Security companies mitigate the risks related to poverty, migration, and contract employment by defining several "proxy" factors that are used to signal the reliability of the people they hire as guards, such as an army background. They also provide training reminiscent of militaristic discipline and ethos. Given the multifaceted skills required of security guards, the occupation's wage levels are recognized by both workers and contractors as insufficient, and many managers and vendors lament a shortage of appropriate applicants for jobs. Yet this widespread acknowledgement of labor scarcity has not led to an improvement in wages or working conditions for guards.

Service jobs within multinational technology companies in India vividly illustrate the ways in which work and workers are continually gendered through organizational practices. Chapter 5 focuses on these myriad practices of gendering. Even though service work globally is predominantly feminized and cleaning in particular is mostly done by poor women around the world, the housekeeping, guarding, and transportation sectors of India's multinational technology industry are all male dominated. These Western and emphatically progressive organizations, which signal India's new relationship to the world as a "modern" rather than "traditional" country, are ironically also sites within which old-fashioned notions of appropriate work for each gender are entrenched for low-wage workers. Only very specific tasks are seen as suitable for female housekeepers and security guards, and men are seen as the default ideal workers. Driving is seen as appropriate work only for men because of the dangers associated with traveling in public spaces, especially at night. Men are criminalized because of their gender but are simultaneously seen to be suitable for the dangerous work of driving because they are men. We trace the process through which work simultaneously is deemed less appropriate for women workers and is feminized, resulting in the emergence of particular forms of feminized masculinity that are mediated by local class and caste dynamics. Within the multinational technology sector, this feminization of masculinity is linked to notions of workers' vulnerability and malleability. It is ironic that India's most modern sector is one in which patriarchal gender norms are entrenched while, at least among the working women we interviewed, these norms are being partially challenged within the so called traditional sphere of the home, where some women exercise a form of breadwinner femininity. We trace the ways in which women workers note shifts in gender expectations within their households as a result of their waged employment in multinational technology firms. At the same time, this waged work results in intense time pressures for women, who continue to assume primary responsibility for childcare and household work.

In chapter 6 we sum up the main arguments of the book, highlighting how workers who support the multinational technology industry in Pune occupy a liminal space between formality and informality. We explore the question of the "impact" of the development of this sector on those who service global multinational firms, arguing that neoliberal globalization has had deeply diverse effects on this heterogeneous group and both has been mediated through existing class, caste, and gender-based hierarchies and has created and reconfigured them in new ways. Discourses of professionalization, compliance, and entrepreneurialism are key avenues of such a reconfiguration, which fashions service workers as the ideal neoliberal subjects, with specific embodied characteristics that make them suitable for this industry. Nevertheless, such constructions of ideal workers are also riddled with many contradictions, which continue to marginalize them in the urban labor market. This book therefore contributes to and expands upon scholarship on entrepreneurship, informality, social reproduction, and visions of development in emerging economies of the global South in the context of neoliberalism.

Endnotes

1. Throughout this book we do not include dollar conversions for the local currency. Instead, we direct readers to figure 0.7, the Pune cost of living index, which provides official INR amounts required for housing, food, and transportation within the local context. This provides a better understanding of the purchasing power of the local currency than U.S. dollar conversions would. One U.S. dollar in 2014 was roughly equivalent to INR 70.

2. The term "neoliberal globalization" or "neoliberalism" has been used to specifically refer to the "free market" ideologies and economic policies of liberalization, deregulation, and privatization initiated by Ronald Reagan in the United States and Margaret Thatcher in the United Kingdom in the 1980s. Some scholars have differentiated between a "rollback" and "rollout" neoliberalism, in which the former is linked to the 1980s dismantling of the Keynesian welfare state in the global North (i.e., the retreat of the state from public sector initiatives and investment and the attendant rise of privatization) and the latter is related to the reconfigured and proactive role of the state in the 1990s that paved the way for market-led initiatives and other institutional and regulatory reform regimes (Peck & Tickell, 2002). More recently, some scholars have coined the term "inclusive neoliberalism" (Craig & Porter, 2006, p. 90), which combines orientation toward the market with some social initiatives in the form of public-private partnerships. In terms of policy, this is characterized by a discourse of rights and responsibilities, social capital, and social entrepreneurship. We acknowledge the breadth of ideas that are included in the phrase "neoliberal globalization" and the reality that in the Indian context neoliberalism does not follow a period of "liberalism" and its accompanying strong welfare state (Gupta & Sivaramakrishnan, 2011). However, we use the term "neoliberal globalization" to refer to two specific trends. The first is the introduction of policies of economic liberalization through which the state encourages the establishment of technology firms, often through tax incentives within special economic zones. While India has never had a strong welfare state, the state has developed labor laws that serve to protect workers. In the context of contemporary neoliberalism, state policies that promote India as an attractive location for foreign capital investment because of labor savings run counter to state attempts to enforce laws that ensure better livelihoods and higher wages. The second trend is related to the increasing importance placed on the entrepreneurial subject in contemporary global capitalism.

3. English-medium schools are schools where the mode of instruction is in English as opposed to vernacular languages. English-medium schools, a legacy of British colonization, have been historically linked to upward mobility and are perceived as a status symbol in India.

4. Scholars note that the impacts of employment growth in other industries have been greater than that related to the technology sectors. Barnes, for example, argues that the impact of the IT sector on output and employment has been "enormously overstated" (2015, p. 88).

5. We use the words "Western" and "West" as discursive constructs rooted in histories of colonialism, imperialism and resulting global economic hierarchies that has led to United States and Europe becoming the normative standard for development, progress, and modernity. These terms were also

used by some of our respondents. We do not intend to homogenize diverse and differentiated regions and communities in the West (or assume an undifferentiated East), and acknowledge that global North and South may not always adequately capture the current political configuration of the world.

6. Figures drawn from https://paycheck.in/main/salary/minimumwages/maharashtra/minimum-wages-in-maharashtra-4.

7. Adapted from: http://www.numbeo.com/cost-of-living/city_result.jsp?country=India&city=Pune

8. A caste system is defined as "the division of people in social groups (or castes), in which the social and economic rights of each individual caste are predetermined or ascribed by birth and made hereditary" (Thorat & Newman, 2010, p. 7). Upper-caste workers include Marathas, who have a hereditary status and own land, which gives them a sense of pride and superiority. Marathas have warrior lineages and are considered rural elites. Some of them are industrialists and businesspersons, but many of them seek respectable jobs in the new urban economy. Members of "other backward classes" (OBCs) come from artisan and peasant communities, and some of them own land. Scheduled castes include a number of caste groups that were oppressed under the ancient Varna caste system. Some of these caste communities were called "Untouchables," as even their touch was considered impure and defiling. The term connoted both dispossession and disadvantage, and Untouchables historically were denied civil and religious rights, including access to education, and were forced into humiliating hereditary occupations like scavenging and menial labor without the chance of achieving mobility or freedom outside the caste system. The constitution of independent India provided fundamental rights to these communities, including freedom of mobility, property, and education, and abolished Untouchability. In spite of this and some positive discrimination in favor of these communities in terms of access to education and jobs, the situation of these communities remains appalling. In addition to workers from these three broad caste groupings, our sample included workers who identified as members of scheduled tribes, which are communities with a history of dispossession and displacement. The denotified tribes are those that were labeled by the British colonial government as "criminal tribes." They still carry this stigma and risk being branded as criminals. Members of the nomadic tribes have traditionally been nomads. Many of these tribes do not possess any land. All Muslims in our sample belonged to artisan and/or small trade backgrounds. Christians in our sample were not landowners and came from families that had historically engaged in informal sector jobs.

CHAPTER 1

Hidden Informality in Multinational Technology Firms

I n India's major cities, the large, glass-faced corporate offices of multinational technology firms symbolize modernity and progress. While these organizations hire software programmers and customer service agents under formal employment contracts, many use labor intermediaries to meet their security, housekeeping, and transportation needs. As a result, a substantial degree of labor informality pervades these architecturally lavish sites. Informal jobs are those in which workers are paid low wages; have little job security; are not protected from being unfairly fired; enjoy few health, safety, and pension benefits; and lack collective bargaining rights (Barnes, 2013). The presence of informal jobs within the formal sector is not a new phenomenon in India (Ghosh, 2015). Contemporary informality within the transnational technology sector is, however, especially significant for several reasons. First, informality fosters a high level of worker precarity by depressing wages, engendering competition between contractors, and deepening insecurity in a sector that has experienced decades of high profits. Second, informality is ironically hidden within discourses of compliance and formality. A higher level of attention is devoted to state regulation and the construction of documentary proof than to maintaining the spirit of the law, which is aimed at providing minimum labor standards. As a result, minimum wage rather than a living wage is used as a benchmark for compliance, despite widespread acknowledgement that the former is not in line with the cost of living (Sampath, 2016). Attention and resources are devoted to the definition of organizational strategies that are compliant with local labor laws even as practices of informalization continue to exist. Third, rather than suggesting that formality and informality are ends of a continuum or different types of employment relationships, our analysis shows that there is considerable slippage between these categories. For example, workers may be promised benefits such as access to state health and pension schemes[1] but may not be given the correct paperwork that would allow them to actually access these benefits. Finally, informality within the technology sector is significant because the service workers who maintain India's lavish transnational firms are required not only to learn new ways of working but also to transform their identities and embodied aesthetics. Despite their weak employment relationships with these workers, organizations exert strong control over service employees' physical and aesthetic labor. By and large, these workers, who are ideologically constructed and socially positioned as the first to benefit from trickledown development, are deeply disappointed when they find that they are caught in much the same cycle of poverty that they have historically experienced.

As a result of labor informality, the potential of special economic zones and the technology companies housed within them to foster local social and economic development is severely curtailed. Ghosh (2015) characterizes India's development as a process of "exclusion through incorporation" whereby marginalized people have been forced to become part of market systems within which they are largely excluded from economic mobility. Growth has led to limited employment generation as well as a fissuring of the economy, whereby even large, registered formal firms rely heavily on informally employed casual and contract employees. Instead of maintaining that the formal and the informal comprise separate sectors, Ghosh argues that low-paid informal activities subsidize the formal sector.

Supporting this view, a report by India's Comptroller and Auditor General in 2014 revealed that there was a large discrepancy between actual and promised job creation within special economic zones, and in many cases, tax incentives subsidized transnational firms (Ananthanarayanan, 2008; Dutta, 2016; Barnes, 2013; Levien, 2018). Dutta provides a fascinating case study of Nokia, a Finnish company, which received £65 million in the form of incentives from the state of Tamil Nadu as well as exemptions from provisions in labor laws. A decade later, Nokia ceased operations in the region after facing union action related to the poor quality of jobs it created as well as charges of tax evasion. Dutta's analysis points to the potential for special economic zones to generate jobless growth and huge expenditures of public funds that might have otherwise been used for public infrastructure projects.

In line with these analyses, we discovered that uniformed, highly regulated workforces mask the fact that informality, typically associated with underdevelopment, pervades India's most visibly affluent, seemingly modern, and apparently progressive corporate spaces. Through exclusions and poor enforcement, state initiatives designed to promote an influx of foreign capital have overridden many of India's existing labor laws. This has given rise to a situation in which, despite unprecedented GDP growth since the 1990s, there has also been an increasing informalization of labor in India (Jhabvala & Standing, 2010). As a result, corporations that are unambiguously part of India's formal sector and are infused with foreign capital that allows them to create lavish "organizational campuses" are simultaneously pervaded by labor informality (Nigam, 1997; Beale, 2017).[2] Saini notes that employers are "devising various ways to subvert the spirit of labour laws; this is often done through strategies suggested by labour law consultants" (2010, p. 3). One widely used strategy in the service sector is the use of contract labor. Despite India's legislative attempts to curb the use of contract labor through the enactment of the Contract Labour Act (1970), organizations frequently sidestep the spirit of the law, which identifies contract relationships as appropriate primarily for seasonal or nonessential employees. As Singh (2010) notes, the Contract Labour Act was based on the assumption that some seasonal industries would require labor flexibility to survive, and in some states, contract labor is considered suitable for an organization's noncore operations. Since cleaners, security guards, and drivers are defined as "noncore" functions within technology corporations, large, profitable transnational corporations are allowed to hire subcontractors rather than establish direct employment relationships with service workers. This is despite the fact that cleaning, guarding, and driving occur on a year-round and round-the-clock basis and that without these services the companies would find it impossible to sustain their "core" functions. Through its weak enforcement of contract labor law, the state sanctions the widespread use of informal labor within formal sectors. Gooptu (2013b) terms such a trend "organized informality," a system in which informal work relationships are regularized and common in firms that clearly occupy the formal sector. She points to an interesting contrast between nations in the global North where there has been a steady erosion of employment norms and an increasing prevalence of informal, precarious jobs and countries such as India where there has always been an extremely high level of informality in the labor market.

Historically, the scale of the "informal sector" in the global South was understood to be a symbol of underdevelopment.[3] In the 1950s and 1960s, economists believed that these regions had dual economic sectors—the regulated formal ones and the unregulated, inefficient, chaotic informal ones. The informal sector was considered transient, and the purpose of development was seen as the transformation of these informal sectors into modern formal sectors like those existing in the economies of the global North. The notion was that over time these activities and the workers engaging in them would become absorbed into the formal economy (Yusuff, 2011). However, this did not happen in most places in the global South, and workers remained trapped in "the informal economy they helped to build, or drifting back and forth between the slums of the urban periphery and impoverished rural hinterland" (Breman, 2013a, p. 130; 2013b). Later scholars refuted the binary distinction between formal and informal, noting that the "informal economy" is complex, heterogeneous, dynamic, and integrated with the formal economy (Raju & Bose, 2016; Yusuff, 2011). Far from being outside the purview of the formal economy, the informal economy actually enables the formal economy to function. As Roy (2005, p. 149) observes, rather than existing beyond the boundaries of the state, informality is produced by the state.

The influx of multinational firms in India has led to the creation of some formal jobs, but most of the jobs that have resulted from global capital flows have been informal, low paid, and insecure (Barnes, 2013). Much of the research to date in India has been on informal work that occurs within the informal sector, with rich ethnographic studies conducted on street vendors, construction workers, domestic workers, waste pickers, street cleaners, and other home-based workers (Bhowmik & Saha, 2012; Chen & Raveendran, 2012; McDougall, 2007; Routh, 2017; Shankar & Sahni, (2017); Shlaes & Mani 2013). Our sample of service workers—the drivers, housekeepers, and security guards who provide key services to India's multinational technology companies—however, did not belong to this group. The workers we interviewed did not fall into the traditional category of informal workers because many had identity cards that tied them to specific vendors or firms, as well as some formal education. While these workers possessed some assets, cultural capital, and aspirational values similar to those seen among India's new middle class (Fernandes & Heller, 2006), they did not belong to this group either. Many of the drivers, security guards, and housekeepers we interviewed had obtained levels of education that were higher than the Indian average but not high enough to allow them to access the professional or managerial-level jobs that the new middle-class professionals like software and IT workers are able to command. A number of workers were rural migrants from landowning families and thus wielded some power in their villages. They were embedded in social structures that theorists such as Patel (2016, p. 11) have referred to as "petty production," whereby they were involved in multiple monetized and nonmonetized market activities with their families and friends.[4] The vendors/subcontractors who hired them may be considered "self-employed" workers in the informal economy. It was through these subcontracting networks and attendant experiences of work and the workplace that such workers and their vendors were ambiguously tied to both the formal and informal sector in unique ways.

Thus, although workers who provide services for multinational firms do not fit within traditional definitions of informal workers in India, neither do they quite belong to the category of formal workers. Chandrashekhar (2014) has identified three basic features of formal employment: a written formal contract, the provision of social security (pension), and eligibility for paid leave. Some of the workers we interviewed were promised health and pension benefits, but the programs that provided them were not well implemented, and the benefits themselves were not available universally. Very few reported having written contracts, and no one reported receiving any provision for paid leave. Not all the service workers we interviewed had bank accounts. Only some received pay slips.

According to ILO statistics, workers who are informally employed within formal sectors comprise 16 percent of informal workers in India (ILO, 2012).[5] Nevertheless, their importance derives from the fact that the individual success stories of workers associated with multinational technology firms have come to symbolize new discourses of development, progress, entrepreneurialism, and modernity linked to neoliberalism in India. We explore the diverse manifestations of informality and varied employment relationships in the lives of three groups of workers who work within formal sector multinational technology firms—drivers, housekeepers, and security guards. We argue that these workers share characteristics of both formally employed and informally employed workers, fitting into neither of these categories. It is in this sense that their informality is "hidden." It is also hidden because these uniformed, highly visible workers and their work are widely described using a strongly articulated discourse of compliance and state regulation.

Informalization Through "Compliant" Contract Labor

Subcontracting regimes[6] involve the severing of the employment relationship between workers and their organization of work, which Weil (2014) refers to as "fissuring." Fissuring involves outsourcing all work not deemed related to an organization's "core competencies." As outsourced work is further outsourced, workers' conditions diminish as incentives to cut corners rise. Such fissuring facilitates an increase in the distance between employer and place of employment and in turn allows for the evasion of provisions regulating hours of work and wages while at the same time allowing transnational corporations to promote a discourse of compliance. Ideologically, the emphasis placed by multinational technology firms in India on compliance allows officials to promote their organizations as progressive, fair workplaces with more in common with head offices in the global North than with local Indian firms in terms of labor practices. Indeed, many observers viewing the uniformed service workers employed at technology firms would likely assume that they were hired under formal contracts. In fact, many managers of technology firms and even some contractors were emphatic in their claim that despite the use of subcontracting, conditions of these service jobs met the requirements of local labor laws. Our visit with Jaidev was typical of such a discourse of compliance. Jaidev, a regional manager for a large security company, told us that the aim of his company was to maintain high labor standards. He outlined in English laws and regulations related to wages and working time that his company had documentary proof that it followed and observed:

> Normally we work mainly with the multinational companies and big houses since we are very particular about the payment structure. . . . Only big multinational companies, big corporations pay as per the

government's minimum wages. . . . Whatever the statutory dues and regulations that is there, IT is very much particular for maintaining those compliance parts. . . . We need to be very careful about paperwork, because unless and until we are compliant we cannot reply to the clients because it is all in papers. So that is the way the IT companies are. . . . Since most of the IT companies have got international tie up, so this is accountability for the respective unit to their parent body. They are more conscious about the worker's interest.

It is significant that the benchmarks of "compliance" universally used by managers at transnational firms are adherence with India's minimum wage legislation and company payment into health and pension benefit schemes (PF and ESI, see note 1). This is despite the fact that many managers and officials openly acknowledge that minimum wage levels are insufficient given the rising costs of rent and food in the city, and that government benefit schemes are severely lacking (Jhabvala, 1998). This widely held belief is supported by numerous social statistics. Abraham, Singh, and Pal (2014) note, for example, that minimum wage levels are significantly lower than other measures, such as fair wage or living wage calculations, that are more accurately indexed to the rising cost of living. The Tripartite Committee on Fair Wages defines the living wage as the amount that a human being needs to secure the basic essentials of food, shelter, clothing, protection against ill-health, and security for old age. A fair wage is lower than this level, and the minimum wage is even lower (Sampath, 2016). Workers paid minimum wage cannot live at more than poverty levels, and accompanying benefit schemes are fraught with hurdles related to access. As a result, even if workers were "formally" employed, this would only marginally improve their prospects given minimum wage calculations' gross underestimations of the cost of living. Nevertheless, transnational corporations in India use both their focus on compliance and their adoption of minimum wage (rather than living wage) rates as measures of this compliance to position themselves as fair employers and benevolent globalists.

Insufficient as they are, however, provisions related to minimum wages and benefits are themselves not always followed, according to the workers we interviewed. This lack of compliance occurs on numerous dimensions along which informality occurs. Drivers, housekeepers, and security guards all experience job insecurity, work irregular shifts, and are subject to income fluctuations. They are hired through subcontractors (also referred to as vendors), and some are deployed at the same worksite for years, while others are continually shifted from site to site. Workers at the architecturally lavish sites of multinational technology companies do not typically have written contracts that specify the terms of their employment. Across all three sectors (security, transport, and housekeeping), vendors discussed the aggressive competition for contracts. Many vendors operated out of small, densely used offices, apartments within residential buildings, or shophouses. Old furniture, sparsely decorated rooms, and stained walls were not uncommon. Contract turnover was reported to be high—vendors noted that they often won or lost contracts because of small price differences in quotes. As a result, there is considerable pressure to cut labor costs. Workers noted that long shifts and the failure to pay overtime were common. Housekeepers were the poorest paid of the three groups, and a number of workers interviewed were paid less than minimum wage and in cash. A significant number of drivers were in fact owner/drivers (or small entrepreneurs) and as subcontractors were not subject to legislated minimum wage standards. Security guards were by and large better paid (and required more education and better literacy skills) than either drivers or housekeepers, but their fines and uniform costs frequently depressed their actual wages.

The rhetorical assertion of compliance by multinational firms together with the widespread prevalence of practices of informality also occur in the context of extremely poor enforcement of labor laws. A labor official we interviewed, frustrated with the limited resources allocated for labor inspections and computerization efforts, informed us that officials were unable to even maintain a complete list of vendors who had been licensed. Indeed, the mammoth scope of the task of labor law enforcement was clearly evident during our interview at the state labor office, which had wall-to-wall filing cabinets and stacks of papers piled from floor to ceiling. The office contained paper documentation of the 450,000 establishments in Pune. We were told that it rarely received complaints from workers, and that enforcement of labor laws primarily occurred through proactive inspections of workplaces. Funding was allocated for 75 inspections per month, and given the host of other industries in which widespread labor law violations exist and state policy linking national economic progress to foreign investment, inspections at transnational technology firms were rare. Consequently, limited inspection resources were generally devoted to local industries with known violations and without unusually large managerial and legal resources to challenge labor inspectors' findings. Even when violations were identified by the labor department, however, firms faced fines as low as INR 500 (about US$7) for minimum wage infringements (Shyam Sundar, 2010). Despite his long tenure with the department, the official we interviewed could not remember a single inspection that involved a transnational technology company. In line with this, a report by the All India Organization of Employers reveals that across the country there have been an extremely small number of convictions for violations of the Contract Labour Act (Breman, 2010, p. 348). At the same time, the state's depiction of India's favorable climate for business investment depends on the promotion of labor as both inexpensive and flexible. As a result, the construction of employers as nonexploitative, together with the nonenforcement of labor laws, is a necessary part of India's appeal to foreign transnational corporations. As Agarwala (2007) has noted, informal workers are often portrayed as the "ideal" workers to support India's quest for global capital.

Hidden and Varied Informality

Not only is informality masked by a veneer of assumed compliance, but it is also a heterogeneous phenomenon. Although each group of workers we interviewed experienced similar patterns of informality, the employment relationships within the housekeeping, security, and transportation sectors reveal some examples of the different ways in which contracting relationships are manifest in the contemporary global economy.

The Housekeeping Sector

The "professionalization" of cleaning and its transformation into a highly controlled, mechanized industry has been accompanied by the rise of a labor process based almost entirely on the use of subcontracting and the severing of the employment relationship between workers and their place of work. Ethnographic research in multiple countries reveals that the prevalence of subcontracting in India's corporate cleaning industry is typical of other countries as well. In their case study of the practices of ISS, a large multinational cleaning contractor, for example, Aguiar (2006) reports that the emergence of subcontracting has led to an intensification of work for workers, with nine-hour shifts, wages that rarely rise above the minimum, the disappearance of unions, and a reliance on short-term contracts. ISS workers interviewed in Australia also reported working conditions that violated local labor laws, including underpayment, cash payments, and avoidance of leave entitlements (Campbell & Peeters, 2008). Similarly, in Chile, Tomic, Trumper, and Dattwyler note that "the concept of cleanliness as an expression of the modernity claimed by neoliberalism for a small part of Chilean society comes at a high human cost, in the form of precarious labour under harsh conditions and low wages" (2006, p. 525). In a study of janitors in Toronto, Soni-Sinha and Yates (2013) note that cleaning in many global cities is done by immigrant workers. They show that "cleaning work is poorly paid, has low social value and is invisible work, often done in the dead of night when clients are gone. Under the cloak of invisibility, employers subject these workers to harsh, often abusive, treatment as though somehow doing dirty work justifies this behavior" (p. 3). Aguiar's (2001) study of office cleaners in Toronto reveals that technology can masculinize work, draw attention to the fact that such work requires skill, and also be used to intensify work. For example, the "backpack" vacuum cleaner can not only place physical demands on workers to carry a heavy weight but also require them to cover more cleaning space than would be possible with a more traditional cleaning technique (p. 254). Søgaard et al. (2006) find that Danish hospital cleaners report health-related problems and the negative impact of technological equipment on their bodies. Similarly, in a study of cleaners at a university in South Africa, Bezuidenhour and Fakier (2006) note that the end of apartheid in 1994 was followed by the proliferation of neoliberal policies that led to increases in outsourcing and subcontracted work. Not only did more than half of the university cleaners lose their jobs, but the remaining cleaners had their wages slashed to one-third and lost their nonwage benefits. These strategies were justified on the basis of the use of more machinery and management efficiencies. These case studies from countries around the world suggest that the cleaning industry is notorious for its poor labor standards, regardless of whether contractors are large multinational firms or smaller local operations.

The subcontracting out of housekeeping services is the norm among companies in the multinational technology sector in India. Housekeeping contractors providing services range similarly from small, newly established companies led by local entrepreneurs to large transnational cleaning corporations (see figure 1.1).

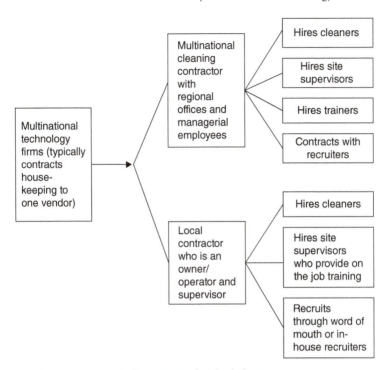

FIGURE 1.1 Subcontracting in the corporate cleaning industry.

Global Cleaning[7] was a large multinational cleaning firm where we met a manager, Akash, in a small conference room that was part of the company's office space in a walk-up building close to a special economic zone in the city. Akash informed us that his company hired over 1,000 cleaners in Pune alone, 70 percent of whom were male. Despite the significant size of the corporation, a small inconspicuous signboard signaled its presence. Independently, we interviewed Manas, a facilities manager at a large glass-faced, multistory multinational technology company that contracted the services of Global Cleaning. Through separate recruitment methods we also interviewed five male (Navin, Viresh, Surya, Vivek, and Rohit) and one female (Megha) Global Cleaning housekeepers who were deployed at a variety of multinational technology firms.

Five years ago, 34-year-old Megha joined Global Cleaning as a housekeeper because of her family's financial needs. Members of the research team met Megha in her one-bedroom home, which she and her children

shared with her brother-in-law and his family. She told us that she had
sought housekeeping work to supplement the family income, although
her first few weeks on the job had been very hard because she had had
to adjust to wearing a "shirt and pant" instead of the sari she had been
used to. She said, "I felt shy. . . . I found it very dirty work, I did not
want it." Over time, however, Megha discovered that her housekeeping
job was quite different from domestic cleaning. She listed off what she
had learned about chemicals: "R2 is for computers. R3 is for glass. R4
for wooden things, for polishing. R5 is an air freshener. We spray it in
washrooms. R6 is used once a week. That is used only for the WC and
washroom. . . . To clean taps we use D7." With pride, she said, "In the beginning I had no knowledge of these chemicals. I could not understand
their use. I thought I would not be able to do this work. I could not even
hold a dry mop. Everyone used to laugh and ask me if I am capable of
doing anything. I said, No, let me try, and over time I learned. Now I
do fine. Other women gave me confidence, saying, 'Do it, you can do
it.'" Megha valued the camaraderie and community that accompanied
her job and emphasized that she was proud to be working in a job that
provided her a uniform and identity card. At the same time, she had not
informed anyone except her immediate family about the nature of her
work. Rules she had to follow included always being "nice and clean,"
having an unstained uniform, wearing no jewelry at work, and minimizing her conversation with coworkers. Megha lamented that she had
pain in her hands, legs, and chest because her job required her to stand
continuously. While she was well aware of the challenges of this kind
of work, it had also given her a new sense of belonging and identity. A
year prior to our interview, Megha's husband had passed away. After
his death she used her earnings of INR 6,300 per month (INR 5,700
after deductions for state pension and health benefits) to support her
family, including paying the school fees for her two children, which cost
over INR 10,000 per year because they both attended private English-
medium schools. She told us that she wanted her children to be educated so "they won't have to do the same things that I have done." Megha
belonged to the scheduled caste community of Mahars, who have historically valued education as a key instrument of upward social and
economic mobility. Although she had attempted to access her health
benefits, she had been told that her registration process was incomplete.
She was sometimes required to work "double shifts" when another
housekeeper was absent, and she was paid a flat sum of INR 150 per
five-hour overtime shift. She reported that many of the housekeepers in

her workplace complained about the low overtime pay. Indeed, in the housekeeping sector as a whole, overtime work occupies a gray zone in which legally sanctioned guidelines for remuneration are rarely followed, even in companies such as Global Cleaning, which is one of the larger and better-established cleaning contractors.

While Megha was a local resident, the five male Global Cleaning workers the research team interviewed were all migrants from rural areas. They were employed at different firms, but all reported earning just over INR 6,000 per month, with deductions for state pension and health benefits. All worked eight- or nine-hour shifts, with some overtime shifts and one day off per week. Surya and Vivek reported that Global Cleaning paid INR 700 to the agents who had recruited them in their respective villages. They lived in company-provided residences in the city. Both were young single men (21 and 23 years of age) who had completed nine years of schooling. Neither had been told about the kind of work he would do in the city, and both said they would not have come if they had known it was cleaning work. Surya stated, "This job doesn't have any dignity. Back home we can't tell anyone about the nature of our jobs that we do, like toilet cleaning work." Yet when Surya compared his current employment with his previous work, he noted, "In the village the salary is lower. . . . We have to work under the scorching sun in the fields, but here we are working in air-conditioned environments in nice, tall, glass buildings." Their employment in nice, tall, glass buildings, however, involved the possibility of the erosion of their wages through fines and the requirement of poorly paid overtime work. Navin explained, "We have to tuck our shirt in, wear black socks, trim our hair. Shoes have to be polished, and we have to shave every day. We have a pouch that contains a duster and a pair of hand gloves. If we forget these things we are fined INR 100." Workers told us that they received INR 23 per hour for overtime work, and that overtime shifts were eight hours. This was less than the wages they received for their regular shifts, even though they were legally entitled to twice their regular wages for overtime work. Navin noted, "Overtime is compulsory for the housekeeper on the second shift." He described his most recent workday as follows:

> I woke up at 5 a.m., got ready at 6 a.m. and came to the office at 6:30 and signed in at the security gate and started work at 7 a.m. After the prayers, the supervisor gave us the list of tasks for the day. . . . I had to handle north and south wing on the second floor. There are four washrooms in total. I cleaned those. At 4 p.m. I started my overtime duty. This is compulsory. It was over at 10 p.m.

In addition to poorly paid overtime, not all of the workers were able to access their benefits. Vivek described a trip to the hospital during which he attempted to make use of his health benefits but was unable to do so because he was told that the correct paperwork was not in place. In contrast to these accounts, Akash, the manager we met at Global Cleaning, informed us that unlike many other cleaning contractors, his company "has everyone on the rolls." He reported that cleaning in the technology sector was easy because company employees were "sophisticated" and had very high cleanliness standards: "Every washroom should be smelling good and clean. . . . Cafeteria should be neat and clean, their workstations should be neat and clean, their desktops and keyboards should be dust free." Akash told us that the influx of multinational firms into India's labor market has led to radical changes in approaches to cleaning. A decade ago, he said, "people never used to look at [cleaning jobs] with dignity, but today [a lot of] people are working in housekeeping. People know what a housekeeping job is. Earlier it was just a *jharu pochha* kind of a job [like domestic work]. People never used to take it so seriously, but now cleaning is a science." Akash insisted that in line with "government circulars," the company officially paid workers INR 6,000 for eight hours of work. State health and pension benefits to workers "start[ed] from day one," since, as Akash noted, it was "120 percent mandatory" that the company comply with labor law. Global Cleaning contracted the services of a "labor consultant" who prepared the evidence of compliance for companies and state officials. Indeed, Manas, who was the facilities manager at a large call center that contracted Global Cleaning, noted that the call center preferred to deal with large international companies because they were able to provide all the paperwork required to show that they were in compliance with local laws.

These trends were not limited to those employed with Global Cleaning. Out of the 33 housekeepers we interviewed, only 20 said they received benefits such as PF and ESI and had been given formal documentation showing deductions. Three-quarters did not receive minimum wage when hours were taken into account. None had a written contract, and one-third, predominantly women, were paid in cash. Many workers seemed uncertain about their exact deductions. Sangeeta, a 30-year-old female housekeeper, explained, for example, "We get Provident Fund, but we haven't been given the 'slip' yet. They don't give us the payment slip. They pay cash. I said to the Sir [contractor] that they should give us the slip so that we know how much is being deducted from our salary." Wages could be further depressed because of fines or deductions for uniforms and shoes. These slippages suggest that the focus on compliance and the creation of documentary "proof" of minimum wage and PF/ESI payments ignores the issues of whether benefits reach all workers or whether they result in workers being able to access health or pension services, neither of which was seen to be a concern of contractors or multinational technology firms. Indeed, when we asked about whether workers were paid PF and ESI, many contractors provided convoluted and indirect responses, such as Vallabh, a contractor we interviewed, who said, "There are government rules, but the company doesn't implement them. What can I do? I began my housekeeping contract three months ago. So far we haven't given PF to anybody. [But] the PF file of all the housekeepers is ready with me." Although contractors and facilities managers uniformly noted the advantages of working in the cleaning sector, such as working in air-conditioned spaces, and emphasized the importance of wearing gloves and masks when using chemicals, many cleaners in fact noted the health hazards that accompanied their work. Sangeeta reported, "My legs hurt because of my work. I have to stand the whole day." Sapana, who frequently worked night shifts, complained of chronic acidity and indigestion. Viresh admitted, "I get very tired. I sleep as soon as I get home." Bharat suffered from "hand pain and leg pain." Prashant was given one day off, which he referred to as an "ESI holiday," because chemicals splashed in his eye and he could not see. Vivek complained of problems with his eyes and skin because of the chemicals he used.

A significant dimension of informality in the housekeeping sector concerned hours of work. Overtime was expected and compulsory for 40 percent of the housekeepers we interviewed, and workers unanimously noted being poorly paid for overtime hours. Often overtime was unscheduled—that is, workers were required to stay for another shift if their coworkers were absent. Manoj reported, "If the payment for one shift is INR 6,000, then we get half of it for overtime. Now I am receiving INR 5,000. If I do OT, then I get 7,500." At times, extended workdays were not even recognized as overtime work. Manish explained, "There is no concept of overtime at all. If there are visitors such as the GM or the manager or some foreign guests we have to stay for two hours extra. For the last four to five days we have been staying longer at work. But we are not paid for it."

Workers also reported being asked to adjust work times to accommodate work intensification. Vijaya, who worked for an organization with 500 employees, described her experience: "At first there were three of us, but then they dismissed the third person. I told our supervisor, 'If you have dismissed that person, then at least raise our salary,' but he didn't listen." As a result of her workload, Vijaya said she had to arrive half an hour early (without overtime pay) to complete her tasks. Indeed, even the labor official we interviewed recognized the widespread violation of hours of work laws and told us, "In one of the IT industries I asked one of the workers, a housekeeping worker [about hours]. . . . I was shocked to hear that they are asked to work for 10 hours and . . . [the company was] paying them for 8 hours. So that is paying less than minimum wage."[8]

Overall, housekeepers received lower monthly salaries than security guards or drivers. They were more likely to have benefits than drivers but less likely than security guards. Of the three groups of low-wage service workers we interviewed, housekeepers also had the fewest other job options, since the majority of them were from scheduled caste communities of poor to modest means and their educational qualifications were limited. Few could amass savings or envision any career mobility. As we will discuss in chapter 2, however, despite their economic conditions, housekeepers are at the forefront of creating and maintaining the spaces closely associated with wealth and modernity in postliberalization India.

The Transportation Sector

The nature of informality within the transportation sector is vastly different from that in the housekeeping and security service sectors, as shown in figure 1.2. We found no multinational transportation companies in Pune. Local firms predominated in this sector, including some that were quite large (with up to 1,500 cars) and others with only a few dozen cars. Smaller firms contracted their services directly to multinational technology companies or to larger subcontractors. All companies we studied included a mix of hired drivers for company-owned cars and contracts with "owner-drivers." The larger subcontractors provided loan schemes under which they served as guarantors on loans to drivers, who after three years of repayments could become car owners.

One company that we will call Flight Cars provides a vivid illustration of subcontracting arrangements within the transportation sector.

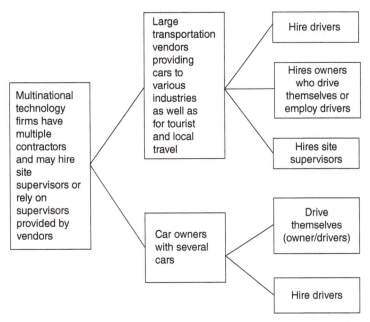

FIGURE 1.2 Subcontracting in the corporate transportation industry.

Members of the research team separately and independently interviewed two managers at large IT firms that contracted Flight Cars (Balder and Nidhi), a manager at Flight Cars (Devrani), a site supervisor hired by Flight Cars (Babu), two driver/owners (Hari and Pradeep), and four drivers (Harish, Ravi, Siddharth, and Akhil).

Flight Cars contracted a fleet of 1,000 cars and employed more than 1,500 drivers and owner/drivers in Pune. A majority of its clients were multinational software firms or call center companies, and they provided transportation services for about 30 companies. Flight Cars was one of the oldest transportation companies in the city and started out by providing staff transportation 15 years ago at the start of the boom in the multinational technology sector. Most of its drivers came from neighboring small towns and villages. A significant number belonged to the upper-caste Maratha community, while others were members of scheduled castes such as the Mahars and Neo-Buddhists. On average, drivers had 9 to 12 years of education, although one of the drivers we interviewed had only a third-grade education. Drivers were described by Devrani, a manager at the company, as "lower class" and "addicted to many things," although out of the six drivers employed at Flight Cars whom we interviewed, only one reported "drinking occasionally." Nidhi, the facilities manager at a large multinational company that contracted transportation services from Flight Cars, reported that she had a team responsible for ensuring that subcontractors paid the required employee benefits to workers. Contractors were required to present receipts for ESI and PF payments each month before their invoices were paid.

Flight Cars had 400 direct employees (most of whom were supervisors), comprising about a third of those involved with the company. The rest of the people connected with the company were either car owners who contracted their cars to Flight Cars or individuals who were part of an "assurance" scheme, which a company official described as a partnership between a driver and a company. Devrani explained that driver/owners "are partners in this so when they are the owners they have the responsibility to run the vehicles responsibly . . . because they are half owners, as after three years the car will be theirs." Loan schemes were presented as an opportunity for entrepreneurship, ownership, and class mobility. Individuals could take out loans to purchase cars and operate them under the Flight Cars banner. The "vendors" could then either drive the cars themselves or hire drivers on their own. Hari, who was just 22 years old, had migrated to Pune five years earlier and purchased a car one and a half years earlier. He told us that he received INR 55,000 per month from Flight Cars. He paid nearly INR 20,000 for diesel, INR 10,000 for loan repayment, and INR 2,000 to 5,000 for servicing. The remainder—INR 20,000 to 25,000—was his salary and went toward covering expenses such as car maintenance, cleaning costs, and fines levied by employers for late arrivals, improper uniforms, or cars that did not meet cleanliness standards. Hari's schedule involved an extremely long workday, which he started at 4 a.m. He said, "I have pickups till noon. Then I come home, pick up my tiffin, and eat my tiffin at around 2, 2:30 p.m. Then I rest for one and a half hours. Then there are two or three drops in the evening. Then I go home and sleep. In the morning I get calls about pickups again."

Out of the four drivers working for Flight Cars whom we interviewed, only one reported receiving employee benefits (ESI or PF). Devrani, the manager at Flight Cars, was aware that many drivers did not receive benefits and told us, "We don't know the drivers personally;

those drivers are not on our payroll, we don't know them." Her view was that many drivers themselves were not keen to have deductions taken from their already low salaries. Therefore, vendors might show fewer drivers operating each vehicle than was the case (e.g., even if a car was being operated by two or three drivers, only one might be shown as the official driver for whom deductions have to be taken). Despite having no direct employment relationships with drivers, Devrani explained that the multinational technology sector has high expectations of drivers. She described the ideal driver: "He shouldn't eat tobacco while driving, he should not spit outside the car, car should be clean, and seat covers should be clean." In order to ensure that all drivers met these requirements, Flight Cars had started a training institute. Hari described the training he had received: "We learn from IT Company that being clean and good are good qualities." Site supervisors had the responsibility of monitoring workers' movements, behaviors, uniforms, and cars. Babu, who had a bachelor's of science degree and earned INR 6,000 for an eight-hour shift, described his work as a site supervisor as follows:

> We download all the data, divide it roadwise, and then prepare roster by adding location, area, and timing. It took me three months to learn everything. It is a risky job with high responsibility. The timings of the associate should be perfect, and there should not be any single mistake. Also there should not be any delay in pickup and drop timing of the cab. If there is delay in pickup timing of the cab, then the employees send emails, and they make issue of it. Naturally then the pressure comes on us. So this is an important job.[9]

Despite the stressful nature of his job, Babu hoped to stay with the company and expected to be promoted. In the meantime, he had a second job and his wife was also earning wages.

We found that the subcontracting arrangements in place at Flight Cars were prevalent across companies. We heard many tales of the promise that the sector held for drivers, who had the possibility of becoming owners. The owner/driver model was widely promoted by both contractors and facility managers at multinational technology firms as a form of entrepreneurship through which drivers could become worthy citizens, just like the software and call center workers who were valorized as being at the forefront of economic development.[10] Ashwin, a transport vendor who ran and managed a fleet of 33 cars and 55 drivers in Pune, characterized the transportation sector as following a

cooperative model much like the Amul milk cooperative: "All the vehicles they come and get associated. . . . They get attached with us. Then
we train them [drivers], groom them, and then we ensure their livelihood is met."

Given this potential for significant economic mobility, we met
many workers who had sold family land or entered into loan schemes
to acquire a car that they could then contract out to vendors. Yet, as we
note in chapter 3, many drivers did not share this optimism for their
economic prospects.[11] Our sample consisted of 13 owner/drivers and
18 drivers. Drivers' earnings ranged from INR 3,500 to INR 10,000 per
month, with the latter brought in by drivers working 24-hour days.
Owner-drivers were able to earn more—most reported receiving INR
20,000–25,000 each month from the contractor of their cars. However,
because they were responsible for any unanticipated expenses and drivers' salaries, owner/drivers reported take-home earnings of between
INR 6,000 and INR 40,000, depending on how many hours they themselves drove and the number of cars they owned. Raja described the
breakdown of his expenses in some detail, showing us his most recent
pay slip: "These are the kilometers that I drove. It is 7,749. I got INR
49,043 for that. Diesel charge is INR 18,622; they have added INR 400
charge in it. I was charged fine of INR 1,000, and INR 10,055 is gone
towards [insurance] for the car. I got INR 18,966 in hand. From that I
need to pay INR 4,500 for rent, monthly expenses of INR 5,000 - 6,000,
savings . . . is INR 5,000 . . . quarterly."

Only 4 of the 31 respondents we interviewed received health or
pension benefits, and the remainder therefore incurred health costs and
did not have access to a pension plan. Drivers such as Raja said that
despite owning a car through a loan scheme, they were able to meet
family expenses and pay their loans off only if they worked as a driver
for 24 hours a day. Like him, many drivers worked extremely long hours
in an attempt to pay their loans off, and many recognized the significant
risk, which they were exposed to. Out of the sample of 31 drivers we
interviewed, only one worked eight-hour days. Twelve worked 12-hour
shifts, 8 worked between 12 and 24 hours per day, and 10 worked
24-hour shifts (sleeping between dropoffs and pickups). Most reported
getting one or two days per week off, although many said this time was
spent sleeping given their exhausting workweeks. Drivers also reported
fluid work times—Raghu informed us, "My duty starts at 7 a.m. and in
the evening. . . . There is nothing fixed."

Despite the physically and economically well-established formal enterprises for which drivers provided services, there were multiple intermediaries between drivers and these companies. Such a system not only resulted in many workers being excluded from labor laws because they worked for themselves or for other very small enterprises, but also led to a situation in which laws or practices that served to protect low-wage workers were practically impossible to enforce. As a result, practices of informality pervaded the work done by drivers, for whom the only route to class mobility was one laden with risk and uncertainty.

The Security Sector

In India, the security sector is distinct from other service sectors such as housekeeping and transportation. A unique relationship has been forged in the sector between private companies, the state, and labor organizations, as shown in figure 1.3. There are two reasons for this distinct manifestation of informality. First, security firms play a role in national strategies related to veteran reintegration, with many Indian military personnel choosing to "retire" into jobs within this sector, and public rural development, with unemployed youth from villages entering the world of waged work through security jobs. Second, unlike other industries, the security sector was only gradually affected by India's economic liberalization policies since the early 1990s. India's colonial past played a role in the hesitation to allow the unrestrained entry of foreign security firms into the country. Despite embracing neoliberal globalization in other sectors, state bureaucrats often emphasized the need to maintain indigenous hegemony over security provision. As a result of these unique features, there has historically been a significant level of state, employer association, union, and activist intervention into the security sector. These symbols of formality pervade the sector, yet, as our analysis in this section reveals, security is also significantly marked by informality.

Currently, the security sector in India is governed by a staggering number of intersecting regulations. The sector has its own national association (the Central Association of Private Security Industry), a governing act (the Private Securities Agencies Regulation Act, or PSAR), and in some regions a guard board (e.g., the Maharashtra Security Guard Board and Nashik District Security Board). In some states, such as Maharashtra, these boards long predate the national act or association—the Maharashtra Security Guard Board (MSGB), for

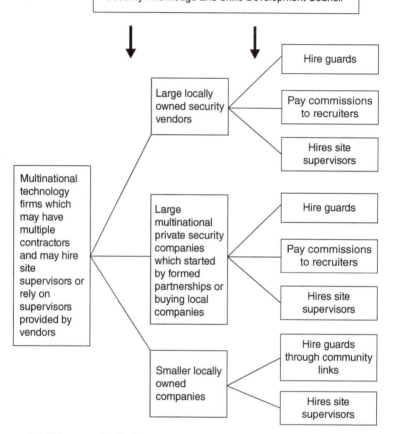

FIGURE 1.3 Subcontracting in the corporate security industry.

example, was established in 1981 (Agarwala, 2013). Despite the normalization of informal contract employment relationships within the security sector, the state has far from receded from its role as a regulator of security work. Instead, the acts and regulations that have been periodically introduced to keep up with the exponentially expanding scale of the industry have led to a maze of regulatory regimes, leaving not only a state of considerable confusion but also ample potential for the misinterpretation of the rules. For example, the relationship between the MSGB and the PSAR in Maharashtra in terms of setting wages and working conditions is still under negotiation (Berrong, 2009), yet the regulations promulgated by both are in effect. Given this regulatory maze, enforcement efforts to ensure that labor standards are being met are by and large few and ineffective.

At the same time, considerable state policy attention has been devoted to dealing with ideological opposition to the foreign ownership of companies that provide security services, given the assumed national aim of protecting assets within India. Although historically there have been restrictions on foreign investment in the security industry, in June 2016 the Indian government announced that 100 percent foreign direct investment would now be allowed in the defense industry (Anand & Kumar, 2016), despite objections from local contractors (Drèze & Sen, 2013). As part of the "Make in India" initiative, the government also simplified the approval process for foreign firms to set up organizations in India (Kumar, 2017). Anticipating these changes, G4S, a $10 billon transnational security company, announced plans to expand its operations in India. Its India-based operations now include 36 training centers and the recruitment of 6,500 guards per month (Srivastava, 2013).

Like the housekeeping and transportation sectors, the private security sector largely relies on subcontracting rather than direct hiring (Gooptu 2013). Upadhyay's field research in the national capital region suggests that the pool of security contractors includes small firms employing fewer than 250 guards as well as large multinational corporations with over 10,000 employees (2011, p. 346; see also Nagaraj, 2012; Kumar, 2015). The use of subcontracting in the security sector around the world has led to attempts to develop global agreements governing the sphere and efforts to engage in collective bargaining (McCallum, 2013).

Security Pro is a company that illuminates the social organization of the sector in India. An Indian company established in the early 2000s, it now employs over 9,000 security guards in a variety of settings across India. About half of its workforce is in Pune. Security Pro contracts its services to more than 100 multinational technology companies, including some of the largest and most established software companies and call centers in Pune. All of the founding members of the company whom we met were ex-military men. The research team independently interviewed six male managers or directors at Security Pro (Vidhu, Inder, Jatin, Dhananjay, Abhinav, and Lakshman), five male guards (Vishal, Raj, Nikhil, Prathamesh, and Veeresh), and one female guard (Anjali), all of whom were employed by Security Pro and deployed at a variety of sites. The majority of the security guards belonged to the Maratha caste. Some were from scheduled castes, especially the Neo-Buddhist Mahars. The security company managers or directors did not introduce any of the guards to us; we contacted them independently. Aside from Vishal, who was born in Pune, all of the guards were migrants whose families owned farmland in villages within Maharashtra and in other parts of India. Independently, we also interviewed a facilities manager at a large multinational call center that contracted security services from Security Pro and a labor activist who described an arbitration case involving Security Pro.

The Security Pro office was in a large building with a prominent sign indicating its location. The company's setup consisted of several offices for the managers, a reception area, and a large room where two dozen people were completing application forms during our visit. The physical space suggested a formal and efficient organization; as we walked to our meeting room, we passed cubicles labeled "compliance," "training," and "payment." We were told that recruitment was a continuous process, since turnover in the sector was high. Managers related the high turnover to the sector's high expectations and low wages. Vidhu told us, in English, that it was not uncommon for guards to have more than one full-time job to meet their expenditures: "A liter of milk is costing INR 47. You must understand a security guard getting an amount of INR 5,800—how can he manage himself? How can he manage his wife, the parents, the schooling, electricity? The cost of living has gone so high. . . . [The companies should] pay a little better than what the minimum wages that government has prescribed." The low wages common in the field were especially significant in light of the numerous skills that security guards were required to possess. Abhinav reported, "In India nobody wants to work in a security field. . . . Today in India security is considered as unskilled profession . . . [but] there are a lot of expectations of the company regarding guards. Companies want guards having knowledge of computers, they expect guards should know driving and many more things. . . . As IT companies receive international calls, companies demand that the guard should know English." In addition to these skills, many companies also expressed a preference for ex-servicemen, although wages were typically too low to be attractive to this group.

Despite general laments about low wages and high cost of living, every manager we interviewed at Security Pro was emphatic about the company's compliance with local laws. In order to remain compliant with the law, the contractor often switched guards from company to company, as Vidhu noted: "One fellow from [IT firm #1] joins [IT firm #2] and vice versa, that is, another fellow from [IT firm #2] joins [IT firm #1]." Indeed, managers discussed the security sector's numerous laws and regulations with precision. Abhinav and Inder explained these regulations and were careful during our conversations to stress that their company followed them to a tee.

Upward mobility was deemed to be possible through career progression. Vidhu noted that two of the company's current directors had at one time been guards, and that guards could follow a clear progression within the company: "Security guard to head guard to supervisor, then after supervisor a coordinator who coordinates all the activities, and then security officer, then [after] security officer, you can go up to the assignment manager level." However, none of the workers from Security Pro reported any career progression. The longest-serving guard we interviewed, Veeresh, had been with the company for four years and aside from being shifted from one location to another had not been promoted at all. His salary had increased in line with the increasing minimum wage rate. He hoped in the future to join the police force. Prathamesh, who had previously worked as a police officer in another state and had left because he feared for his safety given continuous local civil unrest, said that he was planning to return to his place of origin because of his low earnings. Raj similarly intended to return to farming once he had saved some money. Anjali referred to security work as a low-status job and reported that she had not informed anyone in her family about the nature of her work. These workers reported considerable difficulty meeting their basic living costs with their base salaries of between INR 6,000 and INR 8,000, a range in tune with minimum wage levels in the 2010–2014 period. However, these official wage rates were not what workers in fact received. Workers reported paying more than INR 1,000 for uniforms and shoes, a mandatory cost. Furthermore, supervision within the security sector occurs through a harsh system of fines, which serves both to discipline workers and to depress their wages. Anjali reported:

> When I started my job, I forgot to take my walkie-talkie when I went to the washroom. I left it on the table. When I came out, it wasn't there. I kept searching for it. Our supervisor had come and confiscated it, and he told me I would have to pay a fine of INR 500. This was my first day, so I went to the higher-level officer and he said, 'Okay, I will exempt you this time, but be careful.' . . . When you are fined, one day's salary can be taken away. Fines start from INR 50–60. You are fined if you come half an hour late, or if you don't go to your point straight away and go somewhere else to chat, or if you let an employee bring in a cell phone or allow a car to enter without checking. If we argue with the supervisor, he gives you a higher fine. It all depends on the supervisor. . . . If gents come to work without shaving or without hair cut, then there is a fine of INR 150. . . . It all depends on the concerned supervisor as to how much he would charge for each mistake. On duty, if you chew tobacco or *guthka*, then there is a fine for that.

Vishal similarly recounted: "There was a security guard who had a walkie-talkie gadget, and it broke. They deducted INR 1,000 every month from his salary. The total amount deducted was INR 5,000. One guard hit the windowpane with his stick while shooing away flies and the glass broke. He was fined."

Although Vidhu, the manager, reported that his company did not keep guards on duty for more than eight hours, the guards from Security Pro whom we interviewed reported that they were often forced to do overtime. Because of weekly rotating shifts, none were able to take stable second jobs outside the company. Veeresh, for example, told us that he worked eight regular hours and four overtime hours each day. Vishal reported: "Last month I did 30 regular shifts and 28 extra shifts. So I got INR 6,000 extra over my salary of INR 6,000, so totally I took INR 12,000."

All workers reported receiving pay slips and deductions for health and pension benefits (PF and ESI). Despite the seemingly formalized nature of their work, none of the guards interviewed had a written contract specifying their exact pay, benefits, bonuses, and hours. Workers often faced "deductions" from their pay that they did not understand. They also reported significant instability in their jobs. Anjali explained that guards could be dismissed at any time without recourse and declared, "Today every company wants to use and get rid of its workers."

When she first joined Security Pro, she had been required to sign a form that she described as follows: "If you are fired from the job for some reason, then you will not be able to go to any union or organization. Just do your job and go [home] with the money. You cannot complain about anything. Do not say anything." Vishal shared an account of his supervisor, who had fired one of his colleagues for being five minutes late.

Given the presence of a workers' association in the sector, we wondered why workers did not have more recourse to challenge unfair work practices. To answer this question we sought the input of a labor activist, Viju, who informed us that in fact Security Pro guards had made a formal complaint to the local guard board a few years before about not receiving pension, overtime, and vacation pay. At the time, Viju had been involved with the guard board and had helped broker a settlement between the workers and Security Pro. The company had been required to reimburse its guards for unpaid wages. Despite the success of this case, Viju remained deeply pessimistic about the ability of the guard board to challenge unfair labor practices. He noted that most workers felt threatened by their employers and were afraid of lodging complaints, and that bribes were often exchanged between officials and firms. Viju himself had received anonymous threats after making a set of "right to information" requests that revealed labor law violations at specific firms. Overall, Viju noted that the private security firms often strove to diminish labor costs in light of the competitive bidding processes in place at transnational firms.

While Security Pro guards had bank accounts and received PF and ESI, this was not universally the case among all the guards we interviewed. Five out of the 28 guards did not receive PF and ESI. Guards in our sample earned between INR 5,200 for a 12-hour shift and INR 10,000 for an 8-hour shift. Only one guard was an ex-army man, and his earnings were higher than those of his peers. Only two workers received payment in cash. Only one was native to Pune, with the remaining 27 having migrated from villages in Maharashtra or North India.

Two guards—Narayan and Shafeeq—are illustrative of the workers we interviewed. Both had moved to the city and improved their earnings by working extremely long hours but experienced economic insecurity. Narayan suggested that we meet in the cafeteria of the software firm where he worked. Since it was a Saturday evening, the company was closed and there were no company employees present. The cafeteria was largely deserted, with a table tennis table and a television that a few people, likely catering or housekeeping staff, were watching. With Narayan was his colleague, Shafeeq, who was also a security guard. They had met when they had been construction workers in their home state, which bordered Bangladesh and was a six-hour flight or several days' road journey away. Four years prior, Shafeeq, who had heard about employment prospects in western India, had been recruited by a security firm and decided to move because of the hazardous conditions and extremely poor pay in construction. Over the years his contractor had shifted his employment site several times and then fired him after four years. Shafeeq explained that his boss had done this to avoid paying him the benefits that would have been due to him after five years of continuous employment with the same contractor. He had quickly been able to find another employer and had also recruited Narayan, who had arrived in the city four months earlier. Both now lived together and worked back-to-back shifts in order to save as much money as possible. Narayan told us that it was very difficult for him to be in Pune because he missed his family and young child, who were still in his home state. Both spoke longingly about returning to their home and hoped to do so once they had amassed enough savings.

Just over two-thirds of the sample worked eight-hour shifts, and the remainder reported regularly working 12- or 16-hour shifts. Piyush, a contractor, provided us with a detailed account, in English, of industry norms: "Overtime as per labor rate is supposed to be double, but no client pays. I am yet to see a client in India who pays OT exactly as per the labor standards. . . . [Even IT companies are] not ready to pay double. Nobody pays." In this context, he reported that it was much less costly for a company to hire two guards for 12-hour shifts than three guards for 8-hour shifts given the savings the company would realize on benefits. These are classic evasion strategies that corporations utilize to maximize profits.

Several workers said they were encouraged not to take their "weekly offs." Guards often reported unplanned overtime for which they were paid, but not at the rate stipulated by law. Jaidev, a security vendor, explained,

> Security is 24/7 number one. Suppose one guard is doing duty at one post and if he doesn't get his reliever he cannot come out of his duty. This is the major responsibility for the guard, that until and unless he has his reliever he cannot come out of his duty. So how the reliever

will come and do the duty, we at the back office control that, but there are unforeseen issues where even we cannot predict. Because there are unforeseen absenteeism, if suppose a person cannot join duty for some reason, then that guard would have to continue.

In fact, even though we were told by many managers and subcontractors that wages in the sector had risen significantly over the past five years, current wage rates continued to be significantly depressed because of labor relations based on subcontracting networks. Hemant was unique among our respondents in that he had twenty years of experience in the security sector. Aged 60 at the time of our interviews, he supervised a team of eight guards. Hemant told us that he used to earn INR 10,000 when he first started working as a security guard 20 years earlier, noting that "before, it used to be with the company. But that system is no more. So I am with an agency." When we interviewed him, Hemant earned INR 8,000, which was paid in cash and had to cover his mandatory uniform costs as well. Dube and Kaplan (2010) term this situation the "outsourcing wage penalty"—that is, the extent to which wages are depressed due to contract work. Their research reveals that this penalty is equal to 9 to 24 percent of wages in the United States, and Hemant's experience suggests that it might be much higher in India. Hemant also contended that work sourced through agencies was unstable: "You work for 11 months, and if they like your service, you continue. Otherwise you find a new agency. . . . They just remove you. They hire new security." Indeed, on one of our visits to an area of the city with many IT firms, we approached a uniformed young man called Sandeep sitting at a desk at the entrance of a global software company for which he had been contracted to register visitors, create passes, and answer phones. Sandeep told us that he could share his experiences while he worked, although he was not allowed to share any confidential company information. Since there was a steady flow of traffic in and out of the workplace and no one lingered at the desk, he talked freely about his perception of his security job as a dead end with no prospects. He informed us that in this sector, guards could reach retirement age earning the same salary that they had commanded at their time of entry to the sector.[12]

Informality pervades the security sector despite the high level of state involvement in it. Nevertheless, perhaps because of the associations and unions that are present in this sector, we found that compared to housekeepers and drivers, security guards seemed to have much greater knowledge about the laws and regulations that governed their work. Workers at some firms reported receiving better wages and protections. For example, Kalyan and Jitendra worked for a security firm established by a union for security guards that has secured contracts with some large multinational technology firms and reported receiving wages in line with minimum wage law. Owners and contractors at this firm lamented the poor enforcement of labor laws within the sector and noted that evasions by their competitors made it difficult for them to submit competitive bids for contracts. We were told that the local guard board had three inspectors for the whole of Maharashtra, which meant that compliance inspections were rare.

Only a handful of workers we spoke to reported having engaged in collective action or launching formal complaints. Narine, a 32-year-old female security guard, recounted her experience of regularly receiving her pay two or three months late from her contractor—a trend that stopped only after she and her colleagues threatened to telephone the labor commissioner to complain. She had learned about the labor court through her brother, who had won a settlement for unpaid wages from another firm. Narine noted, "Any contract labor worker can go to labor court. They only need proof of employment . . . [but] since most of the people working here are from outside the city . . . they don't think much about these things." Shital worked for another contractor and reported that she was part of a union of security guards. Three years ago, her union had staged a job action in which they set up a picket line outside the firm and also went to the labor court to demand overtime wages in line with the law. She had received a pay increase, and the contractor, a small firm with fewer than 200 workers, had been required to pay double overtime. Despite these gains, Shital emphasized that her employer kept a careful tab on workers who were part of the union. She noted, "If I leave [this security contractor] and go somewhere else, then I will have to remove my name from the union. Only then another company will hire me." Kaveri, a 31-year-old security guard, reported that workers faced reprisals for being union members. She said that she knew about the union but had not become a member because "it is like a mark on you. Anyone who joins the union can't get respect in the IT company. . . . Company gets a call from the vendor and the vendor informs the company that this person is a member of the union and to be careful."

The poor enforcement of laws and regulation has led to a unique manifestation of informality within the security sector. Contractors, multinational technology company managers, and workers tend to be more knowledgeable about the rules that govern work within this sector. However, workers continue to experience significant evasions of the law. Multinational technology companies as well as subcontractors devote significant energy to identifying loopholes in the law that will allow them to engage in behaviors that will be difficult to detect (e.g., hiring vulnerable workers who fear reprisal, reporting fewer workers on the books than are actually working, or shifting workers from site to site). There is also a large focus on the production of documentary evidence of compliance, and through the liberal use of fines, workers are made aware that they are continually being watched and are subject to discipline.

Conclusions

Within the multinational technology sector in India, informality occurs alongside discourses of formality and compliance. Claims of compliance are bolstered by the image of the sector as one in which international standards pervade, profits are earned in dollars, and infrastructural wealth abounds. The buildings that house these companies are built with little regard for expense and rarely suffer from poor sewage or intermittent power. Service providers are uniformed and required to follow strict schedules. Companies possess rosters that contain the names of contracted employees as well as bank details, wages, and benefits. Yet loopholes exist—a fact that contractors and facilities managers themselves admit. Our interviews suggest, however, that these loopholes are far from exceptions. Indeed, subcontracting arrangements in each of the sectors examined here normalize informality, which can occur precisely because compliance claims are made so strongly. For housekeepers, rosters may indicate that workers are earning the legislated minimum wages. Yet rather than 8-hour shifts, some are required to work 12 hours for the same wage, and others are required to work overtime hours without payment at the required overtime rate. Rosters can also show deductions for benefits, but as long as the onus remains on contractors or workers to complete the paperwork or solve the bureaucratic hurdles these claims require, payments often remain far from workers' reach. In the case of drivers, compliance is only seen as relevant for those classified as drivers employed directly by larger companies, and the multiple chains of subcontracting that characterize this sector ensure that this group remains a minority, subject to highly malleable hours of work. Security guards, too, are often required to work double shifts for which they receive single-time rather than double-time pay, face fines that depress their wages, and often fail to receive benefits. Guards can lodge complaints with the local guard board and union, but they have little protection from reprisals. Furthermore, even these institutions do not always challenge job informality. In 2012, a newspaper article in the *Indian Express* reported that a security guard board inspector had been arrested after being caught on camera accepting a bribe. A footnote to the story added a year later reported that the inspector had been acquitted (Express News Service, 2012). In all three sectors we researched, workers' migration status also made them particularly vulnerable.

Our interview with Mohan, a facilities manager at a large call center, illuminates the ways in which the rhetoric of compliance is often used to mask the evasion of laws. Mohan explained that his company expected full compliance from the contractors it hired to provide transport, housekeeping, and security services. When we asked whether he reviewed the payments made to cleaners, drivers, and housekeepers, however, he cast such monitoring as beyond the scope of his responsibility:

> No, we don't see the pay slips, but while passing his [contractor's] bill we do check whether last month's statutory compliances he has done. That is whether I have 75 housekeeping boys and 50 guards on my contract; I don't see their physical presence, whether 75 housekeeping boys were there or whether 50 guards were there, we are not bothered. As far as we are concerned, the services that you have committed and the cleanliness level is maintained. So you get it done through overtime or absenteeism, that we are not bothered. . . . Our contract is based on the work, not on the number of people. But at the same time . . . any contractor who is doing this type of work, he has to provide us his last month's labor taxes paid, last month's ESI paid, PF paid, all those *challans* [official notices] he has to submit to me this month to get his bill cleared. . . . My duty [is] to clear his bills only after he has complied with these, and if he has not done, then as a principal employer we are liable to pay that.

Mohan oscillated between task-based evaluations of work (as long as the required cleanliness level was maintained, the company did not care how it was done) and concerns about accountability for workers (if ESI and PF were not paid, then his company, as the principal employer, would be liable). Despite the recognition that his company was responsible for unpaid wages or benefits, Mohan admitted that it did not keep track of the actual number of contract employees being deployed onsite:

What I am saying is, as far as payment is concerned, it is not counted. We are not giving money on man days that is present. See, there are two ways of looking at this particular problem. I check contractor's bill based on the number of man days he has supplied—that is one source. Here, I will have to actually keep checking every working boy and his working hours, his payment, and so on. We are not doing that. We have a lump sum contract, like seven lakh rupees a month will be giving you for housekeeping, which also includes not only the labor part of it, but the housekeeping material that is required and everything.

When we expressed our confusion during the interview about how the organization could confirm that every worker was being paid correctly if it was not sure about the numbers of workers who needed to be paid, Mohan responded by saying that there was only so much a company could do, as the onus was largely on the contractor to monitor and pay the staff on its payroll. He also emphasized that there was nothing that a company could do when workers did not have the correct documents to allow for the payments of benefits. He recounted:

We had one case of an employee, a housekeeping boy, who came after about a year of leaving the company that he didn't get his PF money. He came to us with a complaint of the contractor that he had not paid him. We could have said, 'You were contractor's employee, so go and talk with them.' [But] we said, 'Okay, we will find out, we will talk to the contractor and will call you later.' The thing was that this employee, though he was given a letter by the concerned person of that housekeeping agency saying he should submit his papers in this format and he should open the account in bank, because the money doesn't come to anybody's name, it goes directly to bank. He never did that. When he came to us, he didn't say that 'I have not opened the account.' Then we asked him that, 'Why you didn't open the account in the bank?' He said bank people told him that you have to keep the minimum balance of 1,000 in the bank.

Mohan noted that in rare cases of worker complaints such as these, he would instruct the contractors to pay workers: "We told [the] contractor to give him money from some sundry account and stop the issue. Why waste so much time and energy on an amount so little?" It is through these "little amounts," though, that informality is exercised in the context of large, formal multinational firms.

Overall, the rhetoric of compliance supports and props up the varied and hidden manifestations of informality that exist within the housekeeping, transport, and security sectors. It allows facilities managers and multinational technology firms to limit their concern for workers to the creation and review of documents that do not actually record whether workers are paid appropriately or not. It allows contractors to focus their energies on the creation of compliance ledgers and engage in creative accounting to ensure that they meet their contract obligations. As a result, some contractors pay workers in cash, others pay benefits only to those with bank accounts, and still others demand that their employees work overtime on a last-minute, as needed basis. Workers themselves, who often earn barely enough to meet their needs, do not always object to cash payments or no deductions, even though these practices may expose them to future hardship. Even those workers who receive pay stubs, have their salaries deposited into bank accounts, and possess health cards and pension statements often do not receive double pay for overtime hours or are unable to access health benefits when needed.

The rhetoric of compliance serves several important ideological purposes for the services sector within the multinational technology industry in India. First, it furthers companies' attempts to claim that they meet "international standards" of treatment of workers. In the context of well-publicized accounts of manufacturing and assembly firms that set up global sweatshops, multinational technology firms can claim to be engaging in projects of local development rather than exploitation even as they seek to minimize their labor costs through the payment of minimum wage, rather than a living or fair wage. Extravagant buildings and uniformed workers promote the image of employers who are self-regulating and not in need of external scrutiny. Second, this rhetoric of compliance masks contractors' efforts to find loopholes through which the letter but not the spirit of the law is followed and makes enforcement complicated and time-consuming. The chronic dearth of resources for labor law enforcement has led to a situation in which the risk of violation is low for contractors. Third, given that multinational technology companies place so much emphasis on the perfect compliance record of contractors, workers know that they will face significant reprisals for raising any issues related to their wages or working conditions. In the final analysis, informality in the services sector depresses workers' wages. Furthermore, the focus on compliance skirts another central issue that fundamentally structures workers' lives: the fact that legislated minimum wage and benefits do not allow workers to meet their basic needs. Palash, a housekeeper in a supervisory role, summarized the problem as follows: "This contract system should be stopped. . . . IT companies are earning a lot of profit, but we don't get anything. We don't have any advantages. An employee working in an IT company gets a salary of INR 100,000, but people like us don't even get 10,000."

Not all IT employees receive wages of INR 100,000, but Palash's comment reveals the key characteristics of the political economy of the subcontracting system that are so central to neoliberalism, under which transnational firms depend on depressed wages within certain countries to reduce their own labor costs. Rather than wanting to put an end to low-wage jobs, they often have a vested interest in keeping labor costs low. The continued growth of the security, transportation, and housekeeping industries depends on the proliferation of perceptions of risk, unreliable transit, and dirt, all of which exist because of wealth inequalities and the resultant uneven infrastructure investments in countries of the global North and global South.

Interestingly, even though workers' status as contract workers means that multinational technology firms make little investment in their well-being or future prospects, workers are in fact expected to commit wholeheartedly to their organizations. Kaveri, a security guard, recounted a training exercise in which workers were led to believe that there was a fire. She explained,

> They did not tell me that it was a trial. . . . I thought there was a real fire. Two hundred to 250 employees were present. At the end, they told me it was a part of the training. . . . I was sitting at the reception desk, and people started running. I heard the sound of the alarm. I got slightly scared; I thought about my young daughters and their future. I asked the field officer, 'If I die, what will happen to my family?' He told me the company gives some 2 lakhs rupees (INR 200,000) to the family as compensation. Once I got this confirmation, I remained, as the company property is the responsibility of the security guards.

I was the only one sitting at the desk. At that time not a single guard was present at the reception. I was the only lady guard present at that place, and along with me there was one supervisor who was checking whether all the employees are gone or not. Afterward all the employers came and congratulated me.

Kaveri recounted this accolade wistfully; she was unemployed when we met her in her home because her contractor had lost the contract at the firm where she had been so highly regarded and where now she was only able to work night shift as an alternative. In this way, service workers are required to be willing to give their lives for the companies that contract their labor, just as army or police officers may be required to, but their lives are viewed as disposable, with few of the social and economic privileges that accompany such high-risk jobs.

Endnotes

1. There are two state-sponsored schemes under which contract workers are covered: the Employees' State Insurance Act (ESI) and the Provident Fund (PF). ESI is an insurance scheme under which all workers pay a premium and then receive medical or cash benefits when required. Employers are required to contribute 4.75 percent of employees' wages and employees 1.75 percent to the scheme and are required to maintain their contribution continuously for a six-month period to maintain eligibility during the period. Workers who are sick can access specified medical facilities and receive a portion of their wages. Families also receive a cash payout if the worker dies or experiences an injury that results in a long-term disability. However, ESI provisions are poorly implemented, and there are problems with documentation and records that prevent workers from properly accessing their benefits (see Kumar, 2010 for more details). PF benefits are linked to practices of informality (see Gandhi, 2011 for details on the "informal moral economy"). Employers, who are often small contractors, are required to verify correct payment of PF amounts to the Provident Fund Office but often do not. To receive benefits, workers must have bank accounts. See Singh (2010, p. 102) for other problems with PF, especially for low-income contract workers, who are rarely able to retrieve the money that is cut from their already meager salaries for this fund if they change employers. The deduction of benefits from workers' salaries is therefore not always an indication that workers actually receive or are able to access these benefits.
2. The identification of sectors as "formal" or "informal" has limited these terms' utility in the context of India. Only a small percentage of India's

workforce is considered to be formally employed. In the services sector, for example, about 80 percent of workers are informally employed (Srivastava, 2012). Agarwala estimates that this figure is closer to 93 percent when it includes agricultural workers (2007, p. 145). Overall, scholars have noted that India is experiencing a growing informalization of its labor force across the agriculture, industry, and service sectors. See Srivastava (2012) for more details. Some scholars have argued that globalization has created a growing class of "precariously employed workers," or the *"precariat"* (see Jhabvala & Standing, 2010).

3. Informal workers have always been an integral part of the global economy, although their relative preponderance across countries and regions has been varied. Even the definitions of informal work and informal workers vary across different national contexts. According to the International Labour Organization (ILO), informality exists in both overdeveloped and developing economies around the world but is more common in the latter. Theoretically, there has been a transition from the notion of the "informal sector" to that of the "informal economy" in relation to perceptions of underdevelopment in the global South. In the aftermath of the 2002 International Labor Conference, the notion of informality was expanded beyond its narrow scope within the informal sector to include workers who operated within informal employment conditions even in the formal sector. According to the ILO, "employment in the informal sector" refers to employment in informal enterprises, and "informal employment" refers to employment in informal jobs both inside and outside the informal sector (ILO, 2013, p. 2). The informal economy is thus made up of a wide variety of workers and entrepreneurs who remain unrecognized in and unprotected by national legal and regulatory frameworks. See the ILO (2013) report for more details on characteristics of the informal economy, such as limited access to social protections, denial of labor rights, and lack of organization and representation.

4. Because many workers we interviewed had moved from neighboring villages to Pune in search of work (in the context of a wider agrarian crisis and chronic environmental problems like seasonal drought), both their employment and their residence were intermittent, and they could be accurately characterized as "footloose," a concept that recasts the experience of rural-urban migration as a process of circulation (Breman, 2010, p. 3). A family illness or job loss would result in the worker returning to the village for a period of time until cash earnings were necessary and the process of migration had to be undertaken afresh.

5. Demonetization is likely to have reduced cash payments made to workers (Shepard, 2017).

6. There is widespread consensus that the use of contract labor diminishes working conditions for workers. See Nigam (1997) for an example of a case in Delhi that shows how the very nature of contract work is structured around the attempt to skirt labor laws. In general, services are provided by some struggling entrepreneurs and a number of large transnational firms, all of which win and lose contracts on the basis of their ability to provide low-cost workers who meet employer demands. Indeed, this is a classic example of what Stiglitz (2002) has called a global "race to the bottom," whereby the ability to attract contracts is based on how "competitive" the package is for the multinational technology companies, with cost cuts achieved by lowering wages and other social safety nets (like healthcare) of the workers themselves. See Bezuidenhout and Fakier (2006) for a similar example of how outsourcing and subcontracting have significantly diminished the quality of cleaners' lives in South Africa through lower wages and work intensification.

7. Pseudonyms are used for all individual and company names.

8. Despite the numerous health, work hours, and pay grievances that workers mentioned, none of them belonged to an association or union. In other countries, subcontracted corporate housekeepers have been successfully unionized through efforts such as the Service Employees International Union's Justice for Janitors campaign (Aguiar & Ryan, 2009). Subcontracted office cleaners in California, for example, were successful in increasing their wages and benefits by staging high-profile rallies outside multinational firms that sought contractors who were compliant with labor laws to protect their public image (Zlolniski, 2006). Efforts to organize workers in India have included initiatives such as the creation of the cooperative Saundarya, launched by the Self-Employed Women's Association, which submits tenders for cleaning contracts. However, employment precarity so permeates the housekeeping sector that it is almost impossible for individual workers to challenge the power of employers without risking dismissal. The workers we interviewed noted that while they had to embody professionalism and modernity, they also felt it was best to resolve problems through supervisors, because they were told that the contractor was under constant threat of losing its contract given the intense competition in the business.

9. The words "roadwise" and "risky" were in English, even though the conversation occurred in Marathi.

10. See Agarwala (2008, p. 399) for how informal workers like entrepreneurial drivers construct their own identities as "worthy citizens" and as legitimate claimants for state attention, especially in the state of Maharashtra.

11. Several transportation industry associations have existed or emerged in India in the past two decades, although none of the workers we interviewed reported any contact with them. These include the Centre of Indian Trade Unions' Autorickshaw Chalakara Sangha (which represents drivers of autorickshaws), which has launched several strikes to protest poor working conditions for taxi drivers; the Indian Vehicles Drivers Trade Union; and the All India Road Transport Workers Federation. Subcontracting schemes often make collective organizing among workers along occupational lines difficult. Micro-entrepreneurs or driver/owners may not see their interests as aligned with those of either drivers or larger vendors. While direct employment may benefit workers employed by multinational technology firms, it would undermine the livelihoods of subcontractors. In this situation, it would seem that drivers would be best served by a collective organizing model with expertise in the fluid boundaries between self-employment and employment within micro-enterprises. The Self Employed Workers' Association (SEWA), for example, has developed numerous strategies that may be effective within the corporate transportation sector. Like all SEWA members, one of the most significant challenges that drivers face is access to capital allowing them to invest in the purchase of cars. But aside from informal family group car purchases, no cooperative ownership models exist in the transportation sector. Just as these models have helped other self-employed workers, they may allow drivers to gain control over their schedules and income (Bhatt, 2006).

12. Indeed, the poor working conditions that our respondents shared with us have been reported in a number of other studies involving security guards in India (Upadhyay, 2011; Gooptu, 2013b; Ferus Comelo, 2014; Kumar & Beerepoot, 2017; Kumar, 2016).

CHAPTER 2

Housekeepers

Creating Modern India from the Periphery

The commercialization of cleaning is far from a new phenomenon globally. The past two decades, however, have seen the emergence of an entirely new approach to cleaning in India, as well as in many cities around the world, both in terms of organizational structures and in terms of ideological constructions. Rather than being charged with the task of keeping spaces free of dirt, which has traditionally been the core job of cleaners, Indian housekeepers employed within the multinational technology sector are not only expected to meet new definitions of cleanliness, but also required to themselves embody the spic-and-span modernity of the new India. When we met Lalita, a young human resources manager at a large housekeeping company, in a hotel coffee shop, she explained these expectations to us in a self-evident tone: "Nobody would like to see a janitor cleaning the floor with his beard, with his hair not properly trimmed . . . one who is not wearing the uniform, not shoes. . . . The professionalism has to be there, even in the contractual labor. So it's the first and foremost condition that the grooming has to be completely perfect." This shift represents a remarkable transformation from the notion of cleaning as dirty work, reserved for lower-caste or working-class people whose lot in life is to work with dirt, to the idea that cleaners themselves should be the epitome and embodiment of cleanliness.[1]

In India, progress and modernization are closely associated with notions of cleanliness. Prime Minister Narendra Modi, a vehement advocate of neoliberalism and Hindu nationalism interested in rebranding India as a leader in the global economy, launched the "Swachh Bharat"

(Clean India) campaign in October 2014. Drawing on renowned anticolonial figures like Mahatma Gandhi, Modi professed that the emphasis on cleanliness will benefit the national economy and connected sanitation to "patriotism (*rashtrabhakti*) and commitment to public health" (Modi, 2014). At the same time, the provision of cleaning to transnational firms in neoliberal India is organized through subcontractors. As a result, labor flexibility, deregulation, and informality pervade employment practices within the cleaning sector. In this chapter, we explore how workers and subcontractors make sense of their dual role as both central to the project of India's progress and peripheral in terms of their employment stability and prospects. We explore the ways in which cleaners are trained to become ideal workers who are clean themselves and able to spread cleanliness. We highlight the strategies of subcontractors and facilities managers who professionalize and technologize the cleaning profession by linking cleanliness to good character in order to compete for the contracts of large transnational technology companies that promote standardization. Throughout, we draw on our interviews with housekeepers, supervisors, subcontractors, and facilities managers in Pune to explore and map the landscape of cleaning and cleaning organizations in India today.

Hygiene and Modernity: Dirty Work and Clean Spaces

Links between the project of modernity and discourses of cleanliness are being forged in many cities around the world today. Brody (2006) traces this development to the emergence of Bangkok as a global city and argues that "in the case of Thailand, the notion of hygiene carries enormous symbolic significance and is perceived as marking an important difference between 'developed,' 'civilized'(*siwilai*) places and 'backward,' 'uncivilized' (*la samai*) places. . . . In order for the associations between cleanliness, civilization, and modernity to be kept alive, though, these public spaces need to be constantly maintained and, above all, kept spotless" (pp. 540–541). In a similar way, Tomic, Trumper, and Dattwyler (2006) explore how modernity and cleanliness have historically been intertwined in Chile. During the cholera epidemic that swept through the country in the early 1990s, state and healthcare professionals discursively constructed the illness as a disease of the poor. An extensive anticholera campaign that included public outreach and posters aimed to make women who were defined as economically backward "modern" through techniques such as handwashing, toilet cleaning, and the use of cleaning gadgets. In this context, cleanliness in Chile became "a central aspect of presenting an image of modernity and progress" (p. 518). Rogaski (2004) similarly traces the manner in which imperial discourses of modernity in twentieth-century China were instrumental in constructing a "hygienic modernity" that marked a significant departure from multiple pre-twentieth-century understandings of individual health. She argues that "by the early twentieth century, a powerful new set of meanings coalesced strongly around the word 'weisheng,' causing it to split from its earlier associations. The term became one of the most significant ways of naming the modern condition: a hierarchical principle that determines who would be included or excluded from the realm of civilization, a discourse that defined the difference between a sovereign nation, and a subjected tribe" (p. 23).

India has a similar discursive history of aligning modernity and cleanliness. As Chakrabarty (2002) notes, colonial space in India was historically constructed as "dirty" and "disorderly" (p. 76) and contrasted with Western imperialist practices of maintaining unpolluted, hygienic, and regulated spaces that were assumed to be "incapable of producing either disease or disorder" (p. 77). Ray and Qayum (2009) similarly argue that "to be 'modern' in postcolonial India is to align oneself with projects such as developmental science, progress, invention, and discovery; in turn, to be 'traditional' means to react differently to such aspirations to modernity" (p. 16). These discourses of modernity are being forged anew in multinational technology firms, imprinted on the bodies of the cleaners themselves. However, as our analysis will demonstrate, such discourses are simultaneously accompanied by unfulfilled promises by this industry, making such modernity always an unfinished project.

Two historical trends structure employment relationships within the housekeeping sector. First, housekeeping involves cleaning, which is embedded within gendered norms associated with domesticity and women's work. Both within and outside the household, tasks related to social reproduction are seen to be women's responsibility, and across classes, there remains a stark inequality in the sharing of household work. Women in India continue, for example, to carry out 90 percent of household work (Sudarshan, 2009) and also predominate in the paid domestic labor force (Ray & Qayum, 2009). Second, cleaning jobs have historically been deeply entrenched within the caste system, giving rise to highly exploitative relationships. Caste and gender are inextricably related. Gopal (2013), for example, describes manual scavenging as demeaning work involving "women actually lifting and carrying shit from the dry toilets onto baskets which are then dumped onto carts" (p. 92). This work is reserved for members of the scheduled castes, the lowest groups among the lower castes (Omvedt, 1994). Despite the degrading nature of this labor, there have been few resources devoted to its mechanization or sanitization. Similarly, a study of street sweepers in Mumbai (Chatterjee, 2014) reveals that exclusively scheduled caste women and men do this hazardous and poorly paid work. Jobs are "inherited" by wives and children of workers when they die prematurely, which occurs often, given their routine exposure to disease. Despite the poor wages and working conditions of this occupation, families are trapped within it because of the housing benefit that accompanies it and the near-complete absence of affordable housing in Mumbai.

As a result of these caste and gender dynamics, cleaning is both a feminized and a stigmatized profession, despite the fact that public sector cleaning jobs sometimes have benefits that are desirable. Housekeeping subcontractors servicing multinational technology companies play an active role in challenging the stigma of cleaning jobs by developing a rhetoric of professionalism around cleaning. There has been a concerted effort to distance cleaning done within tech firms (referred to as "housekeeping") from cleaning done in other settings. A recruitment video made by a major transnational housekeeping firm provides an example of this discourse, proudly referring to the international certifications that its workers obtain, as well as particular practices of "mechanized cleaning" that they follow.[2] Multiethnic workers and company employees signify the universality of such standards. Cleaners are referred to as "environmental service managers," with careers and promotion ladders. Workers wear uniforms with gloves and carry identity cards. These bodily markers are distinct parts of their identity as housekeepers but also clearly set them apart from the "regular" employees of multinational firms—that is, software professionals and call center workers.

Housekeepers working for India's multinational technology corporations are the core workforce assigned the task of maintaining cleanliness—both in material and in ideological terms. There is widespread recognition among supervisors, facilities managers, and contractors that not only are these workers engaged in the task of transforming the occupation of cleaning, but an important part of their own work is also to create a workforce who is appropriately embodied and trained to carry out this labor. This idea was explained to us by several contractors, including Balaji, whom we visited at a large housekeeping company located in a building at the end of an unpaved road. When we arrived, we noted the continuous recruitment occurring at a plastic table set up in front of the building. Balaji was passionate about the virtues of the new professionalization of the cleaning industries during our interview and gave us glossy brochures that described the equipment and chemicals his company used. He explained, in English, the differences between general and "mechanized" cleaning: "Suppose it is a general housekeeping, you have to broom and all. . . . You are saying this is clean, but I am saying this is not clean. I will not [check it] with the microscope, but some dust particles would be [still] there. If you are doing mechanized [cleaning], then there are some instruments, equipment for that. Doing it manually and with equipment has a lot of difference." When probed about exactly what mechanized cleaning was, he answered:

> In mechanized cleaning there are lot of chemicals, from R1, R2, to R12. . . . You have to decide which chemical has to be used for which site, which particular location for cleaning. You have to have the knowledge about every chemical. These chemicals are for particular sites—for floor, etc. Similar is with the equipment. Suppose here you need high pressure and here you need single disk, it will not work in that site. We have knowledge about that. . . . Here you have to hire a person who is more efficient.

Given the close association between cleaning and domestic labor, women dominate housekeeping work in many parts of the world. At the same time, ethnographies of cleaners reveal that there are significant divisions within the cleaning workforce. While those engaged in household labor, paid domestic work, and hotel cleaning largely continue to be women, some segments of higher-status cleaning work are seeing more and more male workers. Simpson and colleagues (2012) note, for example, that men predominate in institutional cleaning, while women are more often associated with domestic work (p. 6; see also Tomic, Trumper, & Dattwyler, 2006). According to the contractors and facilities managers we interviewed, between 50 and 90 percent of housekeepers serving multinational technology firms are male. Despite the fact that domestic work and housekeeping both focus on cleaning, workers and contractors did not draw parallels between the skill required for the cleaning of homes and that required for the cleaning of offices. This was somewhat surprising, because the actual tasks involved in cleaning these two domains were remarkably similar—dusting, sweeping, cleaning washrooms, and vacuuming. The disjuncture between domestic and corporate cleaning work is reflective of a set of practices through which this work is gendered and the latter work defined as appropriate for men. For example, associations between cleaning and technology allow cleaning within multinational technology firms to be seen as having a completely different nature than domestic cleaning.

When asked why mechanized cleaning was so important, contractors provided a few explanations. First, we were told that mechanized cleaning is especially needed in the high-cost spaces that have been built by India's multinational companies. When we met Akash, a manager at a large housekeeping firm with a small set of offices next to a special economic zone, he explained in English:

> When we talk about IT and BPO, we only use eco-friendly kind of chemicals. That is harmless chemicals. If someone consumes, also there are no side effects. . . . They are not poisonous. There are certain chemicals which are acidic like toilet cleaners, which cannot be used on this kind of granite floors. It will kill the flooring. Those are more important. There are certain chemicals which have to be used on certain areas. For example, we normally use, you use Harpic at home for toilet cleaning. If you get that Harpic and use it on your floor, it will kill the floor, there will be patch on the floor as that is acidic, so that he has to understand.

Viresh, a 25-year-old male housekeeper who we met outside a large multinational call center, reinforced this construction of housekeeping as skilled work: "What is the difference between cleaning toilets, sweeping roads, and here? That job is a low-status job. This job is of higher level. There are cleaning materials." In this way, through the use of specific cleaning tools and materials, new standards of cleanliness are crafted in these corporate spaces and are critical in constructing such spaces as different, more hygienic, and more "modern" than other workplaces in urban India.

While some housekeeping contractors in India today are small, other cleaning companies are large multinational corporations. Regardless of their size, however, the language of "standards" is pervasive. As Weil (2014) notes, the introduction of standards has played a crucial role in the formation of contemporary fissured economies by allowing companies to manage the dangers that arise from indirect employment. Fissured organizations have "clear, explicit, and detailed standards that provide the blueprint that the enterprises of lower levels must follow" (p. 9). Through these standards, large corporations can exercise control over multiple smaller subcontractors without assuming responsibility for training employees. Standards involve three elements—the setting of clear guidelines, the introduction of monitoring systems, and the levying of penalties (p. 64).

The setting of standards also contributes to the establishment of hierarchies of global and local ways of working. Herod and Aguiar (2006) trace the impact of the emergence of ISS, a Danish company with branches around the world, and note that "in the case of such global cleaning giants' entrance into the cleaning market in developing countries, this discourse of professionalism has been facilitated by long standing and deeply engrained associations between foreign way of doing things and higher quality, and has encouraged a growing standardization of ways of working" (p. 431). Tomic, Trumper, and Dattwyler's (2006) case study of changes that occurred when ISS took over a local Chilean cleaning company is telling in this respect. They note that "ISS contends that its final product is unique because it is based upon 'Scandinavian values' of honesty, initiative, responsibility, and high quality services—values which ISS executives presumably believe are lacking amongst Chilean workers" (p. 514). Approaches to cleaning can thus become a forum within which hierarchies among nations are established and reinforced.

Discussions of housekeeping requirements within multinational technology firms in India position cleanliness as both originating and achieving the highest standards in the West. Naresh, an owner of a software firm, told us that he thought that this association existed "because most IT companies by definition are serving customers in the West. So some of the standards that are in the West are taken for granted. . . . You begin to either get mandated, or at least you begin to absorb those by osmosis. And you reflect those, you know, in your environment as well."

This "osmosis" was clearly evident when we met Reena, a manager at a large housekeeping company. Her company was housed in a modern building with large panes of glass throughout, and she noted the importance of maintaining buildings in India in ways that are comparable to the practices used in the West and acceptable to foreigners from the West:

> [Multinational corporations] are investing so much money over here. . . . Once you enter the facility, you should have security access, everything going through. . . . You should find a very clean desk and

clean atmosphere around you. Ambiance should be okay, lighting should be okay, AC temperature should be there. . . . Washrooms should be clean, hygiene should be important aspect, safety is very important. Then you should have the clean environment to eat. . . . Because there are clients who come from abroad also here. . . . . They will see their facilities over here, so if they are paying so much to that company, they will ensure that you are at that benchmark.

The focus of a majority of the work processes and training in the housekeeping sector was the creation of a "more efficient" worker who met the required "benchmarks." Contractors and managers spoke extensively about the training that workers were provided. They claimed that workers were sent to an offsite training area where they received up to three weeks of paid training. Training was continuous, provided either through daily briefings from supervisors or designated sessions every two to four weeks. Workers were also given opportunities to learn on the job through two-day job shadowing stints during which new employees watched a more experienced "buddy" at work.

Despite the widespread emphasis placed by managers and contractors on training, chemicals, and cleaning technologies, however, it was clear that housekeeping was an extremely competitive field, and that there was considerable pressure on firms to keep their labor costs at a minimum in order to win contracts. As a result, about a third of the workers we interviewed mentioned that they had received no training or had only received on-the-job or informal opportunities to learn how to do their jobs. The remainder had received training for two to three days, with slightly longer training times noted by those who had been recruited from rural areas. Yash, a 22-year-old male housekeeper, was one such recruit. The research team met him at his home, which was in an industrial area where bricks were manufactured. After walking through dust and drain water, we sat in his small room and he told us about the detailed training he had received when he had first started his job two years ago:

> When they taught us about dusting, they told us what duster means, how dusting is done, and which duster is used when. [The trainer] showed us three types of dusters: one, blue-check duster; two, white-check duster; and three, red-check duster. . . . The blue-check duster is used in the office area, the red-check duster is used in the toilet area, and the green-check duster is used in the canteen area. . . . On the second day, they told us about toilet cleaning and how is it done.

When Yash had been recruited, he had been told that the job involved dusting and washing teacups. It was only later that he found out that he would also be required to clean toilets and "trained" accordingly. Despite his characterization of his job as requiring specialized knowledge, Yash noted that he wanted to quit because of the low wages. He hoped to set up a business of his own in the future.

The Mechanized Housekeeper

The fact that workers have to possess bodies that look a particular way or transform their bodies for their jobs has been explored through the notion of "aesthetic labor," which has been defined as the "mobilization, development and commodification of embodied 'dispositions' [that] . . . are to some extent possessed by workers at the point of entry into employment" (Witz, Warhurst, & Nickson, 2003, p. 37). If workers do not possess these bodily characteristics, they have to be taught to assume them through on-the-job training. Such training can be variously perceived as a mechanism of control and as a way for workers to perform modernity such that it is not just restricted to their place of work but simultaneously becomes part of their bodily comportment, behavior, and mannerisms. Some kinds of aesthetic labor, like that required of models in the beauty industry, involve an ongoing production of the body or the self—that is, the physical and emotional effort to keep up appearances (Entwistle & Wissinger, 2006).

Mechanized housekeepers in our study not only had to possess certain skills and training so that they could use the correct chemicals, cleaning cloths, and brooms in different areas but had to look a particular way. Indeed, workers reported that the most substantial training they received was on their "grooming" and "soft skills." There were three requirements that were mentioned: the need to be clean, which included bathing, cutting nails and hair, wearing ironed uniforms and polished shoes, and abstaining from the consumption of alcohol or other traditional recreational substances before coming to work; the need to interact with each other and company employees in particular ways; and the need to be disciplined, particularly in relation to time.

Cleanliness

One afternoon, as we stood by the side of a road that led to an IT park, a young man in a checked shirt with the logo of a large software company and blue pants approached. We stopped the man, whom we refer to as

Anoop, to tell him about the research project, and he invited the research team to his home that Saturday. It was a difficult place to find, wedged between a trash collection site on one side and a public toilet on the other. Inside the tin-roofed structure was a sofa, refrigerator, and TV. A baby slept in a homemade crib, and a woman and a dog were sitting by the child. There were half a dozen young men also present in the small room, and as we introduced ourselves, they told Anoop that they were concerned that we would make a public health complaint about the living quarters, which did not contain a toilet so were not up to code. However, after we described the nature of our research, Anoop decided to participate and offered us a cold drink. He informed us that his brother-in-law owned the home, and that the family occupied a caste in the village that was historically associated with cleaning. However, since there was no work in the village and his wife was sick, Anoop and his family had migrated to the city. He had obtained his current job through his brother-in-law, who was a labor contractor. With no formal education, Anoop had few job options in the city, even though he was deeply ashamed to be a housekeeper. He said he could not bear to tell his relatives in the village that he had a cleaning job, given the stigma he faced because of the association between his caste and cleaning. Anoop noted that although he did not feel that his job was prestigious, it was better than being unemployed in his village. Despite his bare-bones living situation, Anoop described the grooming requirements for his job as follows: "You have to wear suits and wear black shoes, wash your clothes, press them, shave, cut your nails." When we asked about the consequences of not following these requirements, he said, "They pay you half. . . . We get [INR] 170 [a day], so out of that they take away half."

The project of maintaining clean bodies and clothes not only serves to minimize offense to others but also contributes to the creation of notions of self. Lalita, a housekeeping vendor, explained that part of the training related to grooming is about instilling in the housekeepers a sense of self-worth: "Well-groomed is [pause] it's the . . . the person has to feel positive, the person who is interacting should feel positive that the hair is trimmed, the nails are not grown, he's completely shaved, wearing cap, wearing clean uniform with all the accessories in place, then his posture of standing, his way of greeting, is called grooming." In this formulation, being clean leads to feeling positive; cleanliness is in this way constructed as a good habit that both improves one's sense of self-worth and enables workers to better perform their jobs of cleaning offices.

A similar link between cleanliness and moral behavior was made in a story shared by Lalit, a facilities manager at a smaller software company. Lalit was in charge of setting contract terms and supervising the 82 contract employees who provided administrative, housekeeping, security, and transportation services. He described in English the "core values" in place at his organization, which he informed us extended to subcontracted workers. These included "basic things, like they should be clean, they should not stink in the office, they should be polite, they should not be rude." He went on to share an example of an incident that exemplified these values: a housekeeper found INR 10 in the cafeteria and despite the fact that this was a small sum, returned it to his supervisor. In this way, cleanliness was related to the moral value of honesty. The assumption underlying such "civilizational discourses" is that workers do not have these values and thus must be taught them through corporate training practices. In much the same way, Manik, a manager at a large call center, stated that if a housekeeper "has good dress, good turnout, then people coming from front . . . will think he is a genuine person, he is very good." Ameerier (2017) notes that such "sensorial regimes" serve to situate one's self and the "other" and are key components of modernizing projects. Her study of the training provided to some Pakistani immigrants to Toronto found that they were told that they should smell "clean" and "not like Indian food, or masala" in order to be perceived as "clean and professional" (p. 85). In noting that workers should not "stink" and should be "genuine," Lalit and Manik constructed workers as uncivilized and in need of aesthetic and moral education that would allow them to fit into the neutral, smell-free environment of multinational technology firms.

Achieving such "cleanliness" comes with a cost that is borne by workers. Although some companies helped workers maintain these standards of cleanliness by providing access to laundry facilities, this was certainly not the norm. Karthik, one of the only workers we interviewed with access to company-provided laundry facilities, noted: "Daily shaving is necessary, hair should be short and properly cut, uniform and shoes should be clean. After wearing it once, we give our uniform for laundry. . . . In the company there are laundry facilities. . . . We get [the uniform] back washed and ironed. Even shaving facilities are available in the company, [but] we have to pay for shaving." For most workers who have long hours, significant household responsibilities, and a lack of regular electricity and water in their own homes, the requirement of maintaining cleanliness was often a source of significant stress. A housekeeping contractor, Satish, noted the hidden cost associated with "cleanliness" for workers: "A proper haircut and short nails, clean uniform, polished shoes, etc. [are required]. At least once in a week workers should polish their shoes. The salary they get is INR 5,000–5,500. It's not possible to polish their shoes every day on this salary."

Subservient Interactions

There is a close connection between subservience and caste relations in India. Workers of certain lower castes were, and often continue to be, assigned the dirty work of cleaning by virtue of their assumed contamination and inferiority. Cleaning is an example of a historically caste-based occupation deemed appropriate for the least clean and most poor. As Ray and Qayum (2009, p. 153) state, "The servant body is considered to be weak, susceptible to illness and unclean, but servants are expected to do work that requires them to be strong, healthy and clean." Modern-day housekeeping is characterized by a full reversal of this notion, with unclean workers deemed to be inappropriately embodied for the work of cleaning. Part of the project of creating the new breed of "mechanized cleaners" involves challenging the spatial segregation that continues to accompany cleaning in the context of domestic service in India. Practices of distinction are key to the culture of servitude in India and are not therefore entirely new to the mechanized housekeepers working for multinational technology firms. Distance has historically been maintained between those involved in cleaning and domestic work and their employers through the creation of separate spaces for eating, sleeping, and bathing. This notion of separate spaces is inherently tied to the concept of caste contamination. Upper-, presumably purer, caste members are said to become "impure" if they touch individuals of lower castes, who are seen as the performers of inferior labor. Ray and Qayum explain, "In upper-caste house-holds members of the low castes were traditionally not allowed to touch certain things and enter certain sacred or ordinary spaces. In order to overcome the ritually imposed caste barriers in daily life, the women and girls of observant Hindu households practiced routine and ritual procedures, such as pouring (clean) water over the (unclean) *jamadar's* hands" (p. 153). Anecdotal narratives of caste contamination describe how some upper-caste Brahmans felt the need to bathe if they inadvertently touched even the shadow of a person who was considered lower caste.

Workers, contractors, and facilities managers we interviewed went to some lengths to specifically differentiate the interaction norms within their firms from these traditional caste stigmas. Many noted that workers were allowed to share the same spaces as employees, often using the same washrooms. The staff canteen was accessible to most housekeepers. Ironically, however, many workers could not take advantage of the same catering facilities used by software programmers or call center workers, but not because of social taboos. Rather, the food prices were beyond their budget.

In describing their jobs, many workers noted that their workplaces did not follow segregation norms traditionally associated with caste and that subservience related to one's caste position was not required. One afternoon, we arranged to meet Nabanita outside the gates of the large software company where she worked as a housekeeper. As we waited, we watched white-collar office employees and housekeepers stream out of the same elevator and saw Nabanita appear in an elegant *salwar kameez*, clutching a purse. We sat on a bench next to the company gate as she told us about how she became a housekeeper seven years earlier after dropping out of university. Nabanita informed us that she lived in a one-bedroom home with her in-laws, daughter, and husband, whom she described as an unemployed alcoholic. She recounted a recent visit to her workplace by a high-ranking training official from the head office who had told the housekeepers that they should not feel inferior. Nabanita noted with pride that it had been the "madam's" birthday, and that the official had accepted a piece of cake from her, subverting caste taboos. She noted, "I am a housekeeping lady, I clean toilets, but she ate cake from my hands." The significance of the executive's actions lay in the fact that they challenged traditional caste norms, which are specifically based on the prohibition of food exchange from lower- to higher-caste members. Despite the pride with which Nabanita reported this incident, she emphasized that only her immediate family knew that she performed the job of "toilet cleaning." She also noted that she preferred to work inside a glass building rather than in a mall or public space because she was embarrassed to be doing cleaning work. Clearly distressed, she revealed that she even lied to her own brother about the nature of her job. While Nabanita noted that her subservience was not structured by caste taboos, as she was allowed to offer an upper-caste woman food she had touched, she continued to be extremely deferential. She consistently referred to the training official as "Madam" and recounted her advice that nobody in the company was inferior to anyone else, despite the obvious fact that the trainer clearly wielded considerably more power than she did and that she was required to be deferential in her interactions with her.

Such "rearticulations" (Ramamurthy, 2011) of caste hierarchies are occurring at multiple sites in contemporary India. Analyzing why farmers who own small plots of land in rural Andhra Pradesh prefer to cultivate cotton even though they could earn more as wage earners, Ramamurthy shows how they construct cotton as an "aspirational crop" that promises farmers that they can transcend caste hierarchies and fashion better livelihoods for their children (even though these promises are only occasionally realized). Like the rural farmers interviewed by Ramamurthy who experience autonomy and pride because they are no longer expected to remove their slippers when addressing higher-caste moneylenders, the opportunity to offer food to her manager signified a shift in social relations for Nabanita, even though it did not diminish her shame about being engaged in low-status cleaning work.

Rather than being told that they had to use separate washrooms or sit in segregated spaces, workers were nevertheless asked to be subservient in other ways. Similar to the requirement to be "clean," workers were told that they must be quiet and invisible. Lalita, the contractor quoted earlier, described the training that workers receive as follows:

> They are given the training wherein they are not supposed to interfere in anybody's sphere of work. They just have to do the housekeeping and come out of that place. They're not supposed to stand there and listen to somebody's talk or, you know, be vigilant about something. We call it as, again . . . bad manners, you know. So they are trained in a way that they are not supposed to have any fights with the customer, they're not supposed to cross-question, they are supposed to obey the orders of their team leader, the supervisor. Whatever they want to communicate, it will be communicated through the supervisor.

Workers noted that they were told that silence is a form of respect and proper behavior appropriate for the professional spaces they occupied. The segregation of housekeepers thus was enforced not through taboos around physical contact, but through the prohibition of auditory contact with employees and one another. Workers were required to be present but invisible at work. When members of the research team met Megha in her one-bedroom flat that two families shared, she told us that she did not like her housekeeping job but did not think she had other job options. She noted that cameras ensured that housekeepers did not talk to one another on the job and reported, "We are not allowed to talk on the floor. They don't like it if we talk too much. If we are talking, sooner or later supervisors will find it. Therefore, we do not talk. . . . If someone catches us talking, then they tell the supervisors. So we have to work alone as much as possible." Like cleanliness, working alone and working quietly are constructed as signs of moral traits such as self-control and good manners.

Long working hours together with the requirement to be silent during work led many workers to feel socially isolated despite their dense living arrangements and numerous colleagues. Priyanka explained this to us when we went to her home on her day off. She shared her small two-room flat with her son, in-laws, brother-in-law, and his wife. Priyanka commuted about an hour each way to work, walking for about half the distance and then taking a bus. The flat had a fridge and television. The quietest place to have a conversation was the stairwell outside the flat, which is where we sat as Priyanka told us that she had not had the opportunity to pursue an education but after her husband, who had been an alcoholic, had died six years before, she had been determined to give her children the opportunity to do so. When she had first been "sent" by family members to the housekeeping job, she had never worn pants and a shirt before and had been scared to even leave her house. Priyanka recounted, "Initially, I felt very bad, I cried when I was doing this work. I never did this kind of work, but I just gathered courage and did it." Later, she had gotten used to the uniform and realized that it was useful because she was never harassed while wearing it, even when she walked home after dark. With pride, she reported that her now-married daughter had completed her bachelor's degree, and that her son was currently completing his high school in an English-medium institution. She lamented, however, that because of her long working hours she was estranged from her son. She talked about being socially isolated, saying, "I do not get time to visit neighbors' houses. I am busy with my work and house. Maybe making such friends is not a part of my nature, because I do not get that much time." At work, she was encouraged not to speak to coworkers. She reported, "In the company, we generally do not much speak with each other. . . . [When we sit] we have to sit alone. We cannot sit with anyone. Each one of us has to sit on our floor, and we are not allowed to leave our floor." When we asked about her relationship with her coworkers, she said, "We finish off our work and go home. There is no time to make friendships."

Discipline

Determined that his son become a manager at an IT company, Rahul, a housekeeper, informed us during our conversation that he had to work three jobs to make ends meet. He worked from 6 a.m. to 10 p.m. Aside from his full-time housekeeping job, he made deliveries for his wife's tiffin service, helped a vegetable vendor, and delivered milk every morning. Recently promoted, he was now in charge of supervising other housekeepers at the large call center where he worked. Rahul described a recent visit from a "foreigner" who came to instruct the housekeeping staff on the requirements of their jobs. According to Rahul, the visitor wanted things to be done as they were in the United States, declaring: "The ideal housekeeper should be present for duty five minutes before. . . . He should ask the supervisor before performing his duties. He should be able to complete his work before the scheduled time, and that too neatly. He should be well groomed, in uniform, and his hair should be properly cut. His nails should be short." Despite housekeepers' extraordinarily long workdays, time discipline was seen as equally integral to being a good housekeeper as looking and interacting according to the established rules. Indeed, Pratap, who worked for a large call center and had recently received a "Best Housekeeper" award, told us that his responsibilities included taking attendance during shifts. He emphasized the focus on time: "A good housekeeper should know the importance of time. He should come to duty on time. He should maintain personal hygiene. He should shave every day. He should take care of his nails. He should wear the proper uniform. He should use safety gear like hand gloves provided by the company. He should respect his seniors." Silence, deference, time discipline, and cleanliness are all central "soft skills" required of the mechanized housekeeper in India today. In identifying these qualities as important for the job, employers socially construct workers as ideal, trainable, or inappropriate depending on their embodied qualities and demeanor. The focus on aesthetic labor, or the need to "look" and "act" in a particular way, defines ideal bodies for jobs and in this way enacts particular forms of exclusion.

Creating Modern Cleaners

Transnational firms and their contractors in India have not simply found a ready-made subservient, appropriately aesthetically endowed, low-wage service workforce. Rather, through training and organizational protocols, such workers are "made" (Salzinger, 2003). These companies' efforts are supported by state and media practices through which links between modernity, progress, and cleanliness are forged. Our interviews revealed that distinctions between clean and unclean workers were drawn continuously within the housekeeping sector. Certain groups were deemed more unclean and therefore in need of substantial training to be made clean. The transformation of workers assumed to be rural, backward, and dirty into professional housekeepers was achieved through an elaborate process of training. During one of our interviews with a housekeeping vendor, we were given a spiral-bound training manual entitled *Guide to Green Cleaning: Textbook for Professional Cleaners*. The manual, written in English, is authored by an organization called the American Institute for Clean Technology, and the text notes collaborations between this organization, the Canadian Cleaning Institute, and a multinational cleaning chemicals and supplies distributor called Miraclean. The 100-plus-page manual contains a section on "Ground Rules for Custodians," which lists rules in terms of "dos and don'ts." Don'ts include don't argue, don't steal, don't be late, don't swear or be vulgar, don't bring dirt to a jobsite, don't wear dirty shoes, don't eat food left behind by others, and don't chat with the client. Dos listed include be clean, be cheerful, be punctual, and be well groomed. Detailed instructions are provided on how to clean different parts of offices and how to use certain equipment. It is through such documents that the professionalization of the cleaning profession is achieved. Affiliations with American and Canadian institutes signal that these standards are global and justify the extensive training given to local labor forces, such as rural Indians, to meet required benchmarks. The collusion of Western training institutes and multinational cleaning chemicals suppliers is clearly evident in the setting of such standards.[3]

Workers defined as "rural" or "from the village" are seen as requiring the most training to become modern Indian housekeepers. On a visit to a special economic zone, we met Surya by the side of the road, and after hearing about the project, he asked us to come to his home at a set time the next day. He said that he lived in a nearby building where many migrant housekeepers lived. We found that Surya lived in an apartment that had two rooms. The floor was lined with mattresses, and uniforms hung on clotheslines strung from wall to wall above them. Several men played cards at a table in the corner while we interviewed Surya. With him was Vivek, who had been part of a group of 20 boys who had been brought to the city from the same village a little less than a year ago. Surya had been recruited by an agent and promised waged work in the city. He described the training he received as follows: "In the training they gave us three booklets. . . . One book was on memory. The other book was based on the information about how to talk with your seniors; then [the third was] information about grooming—like nails should be properly cut, clothes should be clean and pressed, bathing and shaving should be done daily." Vivek, who had attended a similar training program in his village, noted, "They taught us how boys should behave after coming to a city from a village—how to behave in an office area, how to speak, how should you respond if a senior asks you something. Boys from a village do not know about these things, so they taught us." In particular, the need for silence in the workplace was justified by the claim that villagers' social norms differed from those acceptable within multinational technology firms. Vivek informed us of a scenario that had been presented during his training:

> In the exam we were asked: If there are girls and boys [company employees] who have sexual relations, and they are discussing these in front of others, what will you do? What happens usually is boys from village backgrounds will find it inappropriate to talk about sexual relations in front of others, and hence they will start laughing. So, what will you do? This was the question. So the expected answer is: You don't laugh when such discussions take place.

The contractors whom we interviewed constructed those from villages not only as socially awkward, but also as steeped in religious practices that were not in keeping with the time discipline needed in transnational firms. Akash shared his central labor-related challenge as follows:

> Challenge is, you know, absenteeism, biggest challenge. And now absenteeism, when there are festivals, now festivals are going to start like Ganesh Chaturthi, and after that it followed by Dashera, Diwali, Navratri. Navratri they all want to go enjoy the Garba, and in the morning no one wants to come for the work. Ganapati, in every lane there is an idol kept. They all are enjoying whole night sitting in the *pandal*, so it happens absenteeism increases during these festive days. They want to go to their native place, places where they worship. Some people, they don't come for 10 days, they have to go to their native places.

In a similar way, Vikram, another contractor, emphasized that certain people were harder to train than others and such distinctions were closely tied to regional stereotypes with racial and ethnic undertones.

He reported in English, "[My] experience is Maharashtra people are very easy to train. Their understanding level is better than Biharis.... It is not because of the language, but their understanding level is better—because they are born and brought up in the city area. But those who were coming from the villages, they are little bit sluggish. Mostly Biharis are most sluggish." The construction of Biharis as sluggish is reminiscent of colonial discourses that historically used racial stereotypes to describe people from the tropics as lazy (Kukreja, 2017).

In these ways, even while it is subverting caste associations, the emergence of the mechanized housekeeper in India has given rise to new forms of stratification along regional lines. Despite the prevalence of these attitudes toward those from rural areas, only a small proportion of the housekeepers we interviewed were originally from Pune. The majority of them had migrated from villages less than five years earlier. Many contractors noted that they relied heavily on recruitment from villages. Jobs were constructed as "opportunities" through which workers could escape the abject poverty that many faced as rural farmers, construction workers, or domestic workers.

This discourse of housekeeping as a "work opportunity" allows for the management of the dynamics of pride and shame associated with housekeeping work. Despite being described as "professional" housekeepers and being given uniforms, workers do not have control over their work, wages, contracts, or decision-making in the workplace—features that typically accompany professional jobs. In her case study of female service workers in China, Otis (2012) describes the paradoxical responses of women who face forms of humiliation for not following aesthetic rules but embrace rather than challenge these disciplinary practices. She argues that women engage in "virtuous professionalism"—that is, they support managerial attempts to foster work styles defined as professional in order to set themselves apart from service workers who are stigmatized, such as sex workers.

Housekeepers in India similarly embrace such discourses of "virtuous professionalism" to challenge the shame traditionally associated with cleaning jobs. Uniforms are used and often viewed by workers as a source of pride that allows them to align themselves with a "formal" organization. Megha, for example, noted, "I feel respected.... I have an identity card, and I am working with a big transnational company, which is known to others because of the shirt and pant uniform." At the same time, however, she revealed that none of her neighbors knew about the exact nature of the work she did. Indeed, more than half of all the housekeepers we interviewed, including a third of the female house-keepers, informed us that they were ashamed of their jobs and had not revealed the details of their work to family, neighbors, and friends. Anoop said he did not want to tell his relatives in his village about his job because "I feel ashamed.... They ask, What do you do there? You went there to clean the toilet? It would have been better to work in the village then." Vasant similarly told us that he felt that his job had no dignity in society and said that his friends call him a "toilet supervisor."

In their ethnography of three groups of female cleaners in Israel, Benjamin, Bernstein, and Motzafi-Haller (2010) explore how women challenged notions of shame and humiliation in the context of their engagement in "dirty" work. They note that the women rejected their occupational identities as low-status workers and attributed value to their work in terms of the relationships it helped them forge and the contributions it allowed them to make to their communities and families. Skeggs's (2010) notion of "emotional politics" suggests that "cleaning jobs impose two types of emotional experiences on employees: shame, which is linked to the visibility of cleaning and humiliation which is linked more closely to the work process and its embedded forms of control" (p. 347). Israeli cleaners challenged these emotions by constructing themselves as responsible breadwinners who, through their employment, provided for their families and protected their daughters from similar fates. Women also cited the comradeship they experienced through work in order to point to their "respectable belonging" and challenge their feelings of humiliation. Brody's (2006) research too reveals that while janitors recognized the demeaning aspects of their jobs, they simultaneously expressed pride in their work. They noted that it was a step up from agricultural work and allowed them to support family members and children in ways that would otherwise not have been possible (p. 550).

Indeed, many of the Indian housekeepers we interviewed referred to the fact that their job allowed them to fulfill economic needs and aspire for better lives for their children. Nabanita told us that she had initially been very hesitant to take a housekeeping job. Given her level of education, she had felt that she should not be doing a job that involved toilet cleaning. But since she was not treated badly as a housekeeper, she decided to continue in the role. She said, "This is also work, as it gives me my bread and butter. If I don't do this, some other woman will."

Despite noting that cleaning is work, Nabanita revealed that, like many others, she had not shared the exact nature of her job with her brother, in-laws, neighbors, or children. When asked why, she explained: "I feel that I need not tell them about this. If I am doing this, why should I tell others and be a reason for their pain? [pause, sobs] ... My brother will feel bad that his sister is doing this work even after being educated. So I do not let them know about my work. I think that I get INR 7,000 as a salary, and I am okay with it."

Modernity Contracted Out

Many housekeepers we interviewed shared a hope for a better future, not only for the nation, but also for themselves. Housekeepers working in India's multinational technology sector are integral to the nation's modernization project through both the cleaning work they perform and the cleanliness they embody through their dress and demeanor. Yet practices of exclusion structure their day-to-day lives—they have no direct employment contracts and can be fired without reason or recourse. They are trained to be quiet and draw as little attention to their presence as possible. They are constantly asked to prove their worthiness, trainability, and potential for inclusion in the modern spaces of India. Their inclusion depends on their being honest, disciplined, and reliable despite their poor salaries and the lavish wealth that surrounds them. These expectations were described by Ranjit, whom we met at a canteen in a special economic zone. He told us that eight family members were dependent on his work as a housekeeper on the night shift and a plumber during the day. Ranjit described the rules he was told to follow as a housekeeper:

> If you go inside the work area cubicles for dusting, then a lot of employees' valuable belongings are lying around, like their mobile phones. Do not touch anything. Keep all the items in their place. The CCTV cameras are always switched on, so do not attempt to steal anything. I told Madam that I have come here to do my job and I will not attempt any time to steal anything. I will always do my duty and just go home.

Despite being trained to become the symbol of modern India, most housekeepers have not experienced increases in their standard of living or lifestyle, unlike the core "professional" employees who work as software programmers or call center workers in India's multinational firms.

Instead, their experience of modern India is illustrative of the growing gap between rich and poor. Indeed, researchers around the world have shown that lavish infrastructure development in some parts of cities often occurs at the expense of public use projects. In Chile, for example, Tomic, Trumper, and Dattwyler (2006) note that cleanliness comes at the "expense of dirtiness for the majority of the urban areas that lack the means for such perpetual, round-the-clock cleaning" (p. 525). In Silicon Valley, janitors cleaning high-tech firms live in barracks-like apartment buildings, many of which are not up to legal safety codes (Zlolniski, 2006).

Indeed, all of the housekeepers we interviewed told us about the very modest homes they inhabited outside work hours. Neeta described her two-room home, for which she paid more than a quarter of her monthly family income: "I have a TV, a fan, and a mixer. Our toilet is outside the house. It is shared among five [families]." Devika lived with her husband and two children in one room in her mother's house because the family did not have sufficient income to rent its own home. Sneh lived with his mother and sister in a *chawl* (a single-room, low-cost house). Gauri's home, which she described as a "small room" with a television and a fan, had no running water and a public toilet and was shared with her husband and two children. Each month, she spent INR 2,000 on rent, INR 4,000 on food, INR 2,000 on kerosene, and the remainder of the family's INR 11,000 salary on school fees and transportation. Anoop's home consisted of a tin structure that had no electricity, water, or bathroom. He lived there with his brother-in-law's family and children, paying INR 2,000 in rent. Surya, who had migrated to the city recently from his village, lived with six other men in a room. The contractor deducted rent from their monthly salaries for the room, which contained one bed and two mattresses. Tanaji, a recent migrant, lived with 10 boys in a room, where they all cooked, slept, and socialized.

In the context of the links forged during training and on the job between cleanliness, discipline, honesty, and good character, the stark differences between workers' spaces of work and spaces of home are especially significant for two reasons. First, it is within spaces that house multiple tenants and provide only shared washing and bathroom facilities that housekeepers are expected to "groom" themselves and prepare their bodies and uniforms for work during their few nonworking hours. Second, on a daily basis, workers are forced to confront the vast gap between the highly ordered, cleanliness-focused spaces where they work and their living quarters, where multiple family members or roommates share small local spaces that according to the standards that are promoted within their organizations are defined as unclean and disorderly. Manik, a manager at a multinational technology firm, emphasized that he believed that both housekeepers and security guards considered their workplaces to be their "first homes": "They like to stay in the air conditioning. It's clean. Some of them are living in *chawls*. They are poor, so they like it here. It's clean. There is a coffee machine. They get tea. They get to talk to nice people who work here."

Mapping the historical routes of cultures of servitude within India, Ray and Qayum (2009) note that "a culture of servitude is one in which social relations of domination/subordination, dependency, and inequality are normalized and permeate both domestic and public spheres" (p. 3). Inglis's (2013) ethnography of caddies working at India's prestigious golf clubs provides a powerful example of the ways in which servitude, rather than service provision, is required for caddies to develop the personal relationships with members that allow them to supplement their dismal wages through handouts and gifts. Inglis observes, "Two decades of free markets, free trade and mostly jobless growth, combined with underfunding in areas of education, healthcare, and other social service, have left the poor with few other options but to seek out the rich and plead their case for assistance. They do so following not the dictates of religion, community or caste, but rather, the dictates of modern capitalism" (p. 30). Indeed, our analysis reveals that attempts to professionalize the cleaning industry through the use of standards and uniforms on one level represent a challenge to cultures of servitude. At the same time, they give rise to new forms of deference and new hierarchies of power. Despite being integral to India's cleanliness project, housekeepers are largely left on its periphery, required to become modern workers but only able to access modern spaces via exploitative employment regimes. Most insidious is the way in which this access is constructed as a benefit and opportunity for the working poor, who have limited educational and economic capital and are thus expected to do the work of cleaning the dirt generated by those more wealthy than themselves.

Endnotes

1. Such a situation is not unique to India, as neoliberal globalization has had a radical impact on the cleaning industry around the world. As Tomic, Trumper, and Dattwyler (2006) note, based on their research in Chile, the

lives of janitorial workers provide important insight into the global economy because "they are both central to the implementation of the new neoliberal project and because neoliberalism has been quite forcefully imprinted on their lives" (p. 509). Similarly, Zlolniski's (2006) ethnography of Mexican immigrant janitors subcontracted to clean technology firms in the United States highlights the "paradox of poverty in the midst of the affluence that has become a distinct mark of Silicon Valley" (p. 4).

2. This video can be viewed at http://www.youtube.com/ watch?v=WyzWHltXR60.

3. Our findings resonate with those found by Brody (2006) in his study of Thai janitors in shopping malls. Brody's interviews with trainers in Thailand reveal that they justify the need for training by constructing workers as different and rural. One trainer noted, "We need rules because things are so different for people from the provinces (*tang jangwat*). They don't do things in the usual way. . . . [Here] many things are forbidden, such as drinking alcohol at work. Stealing is forbidden. Some people who come from upcountry don't know—they see something nice, and they take it. It's forbidden to eat food upstairs because it doesn't look good in front of the customers" (p. 548).

CHAPTER 3

Model Entrepreneurs/ Violent Offenders

Corporate Taxi Drivers at Crossroads

Social enterprise is often promoted as a developmental miracle drug. Entrepreneurialism is the "fortune at the bottom of the pyramid," in the words of the prominent late Indian academic C. K. Prahalad (Doane, 2014). The celebration of small-scale enterprise is closely aligned with neoliberal state and international agendas. As Freeman summarizes, "The contemporary entrepreneur represents neoliberalism's heroic actor: supple, flexible, and keenly responsive to market fluctuations, always prepared to retool and retrain to advance in unchartered directions" (2014, p. 17). India's corporate taxi drivers are part of the nation's entrepreneurial class, who, with limited resources, few class advantages, and little cultural capital, are said to be leading the country's "development miracle." The driver is both part of and yet, as we argue in this chapter, different from the well-established and ideologically significant figure of the successful poor entrepreneur, occupying a central role in public imaginations within India and around the world. Drivers' work represents a service to the nation, as they are key players in mediating one of India's greatest challenges in its attempt to compete with other emerging economies internationally—an inadequate transportation infrastructure. Their labor allows executives and employees to seamlessly and safely transition from the wide boulevards and tree-lined streets surrounding their organizations in special economic zones to the potholed roads that lack footpaths and where multiwheeled vehicles share the road with pedestrians, hawkers, and livestock. Drivers' jobs involve conquering traffic uncertainty and chaos in order to meet Western corporate targets of timeliness, order, and accountability.

Jobs within the transportation industry have increased manifold since India's economic liberalization. According to the Regional Transport Office, for example, the number of taxicab permits granted has increased from 6,300 in 2005 to 14,600 in 2010 in Pune alone. Out of these, about 11,000 cabs offer transportation services to the city's multinational technology industry (Dastane, 2010).[1] The provision of company-sponsored transportation services is marketed as a significant perk for women and men employed by software firms and international call centers, particularly those that operate on 24-hour schedules. Furthermore, the ability to safely and reliably transport workers to and from work during the day or night allows organizations to circumvent legal restrictions on as well as widely held social taboos against night work, particularly when carried out by young people and women.

Unlike the housekeepers and security guards who service India's multinational corporations, some drivers own the vehicle that they operate, while others aspire to become owners of capital. These "owner/drivers" play an important ideological role as agents who through their hard work, tenacity, determination, and careful planning, have the potential to lift themselves and their families out of the cycle of poverty within which many low-wage service workers are trapped.

Yet these model entrepreneurs and ideal neoliberal subjects, all of whom are men, are simultaneously a group associated closely with horrendous expressions of masculine power—namely, the rape, abduction, and murder of women. Highly publicized cases of driver violence against middle-class female workers has led to the introduction of surveillance systems and inspection protocols in the transportation sector, as well as an increase in suspicion from employers, passengers, state officials, and the public. Drivers, because they are poor and often migrants to the city, are seen to be always potentially on the verge of committing violent sexual crimes against women. Ironically, workers' enactment of masculinity required for successful entrepreneurship within the transportation field has also led to the criminalization of their poverty.

This chapter explores the crossroads at which India's drivers stand—engaged, like other entrepreneurs, in an endeavor that is potentially transformational but also extremely risky. They are model entrepreneurial citizens who are in pursuit of personal projects of upward mobility and national projects of alleviating infrastructure challenges. As self-employed workers, many driver/owners are unprotected by labor laws, and many work continuous shifts in order to protect their capital investment. At the same time, drivers are both physically and ideologically constructed as "outside" workers with violent tendencies linked to their masculinity, high-stakes risk-taking, and limited local ties. These constructions of drivers as both entrepreneurial and violent rely on the notion that they are willing to go anywhere, work any time, take little from the state, and risk everything.

The Risky Promise of Entrepreneurship

In a small air-conditioned office in a central Pune strip mall, Sunil, a local transportation vendor, narrated the incredible story of his business success. He described his entrepreneurialism with pride and deference, saying that his hard work had paid off because he had committed drivers and well-positioned clients. Ten years before, he had slept on footpaths while working 24 hours a day as a driver for a transnational executive. This benevolent employer eventually gave him a loan, which he pooled with money he received from his mother, who had sold her jewelry to help him. He then made a down payment on a car, which he subcontracted to a multinational corporation and drove himself. Within two years, he was able to repay his loan and make a down payment on a second vehicle. He marketed his services to corporations by visiting them on his bicycle and had the good fortune of receiving word-of-mouth recommendations from the executives he served. He received contracts that he fulfilled by teaming up with other owner/drivers who had made the required capital investment for cars. Multinational firms paid monthly fees for these cars and drivers, a proportion of which Sunil retained as an overhead. In this way, one by one, he purchased vehicles and hired drivers and by the time of his interview had become the owner of a company with a series of small offices, which he had purchased one at a time. Not visible from these offices, however, were the 300 cars under his control—225 of which he owned and 75 of which he leased from other owners starting out like he once had—which were parked at client sites. He paid salaries to 40 employees, posted mostly at organizational sites as supervisors, and his company was housed in three air-conditioned offices—one of which he used as his office, a second in which his English-speaking assistant sat and where prospective drivers were interviewed, and a third containing half a dozen desks with computers on which the exact locations of each cab were continually monitored via a global positioning system (GPS) he had purchased from Dubai. Now that he had forged a path to success, Sunil said that he could help other drivers:

> I try to make driver/owners from the drivers I have—those who are good drivers and have been working with me for three years. We select them. We tell them they can put in some money and we will help them. Someone helped me too. Even I had to contribute money from my own in the beginning. Nothing is free. . . . I have had such bad days. I used to have to struggle to look for business. Now this business is established, and these drivers do not need to go and look for business. There is IT park. . . . There is fixed package.

At the same time, despite his phenomenal success and his desire to help others, Sunil was surprisingly circumspect when we asked whether he believed that, like him, others might also benefit from the influx of foreign companies into India. He spoke of the large corporations that provided his livelihood with disdain:

> What a company does is that it gives the contract to those who quote a lower price. Then they also ask you to pay PF [employee benefits] out of that. So their work is done. See, once the British came to India and ruled over us. Today, people at the IT park are taking our profit. They are rising while we are still slaves. They are using us. . . . The [IT] company earns so much money in dollars, but there are no benefits for Indians. They give their employees high salaries, and they have better opportunities. But what is there for us? They are expert in charging us fines. If a car is late, they charge a fine; if dusting is not done, they charge us a fine; if a car is not good, then there is a fine. It is very difficult.

Speaking mostly in Hindi, Sunil revealed that he in fact knew very little English, which he had learned by attending language classes. His English-speaking assistant accompanied him when he responded to tenders[2] at multinational corporations, and the laptop on his desk was really just for show, as he did not know how to use it—after all, he pointed out, he had only completed 10 years of formal schooling. His narrative revealed his deep-seated conviction that there was value in working hard, and he was sympathetic to the challenges drivers faced given the poverty they experienced. Yet he remained deeply uncertain that other drivers could replicate his success. He attributed his economic mobility to the fact that he had pursued opportunities when they were presented to him, but he recognized that such opportunities are few and far between and remained suspicious of foreign capital. Entrepreneurs such as Sunil serve an important role in the neoliberal project in postliberalization India. This project is reflected in the emergence of structural conditions such as the promotion of self-employment over direct employment, as well as in ideologies that encourage individuals to embrace individualism, entrepreneurialism, and self-competition (Ganti, 2014). As Gooptu (2013) notes, the early 1990s marked the emergence of an image of a new set of Indians embedded within enterprise culture—"optimistic, passionate, do-ers in all fields of life" (p. 3). This figure of the "'enterprising self' is goal oriented, self-directed, committed to acquiring skills and competencies required for self-advancement; one who is optimistic, creative, takes initiative, embraces opportunities and seeks autonomy and self-fulfillment" (Gooptu, 2009, p. 45). Risk, in this context, is not only normalized but glamorized. This new kind of entrepreneurship is assumed to cut across classes. In fact, given their potential entrepreneurial energy, India's poor are often depicted in such narratives as "assets." Cast as experts in "creative coping" and as bearers of the strong tradition of "footpath business-men," the poor, with their potential of becoming romanticized slum mil-lionaires, provide hope and promise to Indians (Gooptu, 2013). Indeed, taxi drivers in contemporary India are surrounded by a net of "artefacts of entrepreneurship" (Anjaria & Anjaria, 2013, p. 192), including films, popular fiction, the emergence of citizen candidates in politics, highly publicized rags-to-riches narratives, and foreign and locally funded enterprise "schemes." Together, these have given rise to an increase in drivers' aspirational capital (Gándara, 1995). Instead of improved qual-ity of life or working conditions, such aspirational capital, which mainly involves the ownership of one or more vehicles, is the medium through which drivers hope to climb class ladders and pass on their driving jobs, which are uniformly recognized as stressful and unsustainable, to others who are less fortunate.

The segment of the transportation sector that provides services to India's large multinational firms can be divided into three groups of service providers. Business owners like Sunil own cars and obtain contracts from firms. They are, however, in a minority. Most are part of a second group, made up of individuals who own just one car—the driver/owners—which they drive themselves in order to pay off loan costs and acquire capital to perhaps purchase another vehicle. At the bottom of the economic pyramid is the third set of workers—the drivers who are paid a salary in cash and who hope in the future to purchase a car so they can become driver/owners.

Drivers as a group can be characterized as "on the move" in a variety of ways. Out of the 31 drivers we interviewed for this project, only 4 were born in Pune. The remaining had migrated from neighboring villages. Most had learned to drive on farms as part of their agricultural work, or because they had family or friends who owned rickshaws or tempos (small vehicles). They were part of the literate poor, possessing some education and identity documents, but not enough social capital to access stable, well-paying jobs. We met many drivers while they waited in their vehicles outside the buildings where the executives they transported worked, and many of the interviews were conducted while they were on-call or in between pickups and dropoffs. Amit, who was referred to as "uncle" by employees and colleagues because he was 56 years old, was one such driver. With a fourth-grade education, Amit had come to the city seven years earlier because it had been difficult for him and his multiple brothers to live off farm earnings and he had wanted his children to be educated in the city. One of Amit's sons was now working as a computer technician, and another drove a car owned by the family. Amit himself held two driving jobs—one with a contractor for a technology company for which he worked from 6 a.m. to 6 p.m., and a second for which he drove a bus from midnight to 3 a.m. By pooling their income, the family aimed to pay off the debts they had acquired during Amit's son's wedding and to eventually purchase a home.

Amit's description of his day-to-day tasks also reveals that driving work physically involves being constantly on the move. He provided a continuous shuttle service between two company offices located in different parts of the city, with 30-minute wait times at each office. This continuous movement was typical of the jobs held by drivers whom we interviewed. Contractors and drivers uniformly emphasized the challenges of driving work given the unruly nature of the roads, the unpredictability of weather, and the high consequences of lateness. Contractors also frequently noted the stressful nature of drivers' jobs. Bheem described his own career progression from a site supervisor to a manager at one of Pune's earliest transportation companies serving 24-hour transnational call centers. We met him at his office after many of our attempts to set up an interview failed because he was often on the move dealing with personnel issues (e.g., disagreements between company employees and drivers, absenteeism, or scheduling problems). Bheem's company was housed in a residential apartment building in which bedrooms had been converted to air-conditioned offices for workers at computers. We met in one of these rooms, and Bheem described drivers' work in English as follows:

> It's a hectic duty. They have to be very much cool mind[ed] when they work, because there is the call from the center where from they have been monitored. . . . Because working in this transport section, it is a thankless job and hectic job. And they are actually literally restless, you know. After one duty immediately they have to turn out for the next duty. Bringing the pickup, they immediately go for the drop for the second shift or second section. So they are actually restless, and they get irritated, you know.

What makes drivers' jobs particularly stressful are their work times. In this context, the use of the term "restless" by Bheem refers not only to the anxiety caused by the work but also literally to the lack of rest that drivers get. Drivers are typically employed for 12-hour shifts, but owner/drivers are self-employed, and some work 18 to 24 hours a day. On one occasion we met a driver named Rajiv in a parking lot in a special economic zone. He informed us that his car was also his home. He had migrated to Pune from his village, where there was no employment, and given his long hours had decided not to rent accommodation. He slept in his car and used the washroom facilities at a friend's house. Raza, a 28-year-old driver, also reported working 24 hours per day:

> One can work as much as one wants. They don't say anything. I do this job for 24 hours. Means I can drive as much as I want to. There are gaps every 2 to 3 hours. After 5 a.m. there is two-hour break, then I have to do a drop at 7:30, for example. Then there is again, I have a gap of 2 to 3 hours. Then I take rest. . . . There is no fixed shift in this line of work. There are some who come at 8 a.m. and leave at 8 p.m. But my vehicle is there for 24 hours.

When we first met Raza, he was in a parking lot in his vehicle with his brother, Bhushan, who managed the accounts for the two cars the brothers owned and drove. They invited the research team to their home, where they told us that they were both practicing Muslims and lived with one other brother and Raza's wife, whom he had recently married. The brothers said they could earn more as drivers than they could as security guards, and that during the month of the fast they were allowed to keep their beards, even though at other times they were required to be clean-shaven, which they appreciated. By contrast, Kumar told us that he did not like being a driver. He described his workday: "I arrive at the office at 8 a.m. and return home at 5:30 a.m. I have my breakfast and leave for office again at 8 a.m. I return home around 12:30 to 1:00 p.m. I have my lunch and return to the office at 2:30 p.m. Then I return home around 5:30 to 6:00 p.m. and return to work at 8 p.m." Kumar was deeply affected by the fact that he was continuously suspected of improper behavior and described his occupation as one with no status. He told us that he appreciated the technological tracking devices in his car such as the GPS because it minimized requests from passengers to make unauthorized stops at markets or detours. Kumar's tone was wistful when he described his desired career as a bank manager, and he told us that despite having made multiple attempts to pass his exams, he had been unable to do so and thus had resigned himself to becoming a driver. He was now supporting his wife, who was studying. He felt that he had been held back by his Marathi-medium schooling and dreamed of his children going to English-medium schools, saying, "I studied in a Marathi medium school. I didn't get much knowledge there. I think that children become smarter, they learn manners in English medium schools. . . . That's why I would admit them to an English medium school. I'll work harder and save money for it."

Drivers also reported supplementing their incomes by providing informal transportation, even though this was officially against the rules. On one occasion, as we stood by the side of the road, Raja approached us asking if we required transport. We instead shared information about our project, and he agreed to be interviewed. He told us that he worked 24-hour shifts during weekdays and often supplemented his income by providing transport to individuals while he waited for his scheduled pickups and dropoffs.

These very long workdays made it extremely difficult for drivers to participate in household or childcare work. In fact, out of the 31 drivers we interviewed, only 1 had a wife who was engaged in waged work, although 24 were married and 14 had children. The main contribution of drivers to their households was financial support.

While workers in many professions often work long hours because of the enterprising nature of their work, which requires self-discipline and endurance, corporate taxi drivers do so primarily in order to protect the large investment they have made. Workers who do not meet car loan commitments stand to forfeit their investments. Many drivers become owners through loan schemes, which lead to a situation in which they are, for all intents and purposes, "bonded" to vendors. These bonds are described in contrasting ways by contractors and drivers. This was evident when we met Devrani at her office in a transportation company, where she sat at a desk with a large computer screen. As the sister of the owner and one of the directors of the company, she was responsible for managing contracts, fines, and training. With great pride, she used the term "corporate social responsibility" to characterize her company's ways of working and shared details of the loan schemes they had in place to allow drivers to become owners. When we asked what happened if driver/owners were unable to fulfill their loan commitments, she explained, "If the car meets with an accident or [the driver] cannot run it, then he surrenders [it]. If he says, 'I don't want to do this anymore,' then he can surrender the car back to us, and if there is any deposit . . . then we transfer the car to another vendor." While Devrani characterized the loan arrangement as a "partnership" that instilled a "sense of responsibility" in drivers, it was clear that the risks of ownership were borne primarily by the drivers.

We heard similar narratives from other transportation vendors. It took over a year of telephone exchanges to get an appointment with Hiresh. Numerous times he said he was interested in talking to us but did not have time and asked us to check in with him again, which we did every two or three months. One afternoon, Hiresh himself called and scheduled an interview. Our conversation centered around his enthusiastic support for driver/owner schemes. He spent many hours with us not only telling us about the history of his company but also showing us his parking lot, where the 100 cars he owned and 125 cars owned by drivers he employed were parked. Evidently proud of the organization he had built, he said that his company offered loan schemes to drivers who had been model employees: "We offer them golden opportunity. You are experienced, you have a good record, you didn't misbehave with anyone, so we give them a golden chance. We have hired a new car, and we made the down payment of INR 50,000. If the driver wants, he can drive this car, and he can return the money by paying regular installments to us. So by paying regular installment, driver is benefited as well as we also get profit." Despite this "golden opportunity," Hiresh reported that drivers faced many difficulties. Although the transportation sector had been booming when he first set up his company in 2001, it was now not easy for either drivers or contractors to make a living because American companies expected extremely low-cost services in India and sought to maximize their profits by engendering vendor competition. In fact, Hiresh and his brother, who jointly owned the company, had decided two years earlier to stop providing cars to call centers that required 24-hour-service because the risks were too great. The decision was made after a late-night accident in which a number of company employees were injured because of a tired driver who hit a road divider. Hiresh noted that drivers who did not get a proper night's sleep were often tired and accident prone. He also noted that drivers often did not have insurance and rarely received health or pension benefits.

As independent contractors, driver/owners are paid a flat monthly sum by contractors based on a combination of time and mileage. They are responsible for the payment of their loans, as well as the payment of expenses such as registration fees, uniforms, stickers, logbooks, and identity cards. In addition, they are charged fines as high as INR 500, or 5 to 10 percent of drivers' monthly income, if cars are late or if drivers are improperly attired. Profit margins for those who own and operate one car can be so small that unforeseen circumstances such as a family illness or accident may put them at risk of losing their investment.

Drivers, as a result, were ambivalent about the opportunities within the transportation sector. When we met Raunak, who owned two cars and drove one of them for 12 hours a day, he gave us a vivid description of the risks involved in ownership. He said that he earned 6,000 or 7,000 INR per car after all expenses were paid. He used this to pay for household expenses as well as any extra costs such as accidents. His earnings were low because he did not want to drive himself for 24 hours a day and so had to pay wages to another driver. He said "If you get a bank loan on your cab, then there is no guarantee that you can pay installments. You have to do 8 to 10 trips per day. Not all employee[s] reside in areas with good roads. The car can get scratched while maneuvering . . . and if any accident happens, the driver can't do anything until he gets the claim from insurance and he gets it repaired. In those two to three months he can't do anything. It's risky." Ranuak recounted an incident in which one of the cars he owned was in an accident:

Last week my Indica was parked on the road and the driver was sitting inside. While he was getting out he didn't look in the mirror and opened the door, and some lady was coming from behind on a two-wheeler. She crashed into the door. She got hurt. The driver took her to the hospital. She got five stitches on the head. A police complaint was filed. The police confiscated the car. The hospital bill came up to 12,000 to 15,000. I paid half of it. I also paid the police another 2,500 to get the car back from them. I had to pay all this. If the driver had to pay this, then nobody will work. The driver said he was not paying attention. Drivers are not easy to get, so what can I say to the driver? Even drivers are frustrated after 8 to 10 trips.

Like many other driver/owners, Ranuak undertook what he recognized as a significant financial risk in the hope of providing a better future for his children. However, even drivers who do not have the financial resources to become owners face employment risks because they are employees of very small firms that are not required by labor law to provide workers benefits or protections. As an official with the Labor Department explained, drivers working for vendors with more than five employees are covered under the Motor Transport Workers Act, and those working with vendors who have over 20 employees are covered under the Contract Labour Act. Most drivers we interviewed, however, either owned the cars they drove or drove cars for owners who did not have more than five employees. Kumar, who had hoped to work at a bank, told us that he did not foresee ever being able to purchase a car. He said, "If we are in an accident, even if it happens when car is stationary and we are not responsible, we have to pay for the damage. My boss is a good person. He shares the bill, but still you lose some money. In most cases the drivers have to shell out 90 percent of the money, while the car owner pays only 10 percent." He remained skeptical about the possibility of economic mobility: "If you buy a car—of course, I don't have the resources for it—and employ it in the service of a company, you get a check for INR 40,000 per month. . . . [After calculating expenses] you are left with very little. There is no profit. It can work only if you buy a car with cash." Without any prospect of earning enough to save for the capital investment required to buy a car, Kumar planned instead to try to find employment in Dubai because, he lamented, "I am simply rotting here."

Drivers also face numerous health risks as a result of their employment. In conjunction with their exhausting working hours, the perpetual sense of risk seemed to make even the most seemingly successful drivers and driver/owners circumspect and withdrawn when confronted with questions about their future prospects. They presented personas that were considerably different from the images of enthusiasm and hope that generally accompany discussions of enterprise culture.

Forty-seven-year-old Raghu's experience provides a case in point. He had among the highest monthly earnings of the drivers we interviewed. He had migrated from his village 10 years earlier after droughts had made farming no longer sustainable and had taken a job as a driver. Five years earlier he had used his savings to purchase a car, driving it himself from 8 a.m. to midnight every day. He had been able to save enough to pay off his loan, support his wife and four children, and take out loans to build a home and purchase a second car. He attributed his financial success to the capital he had acquired through the sale of village assets, as well as the fact that he was extremely frugal with his earnings, saving as much as possible each month. When asked about the long hours he spent at his job, he explained, "I am exhausted. And with age my legs and hands hurt. But there is no alternative. I don't get paid like those IT guys. But the cost has gone up. I have to continue to meet my living costs. . . . I have to somehow live day by day." As far as he was concerned, the IT boom in India meant only that the cost of living had gone up because "they pay me so little, it has made no difference to my life." Despite his current household income of INR 25,000 per month, Raghu was not optimistic about his four children's prospects. Because access to better schools and higher education required large payments that he was unable to make, he remarked that he only hoped that his children would complete tenth grade, and that after that, "it's their fate." He concluded that "it's hard for ordinary people to live in cities." As this example illustrates and Anjaria and Anjaria (2013) observe, there is often a gap between enterprising ideals and the actual experiences of entrepreneurship in postliberalization India that gives rise to a situation in which people engage in entrepreneurialism, but reluctantly (p. 197).

Corporate drivers in today's postliberalization India share many traits with "bottom of the pyramid" entrepreneurs such as rickshaw owners (Shlaes & Mani 2013), street vendors (Bhowmik & Saha, 2012), and recyclers (McDougall, 2007). Yet they also differ from them in several important ways. Corporate taxi drivers and driver/owners are expected to engage in a continuous process of what Freeman (2014) has described as the "management of selfhood," a key part of neoliberal entrepreneurialism. In this view, drivers' bodies and identities are seen as "projects" that have to be worked on. Like the female entrepreneurs in Barbados interviewed by Freeman (2014), corporate drivers engage in work that involves an exchange of affect—specifically, reliability and safety. The primary reason for the provision of car transportation services is to facilitate the secure transport of company employees and convey modernity, certainty, and standardization in the face of a chaotic system of road infrastructure.

Drivers reported that they were required to provide documentary evidence of their good character and were asked for identity documents, police clearance, and a valid driving license when they applied for their jobs. Ramesh, a 23-year-old driver who had been driving for multinational technology firms for about six years, gave us a list of documents he had been required to provide: "Xerox of license, two photos, ration card or electricity bill Xerox; in some places, they even ask for reference letter. And then they give us an identity card." Raunak, who was affiliated with one of the larger transport contractors, further explained, "We have to complete a police verification every year. Our fingerprints are taken and sent to the commissioner's office, as well as face recognition. They have an INR 500 fee. We have to pay."

Once they were hired, all drivers reported that they received some training on road safety and employee transportation protocols. Drivers' training, however, primarily focused on cleanliness and, unlike the training received by security guards and housekeepers, placed little emphasis on communication styles or the use of the English language. Unlike many other service workers, drivers as well as, to a lesser extent, housekeepers and security guards were required to be invisible rather than interactive while they worked.

Freeman (2014) notes that the crux of neoliberal entrepreneurialism is the "blurring boundaries between enterprise-as-business and the self-as-enterprise" (p. 209). Indeed, the key to being a successful corporate taxi driver is the ability to transform one's physical appearance in line with "modern" standards of cleanliness. Drivers are required to pay for and maintain their uniforms and shoes, as well as to ensure that their cars are clean. Kapil explained that he was required to "maintain cleanliness and be presentable. Your shirt and trouser should not be soiled." When asked why these requirements were seen to be so important, he emphasized that "the employees wouldn't like it and they would not cooperate if we are shabbily dressed." Sudhir reported receiving training on minimizing smell because when drivers were on night duty, "we sleep in the car while the car windows are shut, and that generates a smell in the car." Kapil's and Sudhir's sentiments were echoed by a facilities manager at a large multinational firm who pointed to the fact that since drivers were often poor, they could not meet the requisite "hygiene standards," such as wearing ironed shirts and polished shoes, demanded by their company headquarters. Ratnakar, a transportation vendor, remarked, "Drivers here are from a totally unorganized and totally uneducated background, so we try to educate them and try to make them as professional as possible." Education here was not only used to refer to formal schooling but was steeped in civilizing discourses emphasizing cleanliness and neatness.

While the self-work required of housekeepers and security guards generally involves learning how to interact with employees in particular ways, drivers, in stark contrast, are asked to "disappear themselves" as part of their job. Raghu stated:

> I don't talk much. When they [passengers] sit in the car, I drive them. That's all. There is no need to talk. Whether it is a woman or anyone, we do not say anything to anyone. . . . There are no words spoken. I bring them to the company office and drop them back home. . . . We are given a computer sheet. It has all the information such as the schedule, timings of pickups for each employee. If she or he is not ready to board at that time, then we leave them. We have to reach the next point of pickup.

Workers are usually instructed not to interact with employees, even if they are spoken to, as Raja corroborated: "We do not speak much with the employees, and if they start talking too much, then we call the transport department and they tell us what is to be done." Kapil similarly noted, "Talking with passengers is to be avoided as far as possible. When you start a conversation on one theme, it can lead to . . . you know. . . . We are supposed to make only necessary conversation because nothing should happen." Ashvinkumar explained: "We don't talk to employee passengers while driving. We have been instructed not to do so by the company. We speak to passengers only if we don't know the way, and they give us short instructions like 'left' or 'right'. . . . When ladies are in the cab with the security guard, we are not supposed to talk to anyone, even the security guard."

Both the provision of safety and the avoidance of the undesirable consequences to which Kapil referred involve disappearing embodiments—that is, the expectation that drivers will become as invisible as possible. Ideal drivers are those who perform their jobs like machines—those who follow schedules with clockwork precision; do not speak; satisfy no bodily needs while they are on the job, such as eating, drinking, or using the bathroom; and do not listen to the radio or chew tobacco, which is said to produce an unsightly red color and smell distasteful to passengers.

The prohibition against any relationship building is applicable not only to drivers, but to contractors as well. As Reyaan, a manager at a transportation company, reported, "We have orders from big IT companies. We have orders from the higher authorities that we should not maintain any relationships with company employees. We are not supposed to talk much. Because you never know [if] someone might not like [it]. We don't talk much."

In contrast to most other service professions, which involve the embodied emotional labors of distancing, caring, or empathizing, drivers are required to diminish any emphasis on interactive labor. As we will discuss in the following section, a sense of safety is conveyed to passengers by nearly new cars (most companies require vendors to provide cars that are less than three years old), silent and uniformed drivers with identity cards, surveillance protocols that include the use of GPS systems and extensive records of employee and car movements. These protocols, which forbid any driver/passenger contact, have developed in response to associations that have been forged between driving work, masculinity, and violence.

Rapists in Waiting: Model Entrepreneurs or Violent Offenders

In 2005 a young female call center employee in Bangalore was raped and murdered by a cab driver who was transporting her home from work. She had been employed by a large multinational company that outsourced its transportation services to a vendor, and her murder was one among other similar acts of violence that had been committed by drivers against young female workers employed in the multinational technology sector in cities such as Bangalore, Mumbai, Pune, and Delhi. Hegde (2011) describes the social and organizational responses to the Bangalore rape, which centered on improving the protection of female call center employees through the introduction of surveillance technologies. The 2005 incident, however, also represented a watershed moment for corporate taxi drivers, particularly those responsible for transporting female employees during nighttime hours. As Ramchandra, a 36-year-old driver with two adult daughters, explained, "Earlier, driving was a respected line of work. But after the case of the rape of the lady employee passenger, people look at us with suspicion." In response to publicized cases of violence by drivers, the professed safety of women working in international call centers was called into question, and numerous protocols were established to provide greater scrutiny and surveillance of corporate taxi drivers. Drivers went from being the facilitators of safety to the embodiment of extreme risk. Their work processes changed accordingly.

The risk that drivers are thought to pose is managed not only through work processes that require them to remain disembodied during work but also through their physical exclusion from their spaces of work. This exacerbates their already existing status as "outsiders," a perception that stems from their assumed weak community ties due to their recent migration. Ironically, drivers' poverty and limited engagement with home and community settings has led to their further criminalization.

Both physically and symbolically, drivers are distanced from their place of employment, as they spend most of their time on the road picking up and dropping off groups of workers. As "outside" workers, they gain only temporary and transitional access to high-tech organizational spaces. Rajiv, the young driver who informed us that he lived in his car, had moved to Pune four years earlier because he could not get a good job in his village based on his twelfth-grade education. He described the organization for which he provided transportation services in the following manner: "The company building is made of glass. You can't really see people. Most IT staff works indoors. There are security guards at the entrance, and they don't allow you inside without a valid ID card. . . . There are security guards, employees of the company, and there is the housekeeping staff. But we are not allowed inside the office. We can go only till the gate. We drive the staff till the gate and pick them up from the gate." Similarly, Saini reported that his company was "made of glass" and that his only interaction with those on the inside was through telephone conversations with the transportation supervisor. Indeed, the glass-faced buildings, which are celebrated as India's architectural symbols of modernity, are experienced by drivers as markers of exclusion, despite the long hours they spend in the areas around or the basements of these buildings. Raja stated, "We can only go up to the parking which is on ground floor. I think there are seven floors above parking. The building from the outside is all covered with glass. We cannot go up above the parking level into the building."

The physical containment of drivers to the boundaries of the organization is accompanied by complex surveillance protocols, which have become standard in the industry. Most of the costs of such technological requirements are borne by drivers themselves, although contractors also report hiring additional personnel for surveillance. Some cars are equipped with GPS and employee "panic" buttons that have to be monitored by vendors. Vehicles that are found to be off-route can be turned off remotely if fitted with the correct technology. Trunks are checked at organizational gates with a metal detector, and drivers receive daily alcohol tests. Raunak summarized that the protocols in place to monitor drivers are the "same as that of a criminal." However, not all drivers experienced surveillance as invasive—as Ashvinkumar claimed, "It's good for the passengers as well as good for our safety. . . . If something happens, we are not responsible. We can ask them to look at the report and find out who is responsible. . . . GPS shows how fast you are driving."

Surveillance protocols also involve passengers themselves. During one of our interviews with a driver in his car, we noticed a prominently displayed list of "dos and don'ts" for passengers. The list included: "Do not call the driver directly for unscheduled pickups or dropoffs; if the vehicle makes a stop at an unscheduled or lonely spot, inform the transport supervisor immediately; inform the transport supervisor if you see any strange person sitting along with the driver and do not board the cab; do not have unnecessary conversations with drivers; avoid discussing your personal or immediate plans while in the cab." A separate list was directed toward female passengers: "Don't sit in the front seat; when travelling alone inform security and also your family members; be alert about anything abnormal, appear confident, do not panic; do not wear noticeable or expensive clothing/jewelry."

In addition, drivers transporting female passengers at night are required to have a male security guard accompany them when there are no male passengers. Security vendors, rather than transportation vendors, provide these security guards. This protocol assumes that, despite the possibility of violent male drivers, men are still required to safeguard women at night. Tara and Ilavarasan's (2012) interviews with female employees at call centers reveal the tenuous nature of this assumption. One employee they interviewed noted, "The guard in our cab does not carry any weapon, and he is neither strong enough to handle any tough situation; most of the time he sleeps during the travel. But my parents feel that I am safe when I am coming with a guard, but I think it is good for nothing." Another call center employee interviewed in this study characterized the driver and guard combination as a "double risk" for women (p. 161). A transportation vendor we interviewed expressed similar sentiments. Ali, who worked for his family-owned transportation company, noted, "The guard is also present in the cab. What he will do? He will . . . try to shoo off the harassers verbally, but [what] if they get surrounded by four to five unruly people who try to abuse the occupants of the cab? The cab driver can't fight with them, and the guard is equipped with a small baton but not authorized to hit anyone with it. It's just like a show piece."

In spite of the widespread introduction in the sector of technologies and work practices of surveillance, acts of violence continue to occur. Driver surveillance serves primarily to signify that organizations have taken some action to prevent violence. This action, however, has not included addressing drivers' employment terms or working conditions. Rather, violence continues to be seen as isolated and random. As the chief of the company that employed the 2005 Bangalore rape victim noted, "What precautionary measures can be taken against a suicide bomber?" (Hegde, 2011, p. 186).

Indeed, while popular among many contractors, not all transport companies have introduced GPS systems. Ali, a transportation vendor who expressed skepticism about the current security protocols in place, stated, "We don't have GPS in every cab. . . . Not every company wants to do this; they don't want to raise cost unnecessarily. . . . My question is . . . why does all the blame fall on the driver? If you check the records, you will at the most find seven to eight rape cases that have been highlighted, but nobody pays attention to the harassment cases that happen inside the company." Ali instead suggested that female professionals be trained about protocols they should follow as passengers to avoid male violence:

> If you treat the driver properly, he will be nice to you and remain calm. As the drivers are uneducated men, for example, if you throw tantrums or start chatting with your boyfriend inappropriately in front of the driver, then his mind gets disturbed. The devil in his

mind gets provoked. If you take simple precautions then things will become easy. . . . At the end of the day, drivers are also human beings. If you treat them well you will also receive good treatment from them. Actually out of 100 drivers only 1 or 2 drivers may be hot-headed, but today what is happening is that every driver has become a suspect.

This coupling of violence and masculinity ran through the narratives of even those sympathetic to drivers' social and economic circumstances. Despite public acknowledgement of the symbolic purposes of surveillance, it does in effect serve to criminalize drivers. The police and the public at large also exercise surveillance. The Regional Transport Office in Pune has made it compulsory for drivers serving the multinational technology industry to wear uniforms and carry government-issued ID cards while on duty. Akash noted, "Even a person on a bicycle tries to bully an Indica with a yellow number plate [signaling assignment to the multinational technology sector]." Almost all drivers interviewed mentioned the routine payment of bribes to police officers. Raunak reported, "Once a guy on a kinetic [scooter] which had broken brakes rammed into my car. We both had to pay INR 100 fine. The police said, 'I will arrest both of you, and then you can fight in court.' So obviously we paid the bribe rather than going to court." Harshal summarized, "Just by looking at the yellow number plate people bother us and abuse us, even if there is no mistake of ours."

This criminalization of drivers is related both to their assumed poverty and to their status as migrants. An official employed with the Labor Department attributed drivers' high level of violence to their poor salaries, declaring that drivers see that their passengers "are using money like anything and they are enjoying themselves." Because these company employees sometimes earn 10 or more times drivers' salaries, this "creates criminal tendencies in the drivers," the official concluded. Such criminalization of poverty is accompanied by the construction of drivers as transient and with few local ties. Reyaan, a manager at a transport company, thus claimed, "These guys come from outside, where the conditions are very bad."

Thus, as we have illustrated in this chapter, corporate taxi drivers transporting India's IT professionals are constantly under suspicion of being violent offenders. They are given written rosters of their dropoff and pickup locations, and many cars have GPS surveillance systems to ensure that they do not deviate from prescribed routes. They are not allowed to interact with passengers and are forbidden to respond creatively to traffic situations by reorganizing routes to meet their required pickup and dropoff times. Since as men they share their sex with violent rapists, they are asked to present themselves as faceless, disembodied extensions of their vehicles. Indeed, they are asked to be decidedly unenterprising in the way they go about their work.

Yet, discourses of masculinity are simultaneously a necessary condition for drivers' jobs given the irregular and long hours and frequent night work. Men are therefore constructed as simultaneously dangerous, and appropriate for dangerous work. By becoming driver/owners they are emblems of the enterprising Indian, who through hard work and only a little capital, can experience transformation, like Sunil, described at the start of this chapter. The promise of enterprise creates aspirational capital for many drivers who hope, in the final analysis, to purchase cars and pass on their poor quality jobs to others, who can in turn hope to do the same. Their experiences provide a vivid illustration of Gooptu's (2013) observation that class assumptions accompany discourses of enterprise that promote systems in which lower-middle-class workers bear the greatest risks and costs. Indeed, all drivers we interviewed reported that they received higher salaries as drivers than they had in their previous jobs. Yet their extremely long hours and high level of stress, in conjunction with the continual suspicion with which they were treated, caused few to characterize their job as sustainable in the long term, unless they were able to take the risk of becoming entrepreneurs themselves. They both aspired to this aim and simultaneously noted the dubious prospects of this path as a route to mobility.

Endnotes

1. There has been an attempt to further regulate the taxicab industry since the rise of Uber and Ola. Between April 2016 and February 2017 alone, 21,835 new taxicabs were registered in Pune (Biswas, 2017). New legislation entitled the Maharashtra City Taxi Rules was enacted in 2017 requiring drivers of such vehicles to pay INR 25,000 in registration fees (Korde, 2017).
2. Tenders are written quotes for proposed services which subcontractors submit to multinational corporations. Subcontractors compete with one another during the tendering process.

CHAPTER 4

Risk Managers at Risk

*Private Security Guards in India's
Multinational Technology Firms*

The visual representation of wealth in India, the gleaming corporate towers of multinational companies, goes hand in hand with the visual representation of risk. The omnipresence of risk in contemporary Indian cities is embodied in the sheer number of uniformed private security guards who work there. With growing economic disparity between segments of the population, the task of managing the boundaries between spaces of wealth and spaces of poverty must be carried out on a continuous basis. It is commonplace for shopping malls, corporate buildings, educational institutions, apartment blocks, banks, petrol stations, and commercial shops to have security guards posted at their entrance. The proliferation of multinational corporations has intensified the security presence in all major cities. Aside from checking bags, frisking entrants, searching cars, issuing passes, and denying entry to inappropriate visitors, guards are also often tasked with keeping detailed logbooks in which they write names or entry numbers. In fact, India is reputed to have more private security personnel than any other country in the world (Gooptu, 2013b, p. 14).

Since economic liberalization, the Indian state has often promoted the multinational technology sector as the country's "sunshine sector" because of its 3.7 million employees and its assumed potential for phenomenal employment generation (Mishra, 2016). However, it is the private security industry that has created an even larger number of new jobs both within India and worldwide in the past two decades. Reports indicate that there are 15,000 security agencies in India that employ 8.5 million guards (PTI, 2018; Berrong, 2009). A staggering 1 million new security jobs are created per year, and the industry is expected to continue to grow by almost 20 percent per year (Ians, 2013).[1] As Gooptu (2013b) summarizes, the private security industry is "by far the most important among the newly emerging services" in India (p. 13).

The parallel growth of India's multinational technology corporations and private security sector has been far from accidental; indeed, the former has been an important impetus for the development of the latter. Global economic flows have not only given rise to the greater need for security guards but also led to new approaches to private security in India and globally. The Central Association of Private Security Industry (CAPSI) has noted that many guards are from villages, but companies want skilled youth who are educated and speak English (Jones, 2012). To meet the anticipated demand for 22 million guards by 2022, guard training has been identified as a significant gap within the sector and has led to the creation of the Security Sector Skill Development Council (PTI, 2018).

This chapter focuses on the experiences of private security workers who are simultaneously at the forefront of the management of risk and at risk themselves. Because security guards' jobs involve interacting with visitors they were easier to contact as research participants compared to housekeepers or facilities managers, whose jobs were based inside secluded organizational sites. This level of access was further improved when researchers traveled to company premises in a hired car, which signaled both our class position and the association of the research project with a "foreign" university. Male researchers from our team often met guards (as well as drivers and housekeepers) at nearby tea shops, and female researchers conducted interviews at bus stops or public benches, since tea shops were often male-dominated spaces. In many cases, we visited technology companies on weekends, when corporate employees were not present but security guards and housekeepers were. Some security guards were even interviewed while officially on duty because their work involved waiting or interacting with visitors at the entrances of organizations, making it possible to engage in conversations inconspicuously. However, guards not only were in charge of surveillance but also often faced considerable surveillance themselves. Many guards made mention of "security cameras" through which they were themselves being monitored.

Guards in settings where they were being monitored directed us to step outside the security cabin or out of the camera's range as we told them about the project and invited them to participate. Our meeting with Jayant was demonstrative. Visibly nervous as we told him about our project while he stood at his post outside a technology company, Jayant said that he wanted to talk to us but would only do so if we could meet him on Saturday, when most managers and supervisors were not present. He asked us to wait for him outside the gate of the special economic zone, which was a couple of kilometers away from his worksite. Once we agreed not to tape-record our conversation, he revealed the source of his hesitation—he had done two years of a bachelor's degree and was now studying for examinations required to join the police force, which he believed was one of the few remaining stable job options for someone like him, given that he had completed his education in Marathi rather than English. He did not want to jeopardize his plans and characterized his supervisors as extremely punitive, providing us with a list of fines he faced if he deviated from expectations. The list was overwhelming— INR 350 for not wearing a cap, INR 300 for not tucking in his shirt, INR 300 for not wearing the correct belt, INR 250 for not wearing the right shoes, INR 150 for chatting with other guards during work hours, INR 300 for reading a book during work hours, and INR 1,500 for leaving a security post without permission. Jayant reported that each month he received only a part of his stated monthly income because of these fines.

Just as drivers working for multinational technology firms are required to epitomize reliability and housekeepers are expected to epitomize cleanliness, security guards are required to embody safety, an aim that uses boundary management to ensure that only those deemed appropriate receive entry into transnational spaces. In this chapter we explore the mechanisms through which workers are transformed into young women and men with the correct embodied traits of time discipline, professionalism, and deference that allow them to ensure the safety of a national asset—foreign capital. We trace the frontiers of risk that these workers manage—risks to employees, risks to assets, risks to corporate reputation, and risks to themselves. At each frontier, security is provided in particular ways. At the same time, the manner in which security guards are recruited and trained and the conditions within which they work also produce specific kinds of workers. Despite the rhetoric of training and skill that pervades the sector, security guards are classified as unskilled, and their minimum wages are set accordingly

(Jones, 2012). State, labor, and corporate officials all justify these wage levels by evoking the discourse of labor shortage. Yet the assumed scarcity of labor has had little impact on the poor conditions and prospects of guards who are currently employed in the industry. In this chapter we highlight the challenges these guards face as a result of subcontracting, which has led to low wages and unstable work times.

The Global Growth of the Private Security Sector

The growth of the private security industry has not been limited to India. Security is now estimated to be a $120 billion industry, with large companies such as G4S, which claims to be the second-largest private sector employer in the world, operating in 115 countries (Abrahmansen & Williams, 2011, p. 171). In line with worldwide trends, in Australia private security personnel outnumber police two to one (Prenzler, Earle, & Sarre, 2009). In China, there are 4 million authorized private security guards, as well as several million unauthorized or unregistered guards (Trevaskes, 2007). Reasons for the recent growth of the industry include the growing preoccupation with global terrorism, which has led to a heightened public perception of risk (Gooptu, 2013b), as well as increasing social and economic inequality, which necessitates the protection of corporate and elite resources from those frustrated by the low or declining quality of their lives.

Much of the global analysis of the security industry has focused on the increasing outsourcing of military and security provision to private companies, particularly in conflict zones. In the Iraq War, for example, 100,000 private security and military contractors were hired to work alongside peacekeeper armies (Krahmann, 2008). Similarly, private security companies have been deployed in Angola, Sierra Leone, Liberia, Colombia, and Afghanistan (Andreopoulos & Brandle, 2012). As scholars have noted, such a trend marks a significant departure from the conventional notion that states hold a monopoly over the use of legitimate violence, as guided by interstate agreements. Not only do state security forces work in tandem with private security agents, but states are also consumers of private security themselves (Krahmann, 2008). Because of a number of highly publicized incidents of violence perpetrated by private security guards in recent years (Higate, 2012a), the frequent deployment of the military alongside private security forces has raised issues concerning the legitimacy of violence and accountability for the sanctioned use of force (Alexandra, 2012).

Outside conflict or war zones, however, there has also been a marked increase globally in the use of private security forces in routine organizational contexts. Security in these contexts, which often does not involve arms, is qualitatively different from security in conflict areas because of the delicate discursive balance that involves the *delinking* of security from violence. Indeed, despite the frequent presence of security in corporate spaces in India and many other global cities, these locations are constructed as spaces where workers face little or no risk of physical bodily violence. In this context, in which political stability is a key pillar of national strategies aimed at attracting foreign capital, the function of security is understood as centering around the provision of safety rather than dealing with violence. Security guards serve to protect organizational members, visitors, and assets from natural occurrences (e.g., fires) as well as material infringements (e.g., theft) by securing the borders around legitimate entrants. As a result, rather than focusing on training militia with weapons and equipment, corporate security relies on workers' "soft skills." Instead of being seen as signs of emasculation, traits such as being neat, remaining calm, and interacting with people with deference are cast as appropriate forms of masculinity for corporate guards to enact (Joachim & Schneiker, 2012b). Although private security remains a male-dominated profession in India, corporate spaces there include a much higher percentage of female guards than are found in traditional security industries such as the army and police. Feminized notions of protecting, caring, and serving are core elements of both male and female guards' jobs. Some feminist scholars have argued that jobs restructured by neoliberalism reconstruct gendered notions of work whereby older male-dominated jobs are being reclassified as better performed by women and traditionally feminine values like caring, loyalty, and empathy are becoming increasingly prominent in the workplace (McDowell, 1997; Salzinger, 2003; Acker, 1990). As we explore further in chapter 5, security service jobs are increasingly being feminized, irrespective of whether they are performed by men or by women.

Risk Management Through Public and Private Security in India

Despite the exponential growth of the private security industry in India in recent years, the industry itself is far from new. Public state security provided by the police and the army has historically been supplemented by private security guards hired by individuals and groups. Security concerns in India therefore far predate the influx of multinational corporations in the 1990s. Although the scale of the security workforce and the traits identified as desirable for security guards have shifted in the past two decades, historically the traditional figure of the *chawkidar*, or watchman, has been prevalent in Indian society and closely related to the militarized masculinities produced within colonial India (Chowdhry, 2013). Indeed, some of the security guards we interviewed were Mahars, who have a long history with the military and have often worked as watchmen in villages. Nalla (1998) notes that these jobs represent stable employment for men and their sons. On one university campus observed in her study, for example, watchmen were recruited from cowherder families, and the position provided stable although poorly paid employment, with housing and health benefits for families. Employers preferred direct employment contracts and expressed significant reservations about the quality of training and the lack of loyalty shown by contract guards (p. 18).

The tendency over the years for private enterprises and neighborhood collectives to hire *chawkidars* points to the fact that the state in India has never had complete control over the domain of security. In the context of India's colonial history, during which public security providers (such as the police and the army) were extensions of British power, local residents often hired local guards for protection. This history has shaped public perceptions of the police and the army, which are seen as extensions of the state that have not always served to protect citizens. A similar dynamic can be found in other postcolonial contexts. In a study of the development of the private security industry in Nigeria, for example, Kasali (2011) traces the country's current orientation toward risk to its colonial past. While traditionally members of the Nigerian elite often made use of the services of brave hunters with close ties to local populations, colonial administrators replaced such systems with a policing system that was detached from the community. Kasali notes that "colonizers designated African police to be an instrument of oppression against the local people with the aim of enjoying continued or unchecked domination over the colonized by the colonizer" (p. 37). This led to a "deep disconnect" between public security and the public it professed to protect, since the central aim of public security was to protect colonizers' interests. This situation gave rise to the perceived need for an extensive private security sector, which continues to flourish. As in India, Nigeria's private security industry includes both small local enterprises and large multinational corporations, and guards are widely used to protect not only private elites but also corporate interests. The Shell oil company, for example, employs 600 security personnel in Nigeria. Yet despite their key role in securing corporate interests, security guards receive poor wages. While Kasali links the growth of private security to the failure of state bureaucracy, Abrahamsen and Williams (2011) note that such growth is also the result of the prevalence of "mentalities of risk" and the valorization of any enterprise (including war) that can generate commercial economic value (p. 173).

Theorists who analyze the relationship between state security provision and the emergence of private security guards suggest that there is no straightforward causal relationship between public and private sector security. Abrahamsen and Williams (2011) use the term "security assemblages" to describe the multiple actors involved in security provision in each context and how they relate to one another. In India, aside from the state, key agents who structure private security provision for multinational corporations include security guards, managers who own or work for multinational companies, contractors, state officials, police, the local guard boards, and CAPSI. The rhetoric of neoliberalism and government downsizing that accompanied India's liberalization in the 1990s gave rise to the language of "public-private partnerships" to describe the relationship between public and private security. As Gooptu (2013b) notes, government ministers have often supported and endorsed the rapid growth of India's private security industry, noting that these services help compensate for India's low police-to-citizen ratio (p. 15). The need for such security has been perceived as increasingly urgent as the influx of transnational capital into India has led to the emergence of extremely visible markers of vast economic inequality in many cities. Accompanying this rise in inequality has been an increasing perception of risk among corporate actors and local elites (Gooptu, 2013b), who increasingly live in gated communities. The management of this risk involves the physical and ideological "exclusion" of those who are deemed security threats—specifically, the poor and less educated. Yet it is only through the labor of these very individuals that security can be ensured. Indeed, Graham and Kaker (2014, p. 13), based on their work in Karachi, argue that "complex interconnections" exist between those within gated enclaves and the rest of the city, giving rise to "uneven patchworks of securitized enclaves." Secure communities can never be truly gated, as they involve the constant coming and going of poorly paid "excluded" individuals who provide the labor necessary for maintaining such exclusions. Complex training mechanisms and work practices are used to convert these marginalized populations into a workforce who can serve the security industry and gain bounded entry across security borders. In this sense, as security is commodified and converted into something that is consumed, those responsible for its production are not only required to create security but also to embody safety themselves.

Security Consumption: Assets, Reputations, Employees, and Guards

The growth of the security industry globally is intrinsically linked to two closely related trends—first, the commodification of security, and second, the construction of the security consumer. On one level, security is constructed as a consumer good, with a buyer and a seller. Like other consumer goods such as cars, vacations, and clothes, it is, as Goold, Loader, and Thumala (2010) have noted, "a key marker of social identity and belonging" (p. 4). Many facilities managers in multinational technology companies in India oversee the provision of multiple services (e.g., housekeeping, security, transport, catering), which are contracted out much like security. At the same time, security consumption is also different from other forms of consumption because security serves to engender a sense of safety that enables other broader consumption patterns to occur. Organizations, for example, engage in security consumption not only to protect their assets and their staff but also to protect their assets from their staff (Goold, Loader, & Thumala, 2010). All individuals who live within securitized space are both targets of protection and targets of suspicion. Guards in India, for example, have to obtain police clearances as a prerequisite for their job and are subject to monitoring and harsh penalties if they are accused of theft. Their primary job, however, is to assess the risk of company employees and visitors, whom they must simultaneously scrutinize and be deferential toward. Rather than operating within a stable, uniform security environment, however, guards' experiences of their jobs reveal that not only are there multiple risks from which they are required to provide protection, but they must also juggle multiple and sometimes competing consumer interests and therefore definitions of security. Security jobs thus involve the careful negotiation of various risks and consumer needs. As discussed in the following sections, guards' jobs involve providing protection from four sets of "risks"—risks to assets, risks to corporate reputations, risks to employees, and risks to themselves.

Risks to Assets

The notion that security is a commodity that can be consumed allows for an analysis of the factors that determine consumer choice. In their approach to security, multinational technology firms engage in a process of creating cultures and marking social relations that give rise to patterns of inclusion and exclusion (Loader, 1999). As Loader notes, "Acts of consumption are preceded by the formation of mental projects in which individuals conjure up a sense of satisfaction they hope to obtain by purchasing particular goods and services" (p. 381). The numerical strength as well as embodied traits of guards at India's multinational technology companies suggest the need to analyze what kind of threat is being imagined in India. Heavily guarded buildings, security protocols that restrict visitors to those who have appointments, and the monitoring of all employees at entry and exit are some of the security features prevalent in India's multinational technology firms. These practices suggest that the unauthorized movement of people and things across organizational borders constitutes the primary threat that organizations perceive.

Gated organizational spaces in India have significant parallels to "gated" housing communities around the world. In Singapore, for example, these communities, which are often housing complexes surrounded by high walls punctuated by gates with security posts, are examples of "defensive architecture" designed to exclude those deemed not to belong. Pow (2013) argues that given Singapore's low and declining crime rates, such architecture serves as a "marker of social identity and belonging, signaling one's place within the prevailing social hierarchy, demarcating social relationships and emphasizing differences in lifestyles and social categories" (p. 190). The boundaries of these communities separate the "sanitized interior" from the "messiness of outside" (p. 190). In line with this, Prabhu, who owned a security company with 1,800 guards deployed at a wide variety of companies, told us, switching between Hindi and English, that new guards were trained by retired army personnel. He described the training of guards for technology companies as "basic" and offered a list of activities that it involved, including procedures for the entry and exit of people and protocols in the case of a fire or lift malfunction. Prabhu noted that most training focused on "how to stop people of different grades—how to stop a laborer and how to stop a top-level person like [a] manager, visitor. Because they [guards] come from native places, basically rural places, so this also we have to teach." It is ironic that contractors teach their guards, many of whom are rural migrants, how to distinguish between and treat differently legitimate entrants to company premises. Krahmann (2008) argues that different notions of being "secure" exist. Security can signify the absence of threat, and efforts to engender security can involve preventing the sources of threats from developing. More often, however, the security industry focuses not on prevention, but rather on deterrence—that is, how potential violators can be dissuaded from acting (Krahmann, 2008, p. 382). In the context of performance indicators such as outputs, costs, and profits, security companies rarely engage in prevention activities because they are unable to provide financial and quantifiable proof that their analysis of the root causes of insecurity or their actions in response to insecurity were successful. In addition, given that security companies benefit from perceptions of risk, they have little incentive to challenge such perceptions. Accordingly, rather than deal with the wider structural issues that give rise to the threat of unauthorized entry and exit of goods and people (such as social inequality), firms focus on creating and securing organizational borders.

Security is not only about perceived threat and anxiety, but also about pleasure (Loader, 1999). The consumption of security allows organizations to take action on potential threats, and in the absence of security breaches, company leaders may experience pleasure and a sense of safety. Accordingly, many contractors note that multinational technology firms require the development of security protocols and systems, as well as the widespread use of technology in security work. Jaidev, a contractor whom we interviewed in English, claimed:

> IT people are very concerned about access control. Why? Because they have so many projects that goes on for a particular company and they have a compulsion to maintain the secrecy, so that access control part is very important. So the main gate part is very important. . . . The security is all about systems. . . .There is no rocket science. The basic thing is that you need to have a system. Suppose, for any IT company, they have a system of access cards, right? I will give you very small example: Suppose a guy have given resignation and he is in notice period for one month, so that is the responsibility of the admin team or HR team that on that particular date, his access should be restricted. His swipe card should be restricted.

Like doctors who diagnose a patient's individual problem and provide a tailormade solution, security firms promise site-specific analysis of security needs, casting the contractor as a consultant (Thumala, Goold, & Loader, 2011, p. 295). Guards as well as security technologies are a part of the system that is deployed to minimize the risks that working in India poses. By securing the physical borders of multinational technology firms, organizational assets can be protected. As we will discuss in the following sections, however, the three groups that frequently cross organizational borders are visitors, company employees, and service workers such as guards, housekeepers, and driver supervisors. Guards occupy the unique position of being responsible for controlling the access of all of these groups while simultaneously being constantly under suspicion themselves. As a result of their roles as both managers and carriers of risk, guards not only are involved in the work of surveillance but also experience significant surveillance themselves in their daily work (Ball, 2005).

Risks to Corporate Reputation

Aside from monitoring company borders, security guards are also required to embody order, safety, and professionalism so that perceptions of security can be maintained. These perceptions are key to organizations as they bid for contracts, given multinational firms' own perception that there are multiple threats involved in doing business in India. As Loader (1999) notes, security breaches often encourage further consumption of security products that are used to "repair" the security system. In India, two areas of security concern have been highly publicized: first, data theft, and second, the rape and violent assault of female multinational call center employees traveling to and from work. These concerns have shaped the current work of guards in the sector.

In the mid-2000s, several incidents of Indian call center employees being charged with stealing consumers' personal banking information affected large corporations such as Citibank and HSBC. These employees were convicted of their crimes, but Western anti-offshoring groups cited such data theft as a sign that outsourcing could leave customers vulnerable (Walsh, 2006; Brignall, 2015). In order to avert a public backlash, many companies invested significantly in the development of new security protocols. A second set of breaches was identified after a series of violent rapes and murders of call center employees, described in detail in chapter 3. Although drivers were assumed to be the most likely perpetrators of these crimes and therefore were most affected by these incidents, the everyday work of security guards also intensified as a result. Several solutions emerged within the industry to respond to these concerns. In relation to data security, employee access to electronic storage devices at work has been tightened. Security guards search bags and sometimes bodies to confiscate hidden flash drives and cameras. Many organizations also now have close-circuit cameras that are watched continuously by guards. In relation to the risks posed by potentially violent drivers, new protocols have been put in place in many companies that require security guards to accompany female employees if they are lone passengers. Also, as noted in chapter 3, cars have been equipped with GPS trackers and panic buttons that are monitored and managed by security guards. The need to protect corporate reputations has in these ways required increases in security, both in terms of personnel and in terms of equipment. Pankaj described the tasks that his security job entailed as follows:

> I am supposed to write down the names of each employee who comes for the night shift after 10:00 p.m. If they have laptops, I need to note it down in the register. Then I check their bags. If there are any electronic devices like pen drives, CDs, cameras, pen cameras, hard disks, I have to note it down and ask them to deposit them, as such gadgets are not allowed in the company. If employees forget their pass, I have to make one after noting it down in the register.

Kalyan, a 27-year-old male security guard who had completed a twelfth-grade education, told us that he had been given a trophy by his company and described the incident for which he had been rewarded: "One day when I was doing my duty, I found a hard disk containing company data in one of the employees' bag. I gave that hard disk to our supervisor. . . . The company suspended the employee."

Goold, Loader, and Thumala (2010) contend that new technology investment has occurred because of the emergence of a new "fear" that justifies the expense. Multinational technology firms use these new investments to market themselves as proactive actors that are able to deal with new and emerging security threats. It is difficult to say whether these protocols have led to a reduction of actual incidents of theft or violence, as such data are not publicized. Tara and Ilavarasan's (2012) interviews with female call center workers in Gurgaon reveal, however, that some perceive the presence of drivers and guards in vans as a symbolic rather than a real form of protection. Our own experience of entering large multinational technology firms similarly suggests that guards typically spend about five seconds searching the bags of those who possess seemingly "correct" embodied traits (dress, demeanor, social status, and position), which clearly may not lead to foolproof security. Furthermore, as we discuss in the next section, guards are nonpermanent employees in precarious jobs who are assigned the task of surveilling those who hold power over their employment.

Risks to Employees

The most complicated perceptions of risk that guards are required to mitigate are the risks in relation to corporate employees. These employees may be managers, executives, senior engineers, software programmers, call center workers, back-office customer service agents, or visitors. In most cases, members of these groups have direct employment or a service relationship with the organization. Given that their own work involves at times exercising deference vis-à-vis their clients and their work is measured using detailed performance and time matrices, many employees expect service workers around them to follow similar norms. In large multinational technology firms, there is a constant movement of employees, bags, and computers in and out of the building, often on a 24-hour schedule. While most of these employees are English speaking and university educated, not all earn high incomes, and many are as young as 19 or 20 years old. Aside from the prospect of stable, salaried jobs, one of the central attractions for these workers is their environment of work—that is, a corporate office that is secure and clean. As Loader (1999) notes, security consumption is a productive enterprise in that it represents "an attempt by people to distinguish themselves (symbolically) from those who remain dependent for their security on a cash-strapped, seemingly unresponsive public sector" (p. 383).

In this sense, security consumption gives rise to new solidarities and organizational cultures based on being protected that represent a significant appeal of software and call center jobs in multinational firms. For many women who work night shifts, these companies' high-security environment is the central factor that reduces family members' safety concerns. Guards are constantly reminded during training that employees (i.e., software programmers and call center workers) are among the organization's most valued assets and must be treated as such. Yet guards are also responsible for ensuring that employees follow rules that prohibit objects such as flash drives and recording devices from being brought into the organizational space. This need to simultaneously defer to employees and exercise surveillance over them results in many opportunities for tension and conflict between guards and employees. Guards and trainers interviewed by Gooptu (2013b) in Kolkata mentioned the importance of saluting as a form of greeting that "is envisaged as an expression of a security guard's deference and servility to his or her corporate boss, clients or customers" (p. 24). This practice is often accompanied by addressing customers as "Sir" or "Madam." Such gestures serve primarily to highlight the low status of the guard. Interestingly, several contractors serving multinational technology companies whom we interviewed noted that they had been explicitly asked to train guards not to salute. Jaidev, a contractor, explained in English: "IT people do not like saluting, you know. What normally we do for security is that they should salute to the management, but the IT people have got an absolute aversion to this. [Why?] I don't know [why] this is. [Pause] They make it a specific [requirement] that no guard should salute the management, even the top boss also. You know, culturally, the IT people are different. They don't write 'Dear Sir' or 'Dear Madam,' they will write 'Hi!'"

Like employees, service workers are also expected to fall in line with "flat" organizational cultures while at the same time ensuring that they themselves are sufficiently deferential. Kaveri described the skill this required:

> We should talk to them with respect. When the employee comes in the morning, we should greet them with a smile and ask, 'How are you, ma'am?' While checking their bags, we should be careful that employees don't get irritated. Sometimes when employees leave their homes they are in a bad mood, and when we ask to inspect their bags they don't like it. We have to make them feel relaxed and make sure that they are calm, then check the bags. That is what we are told. In such situations we are under pressure.

Notwithstanding this need to refrain from acts like saluting that display subservience, it is clear that complaints from employees can have a detrimental impact on guards' futures. Vidhu, a security vendor, summarized, "Employers make false accusations. You want to get down along the route to meet somebody [during dropoff and] the guard didn't permit [it], then what do you say?—'This boy has misbehaved with me. He didn't talk to me properly. He didn't escort me up to the doorstep. He left me in between.' Now the principal employer won't listen to [the guard] at all. He listens to employee." Vidhu advised his guards to record conversations on their phones so that they had proof of employee misconduct if they found themselves in compromising situations.

While it was uncommon, workers who had successfully challenged employee complaints referred to the "victory" with considerable pride. Narine described how her family had faced discrimination because they were from North India. Her husband, who was also a security guard, had been fired because he had been falsely accused of falling asleep on the job. At the time, the family had considered returning to their village, but Narine had been determined to stay in Pune so that her children could be educated, so she had decided to apply to be a security guard herself. At first, she said, things at home had been "uneasy and tense" because her husband was at home while she was engaged in waged work, but then the family purchased a plot of land and her husband built a house with rooms they could rent. At the time of the interview, both were employed and were spending their savings on their children's education. Narine recounted the following incident at work:

> Once I routinely asked a lady employee for her ID, and she said she had it somewhere. Since it was raining that day and she had got wet in the rain, and as I knew where she worked, I let her in. She was pregnant. Next day it wasn't raining and I asked her for ID card. She said she didn't show it the day before so did not need to show it. She ignored me and walked to the lift. I ran after her and asked her again to show me her ID card, and she got angry. She put one foot in the lift and took out her ID card from her bag and handed it to me and said angrily, "Take it and keep it with you. What a pain." . . . I said, "I don't need to keep your card, please take it." She said angrily, "I will get back to you." The next day, when I asked her for her ID card, her husband who was accompanying her came and stood by me and said to her, "You go ahead, she is a slum woman, don't show her your ID card." Then I told the employee's husband, "You are not concerned with where I live—slum or nonslum. . . . Why are you talking to me in this way?" I said, "I will call the manager and make an official complaint. I am on duty, you cannot insult me." I asked him to wait there so that I could call the manager. . . . The woman complained that I had ask[ed] her for her ID card even though I see her every day. The HR officer told

her to use proper language and not say things like "slum people." ... In the evening the HR officer apologized to me while leaving. After that day, that woman started wearing her ID card around her neck when she arrived. Neither of us say anything to one another now.

Narine's narrative reveals the ways in which power is exercised through class, gender, and urbanism in daily interactions between guards and company employees. The vindication she reported was not common, even though many guards noted the continuous emotional labor of balancing the need to scrutinize with the need to be deferential involved in their jobs. This deference–surveillance dynamic was referred to by Jaidev as "soft security" and is the core requirement of security work in the multinational technology sector. He explained:

> In soft security we train them to be assertive; you cannot be offensive, you cannot be defensive. ... That kind of training we give is as per the requirement of the client. ... The people [who] work in IT are much pampered. ... They will forget to come with their ID card. They will ask the security, "Allow me to go," so this kind of situation. If the security says, "No, sir, we cannot allow you," then ... they make a complaint against my security. ... He [the guard] is a class X standard [tenth grade]—I mean, he is a peanut in the whole system, he can be immediately a victim. In this kind of a situation there have been N number of cases where I have to remove my guard on instructions of management where the guard is no way at fault.

Managing this fine line between engaging in surveillance and not jeopardizing one's precarious position is a key part of security guards' jobs and poses considerable risk to them. In this context, part of security work involves mitigating the risks that workers' jobs pose to themselves.

Risks to Themselves

As Krahmann (2008) notes, the shift in understandings of security from a public good to a private one suggests not only that those who have the capacity to pay can ensure greater security for themselves but also that "security offered to some can reduce the security of others" (p. 386). Indeed, many guards shared experiences in which they were in charge of monitoring theft or unauthorized entries but were accused of theft themselves. Guards noted that they experienced constant surveillance while on the job. Jaidev described the surveillance protocol at his firm as follows: "We have night round system. Our managers, our area managers' officers, they go for night round. In daytime normally there is no problem, because everything is open. Night is dangerous. So during the nighttime we also keep tab on people whether they are on duty, whether they are sleeping, or they are off duty. We make some fine if we find that he is not disciplined, his turnout is not right, his uniform is not in the right shape."

Workers noted that cameras were used simultaneously to detect intruders or theft and to monitor their own performance. Anjali, a guard serving in one of the largest multinational technology companies in India, described an incident that shows that not only are guards monitored, but they are simultaneously in charge of monitoring cameras themselves:

> The company can dismiss us at any time. We are security [people], but there is no security of our life. One lady guard who was working at [a big company] was sent home all of a sudden while on duty. On that day the auditors came to the company, and they sent a laptop through the X-ray machine. The company's admin person was standing there. He asked the lady [security guard], "What just went through the machine?" She was not paying attention. She said nothing. Immediately the supervisor collected her cards and sent her home. She had been working in the company for two and half years. Another lady was sent home that day like this.

In response to customer complaints, contractors like Prabhu reported that their company adopted a number of strategies to deal with problems involving guards: "Sometimes thefts take place. Sometimes the person working in night shift is found sleeping. Sometimes they drink alcohol and come on duty. These types of problems [occur].... If they [customers] like that person, then we warn our staff, we keep them; otherwise we change them.... We send them to other site. In case of theft and drinking problem, we terminate them."

While guards are the key agents of security in India, technologies such as CCTV cameras and GPS trackers are also common. Goold, Loader, and Thumala (2010) trace the explosive growth in the use of CCTVs to the 1990s and note that stagnation in adoption of this technology since then has required marketers to convince customers that hardware upgrades are necessary. While such technology is used to monitor security workers, guards also experience technological monitoring as liberating, since it protects them from false accusations. Iedema and Rhodes (2010) note that while surveillance is often seen as a disciplinary mechanism, this is not always the case. They cite as an example a hospital's use of videotaping to allow staff to review their work in order to identify times when they could increase their infection control efforts. Indian guards, too, discuss surveillance in ambivalent terms. In the context of their extremely precarious employment conditions and limited power vis-à-vis software or call center workers, the frequent use of CCTV cameras can serve as a source of protection. Vishal, for example, acknowledged that guards or housekeepers were constantly under suspicion in cases of theft but declared, "It's not risky because there are cameras everywhere."

In order to avoid the "cameras everywhere," Shital arranged to meet members of the research team in a passageway between two company offices in a special economic zone. Since it was a Saturday, there were not too many people around, and Shital described the surveillance systems at the company for which she provided security services:

> There is an operator for checking camera footage, and he writes a daily report. There is also an operator for the night shift. Usually operators don't write anything in their report, but sometimes some operators mention that this particular security guard was taking a nap, and then a complaint gets registered. The company checks the camera to confirm the complaint.... If there are stolen or missing items, they check the cameras. Sometimes employees are also responsible for stolen items, but most of the time housekeeping or security staff are blamed.

During our conversation Shital also recounted an experience with an employee:

> She had put her purse on the table and [her] mobile [phone] was in her hand. After reaching home she found out that INR 2,000 were missing from her purse.... All the admin staff came to settle the matter. They said, "We just can't blame security people for the lost money." ... The admin staff checked cameras in front of all of us, and in footage they found the wallet in her hands. Then admin staff said to [the employee] that there is a possibility that someone from your home took the money from your purse.... After this incidence that madam gave her resignation, and she never came back. She blamed security people. I think this is not right.... According to me, cameras are useful.

Surveillance technologies not only impact work processes but also produce subjectivities. Nayar (2015) notes that neoliberal societies engender "surveillance citizenship," whereby the right to participate in particular spaces is asserted through participation in surveillance mechanisms. By supporting organizational security protocols, contractors construct guards as being at risk themselves and acknowledge that they are often wronged by accusations of theft, just like those who are victims of theft. Yet while surveillance mechanisms both pose a risk to and protect workers, they also signify that security personnel are in fact potential sources of threat, despite their occupational roles. Unlike police officers and army personnel, few security guards see themselves as engaged in high-status, socially respectable work. Instead, as Shital told us, there is no security in a security guard's life. Many experience their jobs as precarious.

Proxies of Security: Creating and Training Professional Risk Managers

As noted in chapter 1, the security industry is organized as a system of contract labor, which gives rise to a paradox in relation to risk. Weak employment relationships increase risks for both workers and employers. Workers in such systems face lower wages and poorer working conditions as contractors are forced to compete with one another and reduce labor costs in order to successfully win contracts. At the same time, because contract workers have weaker connections with their employers, employers may suffer from workers' constant shifts between contractors or jobs rather than having the opportunity to build a stable, long-term workforce. The instability of this worker–employer relationship is particularly significant in the context of the role of private security as an ameliorator of risk. Guards, by virtue of their uniform, are automatically deemed to be trustworthy rather than a source of risk or at risk themselves. In the context of contract labor, however, not only do guards need to be taught how to minimize perceptions of risk, but employers have to simultaneously manage the risk that contract guards hired on short-term contracts pose to the company.

Contractors and facilities managers attempt to ameliorate the intrinsic "riskiness" of contract labor by establishing job processes that require guards to behave in ways that would be recognized as "professional" by international standards and engaging in recruitment and training efforts. Private security contractors and advocates engage in forms of "legitimation work" (Thumala, Goold, & Loader, 2011) to deflect attention from the risk that contract hiring poses. In particular, multinational technology corporations require guards to have a distinct set of traits that serve as proxies for security. Three important proxies for security are army backgrounds, education, and the capacity to physically self-regulate bodies. These traits serve to mitigate fears that frequently stem from security guards' poverty and/or migration status. When we went to meet Shridhar, an ex–air force official who works as a customer relations manager in a security contracting firm, we were shown into a well-equipped conference room. There, Shridhar summarized the ideal characteristics of security guards identified by the multinational technology sector:

> In IT, the person is required to be more educated; he should be [able to] handle computers, phone calls. He should be able to handle all this and speak a little bit of English. [The guard] should be very sophisticated in looks. There is a lot of difference between industrial guard and IT guard. Industrial guard is very shabby: [his] shoes are not polished, not wearing tie, but at the same time, IT security person is very sophisticated, wearing tie, and properly groomed.

Aside from engaging in the aesthetic labor of looking and sounding a particular way (Witz, Warhurst, & Nickson, 2003), guards are also expected to negotiate a delicate balance between their roles as scrutinizers and servers. The standards for security work are set by clients, who demand not only documentary proof of labor compliance, as discussed in chapter 1, but also appropriate training. Vidhu, the managing director of a firm that contracts out 4,000 security guards to multinational technology firms in Pune, informed us, "[The guidelines are] given by the guard board, plus we have two registrations—for example, we have ISO 9001 as well as OSHAS 18001. Now this year we are going for a certification of environment and climate change . . . ISO 14001 and also social accountability 8007/2004." Certifications signify that companies are meeting international standards in guard recruitment and skill.

The possibility of employing risky workers is mitigated by the widely stated industry preference for ex-army personnel. As Nagaraj (2012) observes, there is a close connection between former military and police personnel and private security agencies in India. These personnel are seen not only as ideal guards but also frequently own or manage security companies, serve as supervisors and trainers, or occupy posts in CAPSI (p. 11). Thumala, Goold, and Loader (2011) note that the construction of private security work as parallel to higher-status jobs in the police or army is a form of "symbolic borrowing." Moreover, in Maharashtra,

Marathas were historically members of the warrior caste, and almost half the security guards we interviewed belonged to this community. A significant portion of security guards also came from the scheduled castes of the region, who, as mentioned earlier, also have historic links with the military.

All of the security firms in our sample were owned or managed by ex-army personnel. Contractors noted that multinational companies had a strong preference for guards with a military background, and that while they were often unable to fulfill this request because of a lack of applicants, almost all training was conducted by ex-army officials. In this way, the security sector in India forms an important "second career" path for many men who complete their service in (and continue to draw a pension from) the army. The government has established several incentives that encourage ex-servicemen to start security and training companies and receive support from the Directorate General of Resettlement. Piyush, a manager at a large security firm who introduced himself as a "major-general" even though he was retired from the army, spoke extensively on the importance of inculcating military discipline in guards. When we met Major-General Piyush, he immediately assumed we wanted to "check" his paperwork and presented us with logs showing lists of employee names and dates they had been paid. He lamented the downward price pressure on the sector, which had led to a situation in which many of his competitors paid their employees less through dishonest means, and called for greater state scrutiny and regulation of the security industry. He also told us that his company, which hired thousands of guards and had over a dozen training centers, had a strong preference for ex-army personnel because they were "better trained," were "more disciplined,"[2] and didn't require much training. Piyush described an ideal ex-army guard as someone who "knows how to wear his uniform. He knows what guard duty means. His bearing is better, so that makes the difference. But unfortunately, at present, since last 10 years, we are not getting as many security guards as we want [who are] ex-servicemen.... An ex-serviceman from Maharashtra will never like ask for a security job unless he is compelled, because government of Maharashtra looks after ex-servicemen."

In a case study of private security companies contracted by the Swedish state, Berndtsson (2012) argues that security contractors construct notions of risk as well as narratives about the ways in which their services can ameliorate these risks. Given the multiple actors with whom they work, contractors' narratives are often multifaceted and contradictory. At times, contractors evoke their connections to the military in order to emphasize the discipline of their workers. At other times, however, they specifically distance themselves from this image and instead depict their workers as professionals like those in any other field. Indeed, the contractors we interviewed made little mention of the aggression, hierarchy, and bureaucracy that are frequently associated with the army. Instead, they valorized ex-servicemen because these individuals are assumed to be disciplined and to have traceable, law-abiding backgrounds.

Although they constructed ex-servicemen as ideal workers, the contractors we interviewed uniformly noted that within the security sector, demand for such individuals was far greater than supply. As a result, only 1 out of the 28 guards we interviewed had an army background. Ex-army men mostly occupied managerial, ownership, and training roles. Consequently, there were a number of ways in which security work, particularly during training, was militarized. Narendra, a 22-year-old male guard with a twelfth-grade education and four years of experience in the security sector, described the training he received:

> The duration of the training was 15 days. The training was similar to military training. Trainers conducted an examination after the training. They gave us training on firefighting. In the classrooms there were lectures on duties of security guards. Every morning for around 45 minutes we had physical training. . . . On duty no one is allowed to chew gutkha or tobacco or similar substances. If someone finds you chewing gutkha or tobacco then you are fired. . . . The supervisor checks our uniform, our badge, and we have to follow hygiene rules. We have to shave every day and wear the shoes that the company has provided. These are some of the rules.

Recruiters also spoke of education as a sign of a reliable and safe employee. Contractors universally noted that they sought workers who had completed high school, as such an accomplishment would allow them to fulfill the reading and writing requirements of their jobs. Yet education symbolized more than literacy. Shridhar explained in English, "Take a simple example of standing. You see the cultured person, how he stands, and a low-educated or average-educated person, how he stands. . . . Merely seeing how he stands can differentiate whether he is educated or he is cultured." In this way, education serves as a proxy for the cultural capital accompanying professionalism.

Many contractors we interviewed argued that wages and working conditions were not in line with the fact that the industry required workers who were English speaking, literate, and could provide documentary proof of their character through school certificates and police clearances. Contractors therefore had to "settle" for less appropriate workers and put significant resources into training workers who might not possess all the necessary traits when first recruited. Indeed, several workers were aware that there was a gap between the advertised requirements of their jobs and their own backgrounds. Vishal revealed that he had only completed formal education through grade four, despite a minimum education requirement for his job of having completed schooling through the tenth grade. "You should know how to read and write at least in Marathi," he said. "My brother knows [someone] in the agency, and he helped me.... [The contractor] asked me for the tenth-grade certificate; I gave him one for fourth grade, but he didn't really pay attention to it, and my work was done. He employed me. It was difficult, but I got a job. Now if I need to write something, a complaint regarding AC or something else, then other guards do it for me."

In these ways, since high school completion and army backgrounds are far from standard in the security field given the low wages, companies rely heavily on the rhetoric of training to describe how workers are converted into appropriate guards. Most workers are trained for a period of time ranging from a few days to a month, as well as continuously receiving supervised training on the job. Most male guards noted that their training had focused on firefighting, monitoring cameras, issuing passes, managing the air-conditioning systems, and searching bags. Female guards were also trained in searching the bags of female employees as well as serving, in some cases, at reception. Aside from these tasks, training focused on maintaining correct bodily postures and uniforms that would allow guards to develop the correct professional "look." Tasks, looks, and attitude—all of which are embodied aspects of labor—were seamlessly blended in guards' descriptions of their training, suggesting that these three facets of work are in fact deeply intertwined. Having the right "body personality"[3] for the job of being a guard involves looking smart, being clean-shaven for men, and having crisp and clean uniforms for both women and men. Body personality extends to behaviors—as Jitendra summarized, guards are given "instructions on how to talk to the employees of the company and how to behave with them. We are not supposed to read anything or make noise and chat with each other while on duty. We are not supposed to allow anyone [to] linger in the lobby unnecessarily or leave our post unless there is a reliever in our place." It is assumed that looking and acting in these ways signifies moral virtue and respect. As Kavita told us, her company gave "training about our behavior and manners, how to give respect to our seniors or foreigners, as many foreigners come to our company." The training that guards receive in comportment is supposed to have a transformative impact on workers' lives as a whole. Piyush declared that the female guards his company hired had "to look smart. You'll be surprised to see these women when they are off duty. They are basically 100 percent rural housewives. . . . You can't believe that these girls are working in this company."

The need to be uniformed and well-groomed is, however, often difficult for employees, given that they may not have easy access to laundry and bathing facilities. Anjali arranged to meet us at a bus stop close to her home, and we then walked about 10 minutes to a building where she rented a small room with her brother and shared the washroom with other residents. The room had a small stovetop and tap, as well as a single bed. Only 21 years old, Anjali had completed the second year of her bachelor's degree. Hoping to become a clerical worker, she said she was taking English classes. She and her brother had moved to Pune from a village about 300 kilometers away and now worked in one of India's largest multinational technology companies. Anjali shared the challenges she faced meeting the aesthetic requirements of her job: "They tell us that my shoes are not polished, my body has not been scrubbed properly and has so much dirt. They remind me all the time about my shoe polishing. But they did not give me my shoes with my uniform, even though INR 1,200 was deducted [for the uniform]. I use shoes of another lady who left this work." Gooptu's (2013b) interviews with guards in Kolkata reveal similar findings. There, training for security guards focuses on both the tasks that they are required to carry out and the aesthetic and emotional labor they are required to perform. The aim of the training is to develop "fitness, stamina and endurance," as well as "an embodied expression of regimented discipline" (p. 23). Rather than "a strong, muscular physique usually associated with protection and guarding," workers are often asked to aspire to "smartness"—a trait described as being well-dressed, alert, efficient, and prompt. At the same time, the training emphasizes the importance of treating the customer as a "god" (p. 23). Grooming is important, and "workers are thus tasked with the responsibility of personifying and embodying a suitable corporate ethos" (p. 24). These requirements are viewed as especially important because there is some bodily contact between guards and clients/ employees given that guards must frequently frisk entrants or handle their possessions. Gooptu summarizes that "while all this is expressed in an apparently 'modern' language of professional training, these are also clearly laden with resonances of subservient, deferential, and servile master-servant relationships of domestic work, and they bear the mark of hierarchical caste-based forms of duty and service owed by the lower orders to the higher orders" (p. 24; see also Kumar, 2017). Moreover, since scheduled caste men have historically been constructed as hypersexual, especially in their desire for upper-caste women (Rao, 2009), these practices may be seen as mechanisms of discipline that seek to force lower-caste men to behave appropriately, further perpetuating the characterization of their sexuality as potentially threatening.

What is most interesting in relation to multinational technology firms and other service industries like banking and finance that have been closely tied to neoliberalism is that even among their more upper-class, elite, professional employees, grooming and "soft skills" have become increasingly important (Acker, 1990; McDowell, 1997). Mukherjee (2008b:69) demonstrates how in the software industry, the "social characteristics of the employees have become a key feature of their employability: class, language skills, and appearance"—a claim reminiscent of Bourdieu's (1984) notions of cultural capital. However, within the very same spaces, our research shows that security guards have to embody both deference and discipline. Their job is squarely defined as devoted to keeping these employees, as well as their organizations, safe.

Risky Risk Managers

Across the board, contractors and facilities managers at multinational technology firms who we interviewed lamented the labor shortage within the security field in India. Prabhu, the security vendor who told us that guard training involved teaching rural workers to recognize different "grades" of people, noted that many educated people perceive security jobs as unskilled and prefer other professions, and that as a result, "In security no local good boys are left. They have got other better jobs. People from South India don't work in security; they are educated, but they take other jobs. . . . People of better quality have gone for higher job profiles, that is supervisor level, as they are educated. So whatever people who are ready to work in security, they are kind of . . . [we] don't want to do anything with that kind of people."

Prabhu's notion of "that kind of people" who were unsuitable for security jobs included those who were unable to commit to come to work on time, those who needed to return to their villages periodically, those who were unable to meet the bodily labor demands of the job, those who were confrontational, those who consumed alcohol/gutkha on or before their shifts, and those who slept during night shifts. Despite the training they receive, two factors make security workers constantly suspect and "risky" along these dimensions—their poverty and their migration histories. A labor official we interviewed, Arun, constructed wealth discrepancies between security company employees and contracted service providers and security vendors as the source of potential violence and theft. He claimed, "See, these [company] employees are using money like anything. They are enjoying . . . and getting [INR] 50,000, 60,000 as a salary, and these guys [service workers] are getting only [INR] 5,000 or 4,000. Then that creates a sort of, you know, criminal tendency in them." Such criminalization of poverty—the perception that poor people are more prone to committing crime—was expressed by a number of contractors and company facility managers we interviewed. Vishnu, a supervisor at a software company, told us that the head of facilities had received complaints from employees that sweepers were drinking milk from the company's coffee and milk machine and had been told to ensure that this behavior stopped. Vidhu, a contractor, told us that he had not been surprised to hear a highly publicized news report that a security guard had assaulted a woman and robbed INR 60,000 from her. He stated that guards are "human beings" and declared, "They will face the same problems. So therefore the biggest work of this industry is to motivate these boys [not to] fall prey to these things." Despite the widespread recognition that poverty makes guards a risky population, workers in this sector continue to experience poor wages and working conditions.

Many contractors also depicted security workers as unstable and risky because of their migration status. While migrant workers are often preferred by contractors because they are assumed to be willing to work around the clock, accept low wages, and be reluctant to engage in collective action, such workers are also thought of as having few ties to the local community and as therefore being more prone to risk-taking behaviors. Partha, a contractor we interviewed, explained that many service workers "come from the outside, from nearby villages. When the activities related to farming are finished, they come to city in search of job for six or eight months. Then they . . . do security-type work. When it rains after six or eight months, they return to villages for farming jobs. So you don't know whether they will come back again or not."

Despite these risks, contractors frequently recruit nonlocal workers in order to tap into captive labor pools with few other employment alternatives. Based on her extensive field work in Kolkata, which included participant observation as well as interviews with management, workers, and training agencies, Gooptu (2013) notes that most guards have at least some high school education and migrated from rural areas where they were engaged in agricultural work. Recruitment programs, some of which receive support from the state or village councils, often depict security jobs as respectable and skilled, somewhat akin to police and army work. At the same time, prospective applicants are told that the security industry has high standards and requires dedicated, hard-working, committed workers. Gooptu argues that such "contradictory counselling" serves to "ensure the tenacious and sustained labour market participation of poor youth in low-level jobs, even when faced with un-rewarding and exploitative work" (p. 18). In order to create a captive pool of "meek and pliable" workers, many security agencies ally with national schemes, such as the National Skill Development Corporation, that provide employment training for youth from politically volatile areas (p. 21).

While migrants are valorized as ideal workers because they are perceived as a cheap and captive labor pool, they remain suspect within the security field. Vishal, a security guard originally from Pune, noted, "I didn't have a problem because I am from here. I needed no other verification [aside from his ration card, school leaving certificate, domicile certificate, ATM [banking information], and police clearance]. . . . Outsiders have more problems." Many migrants reported that they lived and formed friendships primarily with others who were migrants. Narayan, who had migrated to Pune from North India, leaving his wife and parents in his village, explained that he could not ask his colleagues if he needed help or support "because we are from outside. Outsiders are not trusted that much." Overall, security guards' livelihoods remain unstable, with few prospects for future growth. As a result, workers continue to engage in cyclical migrations between their villages and the city.

Conclusions: Risk Managers at Risk

Wealth disparities within India are seen as a significant source of risk, which companies have sought to manage through the privatization of security. This approach has benefited private security companies that hire impoverished workers to guard zones of wealth (Nagaraj, 2012, p. 13). Frontline responsibility for the management of risk is allocated to security guards, who are required to transform themselves into professional symbols of security in India. Yet given their low wages and poor working conditions, which arise in part from their contract employment, the commercialization of security provides only limited prospects for precariously employed, low-waged youth (Nagaraj, 2012). As a result, India's security guards remain simultaneously at risk and a source of risk.

Workers are at risk not only because of their poor economic conditions but also because of the ideological exclusion many of them face in relation to the fruits of the economic miracle they are supposed to protect. Sandeep, a 26-year-old male security guard, provides a case in point. On one of our visits to an area of the city with many IT firms, we approached Sandeep as he sat at a desk at the entrance of a global software company. He was registering visitors, creating passes, and answering phone calls. He told us that he could share his experiences while he worked, although he was not allowed to share any confidential company information. Since there was a steady flow of traffic in and out of the workplace and no one lingered at the desk, he talked freely about his work. Sandeep was among the highest paid of the security guards we interviewed. He had completed twelfth grade and earned INR 10,000 for an eight-hour daytime shift. Despite his short (two-year) tenure as a security guard and his limited education, he was recognized as a good worker and had been promoted accordingly. Yet Sandeep was despondent about his future prospects in the field. He claimed that "my worksite can change any time. There is no guarantee that it is going to be here always. I feel proud that I have a job. It is better than not doing anything." He perceived his work as a dead-end job and told us that in this sector, guards could reach retirement age earning the same salary that they had earned upon entering the field. He reported that he was looking for an evening job to supplement his income. When we asked him about his plans for the future, he admitted, "There is no future here. . . . I am very bored with this job. I earn only to fulfil my needs. I cannot do anything else. I cannot have any savings. If I need to go to the hospital in an emergency, no money is left. Whatever I earn is spent."

Thus, as this chapter demonstrates, we heard very little of the promise and hope emphasized in the rhetoric of trickle-down development in the narratives of the guards we interviewed. Instead, like private security providers around the world (Briken, 2012), the guards we spoke to reported that they were perceived by their families and communities as working in a low-status job that involved doing nothing but standing and faced stagnant prospects for upward mobility. While workers were required to learn many skills as part of their jobs, their pay structures and tenuous employment contracts did not reflect the fact that they were part of a skilled occupation, engaged in the important work of protecting international assets.

Endnotes

1. Although this is a large number of jobs, Barnes (2015) notes that job generation related to the IT sector has been overstated, and that there has also been little focus on the quality of jobs created.
2. This association of the military with self-discipline is, of course, not new. Deshpande (2007) notes that a number of *akharas*, or bodybuilding organizations, were established alongside military and rifle schools in the 1920s and 1930s. There, Maratha men who sought to challenge the British engaged in bodybuilding exercises, worked to inculcate values like self-discipline, and committed to spiritual regimes. Nation building and bodybuilding became synonymous with a certain kind of virulent masculinity associated with nationalism and the military.
3. This term was used by a guard, Hemant, and is not a translation. Although Hemant spoke in Hindi during his interview, he used the term "body personality" in English. Such language mixing is common in India.

CHAPTER 5

Engendering Service Work in Spaces of Production and Social Reproduction

Multinational corporations in India do not just impact gender relations but also generate new gendered practices and formations. Service sector jobs within India's multinational technology firms are important sites where new gendered identities are being forged. As Salzinger (2016) notes, rather than describing identities, gender in fact describes contrasts (p. 5). Indeed, our interviews with managers and contractors revealed that these individuals strongly articulated contrasts between male and female workers. This was notwithstanding the irony that was evident when we, as female researchers, were interacting with mostly male contractors or managers. On one occasion, as we sipped tea while we sat on armchairs in an airy open space outside his office, Jaidev, the manager of a large security firm, declared without hesitation that "lady guards have been posted at those places where they are not interacting with the males." After a pause, during which we wondered what he thought about the appropriateness of the cross-gender interaction that we were ourselves in the midst of, we asked, "Why is that?" In an elaborate response, Jaidev explained that security contractors both have to protect workers from the potential promiscuity that could arise from cross-gender interactions and follow the dictates of transnational corporations that express a preference for male security workers. Jaidev concluded by stating in a matter-of-fact manner, "They [lady guards] are not *supposed to* interact with gents or male visitors."

In our numerous interviews with contractors and managers, it was clear that our own position as female researchers interacting with men was largely unproblematic, while guards, housekeepers, and drivers faced deep-seated gender-based taboos. The notions of masculinity and femininity being promoted were in these ways inextricably intertwined with issues of class and caste. Despite the fact that she herself was a career woman, for example, Lalita, a manager working for a house-keeping contractor, told us that female housekeepers made less reliable long-term employees because "in Indian culture, you know, the Indian family, how much ever poor they are or how much ever backward they are, they would not like the lady of the house going to a company where she is surrounded by a lot of other complete strangers.... For men, it's much easier, no?" In her depiction of "Indian culture," Lalita evoked Brahmanical discourses of sexual purity, which were assumed to be internalized across castes and classes (Ray & Qayum, 2009). These re-strictive ideologies were portrayed as actively embraced by lower-caste and poor women as part of their desire for higher social status. For Lalita as a middle-class career woman, and for us as middle-class researchers, such discourses of female seclusion were deemed to be less relevant. Yet with her summation, "It's easier for men," and the rhetorical ques-tion "No?" at the end, she placed herself and us in assumed agreement that while gendered norms may be different for poor and "backward" people, women's experiences across class and caste positions can be con-trasted to men's.

These widely expressed gender contrasts in relation to low-wage service workers are particularly striking given the promotion of multinational technology firms as gender-neutral employers. These organizations are branded as safe, progressive spaces whose aims and values supersede gender biases, which has resulted in the fact that a fair number of women are present in the software and call center professions (Mishra, 2016; Radhakrishnan, 2014). However, alongside the gender neutrality promoted among professional workers, firms foster blatant occupational sex segregation among low-wage service workers based on notions of appropriate genders for particular jobs. In the process they construct masculinities and femininities that are laden with class and caste biases.

In this chapter we explore how service work and workers are gendered in new ways in the multinational technology industry. We aim to contribute to ongoing feminist debates on the gendered nature of work in the context of global capital (Bair, 2010; Desai & Rinaldo, 2016; Chakraborty, 2016; Freeman, 2013, 2014; Ramamurthy, 2010; Radhakrishnan, 2015; Salzinger, 2016). We trace the masculinities and femininities that are produced through daily work practices and argue that these serve to entrench gender roles, reinforce class and caste stratification, promote assumptions about male promiscuity, define cross-gender contact as culturally inappropriate, and reproduce paternalistic narratives of women's need for safety in relation to night work. Collectively, these practices support the construction of men as ideal workers for cleaning, guarding, and driving jobs within transnational technology firms. We argue that contradictory and multiple worker subjectivities are created in the process. Men become ideal workers in historically feminized jobs like cleaning and work involving "soft skills" typically associated with women. In security and driving jobs, masculinities deemed to be appropriate are those that are completely detached from men's sexual desire. Simultaneously, other discourses of appropriate masculinity emerge that are rooted in notions of risk taking, professionalization, and appropriateness for night work. Women are relegated to specific women-only jobs (e.g., cleaning women's washrooms) and do not always earn the same (already low) wages given to their male counterparts.

In the following section, we trace three ways in which low-wage service work is gendered in transnational firms. First, men are identified as ideal workers. Second, masculine sexuality is seen as a liability because of the assumed promiscuity of the poor and lower-caste men employed in these jobs. Finally, skills typically associated with femininity, such as the display of deference, the acceptance of low pay, and the ability to mask one's anger when confronted with unfair treatment, are cast as "soft skills" essential for these jobs. Such feminized masculinity is understood as required for such service positions, and training is provided to teach workers skills that are deemed to be professional, Westernized ways of working. At the same time, we trace the ways in which some women assert a form of femininity different from that demanded by their employers as they begin to challenge some of the traditional gender regimes in their homes. These women assert a "breadwinner femininity" through which they attempt to become key decision-makers in their families; however, for lower-caste and poor women, unlike middle-class women who can hire domestic workers, this new role is generally accompanied by little relief from traditional domestic and childcare responsibilities.

Men as "Ideal Workers"

Our discussions with contractors and managers revealed a paradox related to the gendered nature of the work of driving, housekeeping, and guarding. Specifically, while men were almost universally seen as ideal workers for these low-wage service jobs, masculinity, particularly as it was manifested in assertive or sexually active male bodies, was simultaneously constructed as a liability. The decoupling of practices of hegemonic femininity from female bodies and hegemonic masculinity from male bodies has been the topic of substantial feminist analysis. Feminist ethnographies of gendered labor in the global economy have revealed that while organizations produce hegemonic notions of masculinity and femininity that impact male and female workers, these categories are far from universal or predefined. Salzinger (2003), for example, observes:

> Take sewing leather gloves in a factory: one could imagine a cultural context in which it would be marked as masculine in contrast to work in the home; then within the category of paid work as feminine in contrast to construction work; and still again within the category of garment production as masculine in contrast to sewing lingerie. None of these activities are inherently either feminine or masculine, of course, but the process whereby they become gendered is an inherent aspect of how gender functions. (p. 23)

Not only is the feminization or masculinization of jobs variable across contexts, but it is also dependent on race and class. McDowell (1997) and Mullings (2005) illustrate how older male-dominated professional service jobs like banking and finance in fact have been reconstructed as feminine, with characteristics like teamwork, empathy, loyalty, emotional strength, and patience being valorized in lieu of traditional notions of bureaucratic hierarchy. At the same time, employment in low-wage jobs in global export processing zones has expanded beyond poor women of color, yet these kinds of work were, and continue to be, associated with female workers because of constructed attributes women supposedly possess like nimble fingers, docility, and compassion. Jobs in assembly, garment, and manufacturing plants are often notorious for low pay, routinization, unhealthy working conditions, and job insecurity (Nash & Fernández-Kelly, 1983; Standing, 1989, 1999; Pearson, 1998; Roy, 2003; Wright, 2006) and are filled by both female and male workers who occupy marginalized race, class, or caste positions. As Salzinger (2003) demonstrates, "Feminization emerges as a discursive process which operates on both female and male bodies" (p. v) through the definition of racialized labor as docile and cheap.

Soft skills discourses and the training projects that accompany them constitute one site where such gendered reinscriptions are visible. As Adkins (2001) has observed, "Workers may perform, mobilize, and contest masculinity, femininity, and new gender hybrids in a variety of ways in order to innovate and succeed in flexible corporations. Thus men may perform (and indeed be rewarded for performing) traditional acts of femininity . . . and women may perform (and also be rewarded for) traditional acts of masculinity" (p. 680). Yet while soft skills training might pose a challenge to the static nature of gender roles, it does not diminish the significance of gender as an organizing practice. Indeed, as Freeman (2013) observes, it is telling that the contemporary importance placed on soft skills traditionally associated with women's work has shifted assumptions that these skills are innate, but such shifts have not led to a revaluing of women's jobs, many of which remain poorly paid.

Indeed, despite the prevalence of gender-neutral uniforms, gender vividly structures service sector jobs in multinational firms. We were most surprised by the numerical absence of women from cleaning and security jobs, given historical associations between domestic work and housekeeping[1] and assumptions about the importance of soft skills and deference within security jobs. Managers and contractors estimated that between half and three-quarters of housekeepers working in Indian multinational technology firms were male. In line with this, only 10 of the 33 housekeepers we interviewed were women. Security is a traditionally male-dominated profession associated with protection and closely aligned with professions such as the army and law enforcement. Multinational technology companies are guarded by mostly male security guards, although a small proportion of the workforce—in some organizations up to 30 percent, but more often around 5 to 10 percent— is female. There is a much higher proportion of female guards in these firms compared to war zones or other sectors of the building security industry. In this study, of the 28 guards we interviewed, 6 were female and 22 were male. Finally, driving has historically been a male-dominated profession, and driver positions for the multinational technology companies we researched were entirely populated by men. Managers and contractors provided four explanations for their preference for men for these low-wage service jobs: they saw cross-gender contact as culturally inappropriate, they identified work as heavy and dangerous, they highlighted the necessity of protecting women, and they cited the preference of foreign companies for male workers.

Cross-Gender Contact Taboos

Across the three sectors we examined, we found that a widely accepted and rigidly adopted rhetoric of "separate spheres" organized the labor process such that particular tasks were constructed as appropriate for men and others for women. Additionally, caste-based perceptions also impacted the ways in which work was gendered. While in India social life in general was historically segregated on gender lines, caste-based perceptions and practices of gender differed significantly. Lower-caste and poor women regularly worked shoulder to shoulder with men on farms, in forests, and so on, while upper-caste women worked in more segregated spaces that were strictly defined by caste-based patriarchy. In the interviews we conducted, however, we found that contractors, managers, and the relatively better-off scheduled caste men who worked in the multinational technology sector also used the upper-caste rhetoric of women's seclusion as a way to protect them to explain the reason behind gender segregation.

Cross-gender taboos were expressed in different ways in each of the sectors. The sexual division of labor within the security sector, for example, was justified in terms of taboos against cross-gender touching. Security provision for multinational corporations involves searching bags or cars, checking and issuing identification, and, on rare occasions, frisking entrants. Guards' jobs may also include firefighting, monitoring screens, turning air conditioners on and off, and escorting female employees while they are being transported home by drivers. Only a small subset of these activities were deemed appropriate for women by our interviewees. Shital, a 32-year-old female security guard, stated: "Ladies don't get assigned parking duty. Our duty is limited to checking bags [and] checking visitors' passes." Female guards were hired only because a percentage of employees of and visitors to multinational corporations were female, and women were said to be needed for activities that involved contact with the bodies or possessions of female employees. Such "gender matching" parallels the use of "ethnic matching" prevalent among security firms around the world. Löfstrand (2015) explores the enactment of this strategy in Sweden, where guards of color are deployed in neighborhoods with high concentrations of people of color. Such a strategy allows the police force to counter any possible accusations of discrimination it might face. In fact, Löfstrand notes, ethnic matching "relies on stereotypical use of appearance, language, bodily style and emotion (p. 152). In a similar way, gender matching in security provision in Indian multinational technology firms feeds into assumptions that cross-gender interactions are fraught with the potential for abuse. When we asked Jaidev, a security contractor, why his company did not deploy female guards more widely, he responded, "What is a job of a security? Suppose the frisking part; they [women] cannot do it physically. So it demarcates the whole thing. . . . There are some other issues which may crop up with it, so we need to be careful about it." When we asked Jaidev to elaborate on these issues, he simply repeated that cross-gender guard–client interactions are inappropriate because of local taboos around "touch" (despite the numerous other high-touch professions in which women serve men, such as nursing, massage therapy, and sex work).

A similar rhetoric of cross-gender touch taboos occurred within the housekeeping sector. We were told that female housekeepers were needed primarily because it was inappropriate for men to clean women's toilets. However, men were constructed as more ideal for all other house-keeping tasks, primarily through the discursive distinction attached to this work as being heavy and dangerous.

Heavy and Dangerous Work

All of the workers we interviewed were subjected to various forms of grooming, training, and surveillance, and their working conditions were characterized by long hours, irregular and insecure tenure, low pay, stress, and other health impacts that reflected how these jobs were feminized in multiple ways for both men and women. Yet alongside this feminization was the notion that many service tasks were heavy and dangerous, and therefore most appropriate for men. Within the house-keeping sector, for example, our findings resonate with those of Aguiar (2001), whose research with Toronto office workers discovered that the cleaning industry contains a gendered division of labor even when both women and men are hired. Among the Toronto workers, certain types of work such as dusting, sweeping, mopping, and vacuuming were defined as "light" work and seen as most appropriate for women. Men, by con-trast, were given the work of mopping lobbies and removing garbage, which were perceived as "heavier" tasks, and in general worked in more public areas and were more likely to operate machines (which can sometimes make cleaning easier). A similar division of labor is in place in Indian multinational technology firms. Ramesh, a contractor who was also a site supervisor for housekeeping staff, noted in English that in his organization female cleaners were called "chambermaids" and only assigned the task of cleaning women's toilets. "Every floor has four WCs and four wash basins," he explained. "Two ladies are assigned in one shift. Four floors are allotted to one lady, and five floors are allotted to another lady in each shift. After every one hour, the ladies take rounds. . . . They get salary around INR 5,500 to 6,000. [Housekeeping boys] get salary around INR 6,000 to 6,500." The distinction between housekeeping and toilet cleaning work was used to justify the lower pay given to female cleaners. Soni-Sinha and Yates (2013) explore how male office janitors in Toronto are paid more than women. Women's work is constructed as "light" (vacuuming and dusting) while men's is seen as "heavy" (sweeping, buffering and mopping) even though the former may in fact be more physically demanding and women may often be required to do tasks defined as heavy. They note that men reconcile their masculine subjectivities with the association of domestic work with feminized domestic service jobs through ideologies of skill and toughness. In a similar way, vacuuming and lifting items for cleaning is seen to require men's strength as Ramesh, quoted above, went on to tell us that men engage in multiple tasks: "There are gents toilets to be cleaned, there's vacuuming to be done, every night this carpet has to be vacuumed, so we need gents for that. [Also] in order to lift things or move things from here to there." Housekeepers too reported strict rules around tasks which women workers are allowed to do as part of their jobs. Megha, a 34-year-old working rotating shifts at a large call center, reported that female housekeeping staff were not allowed in the office, and that any cleaning work that had to be done around company employees was done by men. Women were allowed to clean washrooms and pantries. Only during the weekends, when the employees are not on the premises, did women clean the female employees' desks. Interestingly, such restrictions were not imposed on men. Megha explained, "If it's a man housekeeper then he can go to the office and clean there. . . . They also clean the computers and bring bags from outside. . . . They are not allowed to give us any work in the office because women cannot do that work." When asked why these gender norms were in place, many women had little to say, simply noting that these rules were established and enforced as part of their work.

Women's inappropriateness for many tasks related to corporate cleaning work was explained to us, however, by a number of facilities managers who dictated the terms of the contracts. One facilities manager, Lalita, commented: "If big floor is there, women cannot do it. There we deployed men, but for ladies' washrooms and other things, we deploy ladies only." Women's exclusion from many cleaning jobs was justified in terms of their supposed inability to do the technologically "heavy" work of cleaning[2] and the inappropriateness of women cleaning men's washrooms.

In the security sector, similar references were made to "heavy guarding." Kavita, a 38-year-old female guard working for a company that paid the same wages to men and women, told us that the exclusion of women from "heavy guarding" tasks caused resentment among male workers. She said, "In our company usually male security guards check vehicles, and their duty is at the main entrance, where guards have to stand continuously for eight hours. Such points are called heavy points. At such heavy points the duty is assigned to male security guards. Ladies are not given duties at heavy points. . . . Male security guards feel that ladies never have duty at hard points. Also, ladies don't have night shifts, but the salary is same." Not all security guards reported gender-matched salaries. Nitin, a 35-year-old male guard whose job involved checking ID cards and vehicles and who earned INR 8,000 per month, informed us that his wife worked for the same contractor but received "salary of around INR 6,000 to 6,500, as she is working inside the company, and she receives a lower salary than us."

In the transportation sector, women are seen as fundamentally unsuitable for driving because of the dangers associated with night work and public spaces. Interestingly, despite the frequent expression of cross-gender contact taboos and the assumed promiscuity of male drivers, female drivers are still deemed inappropriate. Pratap, a contractor with a large fleet of cars and a large pool of drivers serving multinational call centers, explained that all drivers and passengers face dangers at night, but that women are particularly ill equipped for combating these dangers. He hypothesized:

> What will the woman driver do? Suppose at night in the middle of the road the tire of the cab gets punctured, then there is a spare wheel/ tire and jack, but how can a woman alone do this type of job of wheel changing? How she will manage to lift the heavy wheel? So keeping female drivers is not much success. Our cabs are running 24 hours. So these problems occur regularly. It is the necessity. There are differences in a man's power and ability compared to women.

Night Work and the Need for "Cultural" Protection

Men are also seen as the default ideal workers for security, housekeeping, and driving labor given these jobs' frequent requirement of night work and rotating shifts. Time is a primary domain within which gendered practices are enacted, specifically through the construction of nighttime as a fundamentally inappropriate time for women to be working (Patel, 2010). As Pratap told us, "Our company thinks that most incidents happen at night, so it's better that [women] reach home safely by 8." Another contractor reported that female housekeepers who did work through the night had to be provided transport home, and so men were hired whenever possible to contain costs. Despite the strength of this conviction about the dangers of night work for women, many multinational technology firms—especially call centers, where the majority of employees work at night—do require women to take on nighttime shifts. Night work in these cases is presented as a necessary and unavoidable condition for such jobs. In most cases, however, when women are hired as nighttime security guards and housekeepers, they are assumed to require extra looking after. Jaidev noted, "In fact, the lady guards are not allowed for night duties. In case they go for the night duty, we make arrangements so their transportation is secured, so . . . it's question of how you look after your own people. Until and unless I make them secure, I will not get the people."

In these ways, housekeeping and security firms explain the exclusion of women from most jobs using paternalistic caring narratives. Aside from requiring that special provisions be made for women engaging in night work, managers and contractors also reported accommodating women by "allowing them" to maintain certain local family expectations. Nidhi, an administrative manager at a large transnational call center, explained:

> Housekeeping [and catering] staff can't wear bangles, particularly glass bangles, because there is danger of them breaking and falling into food, but you know, lots of women you see were married, and they were wearing *mangalsutra* [a necklace that is a symbol of marriage]. These are cultural aspects of their identity. Do they agree when you tell them to take it out? Sometimes they say, "My mother-in-law doesn't let me leave the house without these things." So then we tell them, "Take them off when you come to work." Or they wear it and put it inside their shirt. We say, "Don't wear glass bangles. Wear metal bangles."

While such "accommodations" often extend to uniforms and occasionally to women's requirement to perform night shifts, they never extend to women's assumed domestic and caring responsibilities. Women receive no special consideration for their primary responsibility for childcare and domestic work, which will be discussed later in this chapter.

The use of gender-neutral uniforms or rules against the wearing of aesthetic markers of marital status was uncomfortable for some of the women we interviewed, yet these restrictions were assumed to be requirements of working in a "progressive," "Westernized" space. Megha explained, "Nails should be cut, hair should not be loose, and ornaments should be kept in our bags. They can be worn after the work. We keep our bags in the bamboo house, though there is no locker. We keep ear tops and bangles in our bags. Anklets are hidden in socks. If there is a locket, then it is hidden in our shirt. We should not have big bindis."

Even as companies require that such gendered markers be removed during working hours, women continue to be symbolically "marked" as appropriate for a limited set of tasks. These practices provide a vivid illustration of ways in which multinational technology firms use social constructions of gender to achieve corporate and economic advantages, often in the name of "cultural sensitivities" (Pyle & Ward, 2003, p. 466).

Subcontracting Regimes and Gender Preferences

Despite the importance these sectors place on soft skills and deference, guarding, housekeeping, and driving remain largely male-dominated sectors. Subcontracting regimes further perpetuate these gendering practices. This was most evident when we tried to discover the origins of the "rules" in place for the separation of women's and men's work and the stated preference for male workers. Contractors explained that they were required to follow organizational requirements for uniforms, job tasks, and times. They reported that multinational technology firms specified the gender of the workers required right at the beginning of the contract negotiation process. When we asked Praneet, a security contractor, why male and female guards were assigned different work, he responded in English: "Ladies guards cannot frisk gents, so that is the one thing. Again, if it turns out that someone has to be interrogated, a female has to be there. If someone has to be apprehended, a lady guard has to be there, so that is the requirement these days." When we asked whose requirements these were, he replied, "These are the corporate protocols these days. . . . [The multinational technology companies] place their requirement, and based on their requirement, the deployment is actually done. We do not deploy as per our requirement.

We deploy as per their requirement." In a very similar manner, Reena, a housekeeping contractor, told us:

> It depends on client. If the client insists on ladies to wash ladies' washrooms, then we appoint ladies, but if it is all right for the client to appoint men to wash ladies washrooms by putting board outside the washroom, then we appoint men. . . . We have a total staff of 270, out of which 10 percent are ladies and rest all gents. . . . Clients prefer men employees. The reason behind this is sometimes unskilled workers get involved in illegal relations or in unwanted matters, and you don't have any control on them. So they asked us to provide male employees.

Feminized Masculinities and the Desexualized Man

It was common for us to hear views such as those expressed by Reena, according to which men are identified as ideal service workers yet masculinity is referred to as a liability. Hall, Hockey, and Robinson (2007) trace the ways in which different occupations have different expectations for "embodied masculinities," whereby "representations of particular kinds of male bodies play a role in who men think they are (p. 544). The men who are seen as ideal for service jobs within transnational firms are those who display feminized traits such as being calm and deferential, as well as those who do not exhibit any sign of heterosexual male desire. Joachim and Schneiker (2012) note that the security industry often presents two faces of masculinity in its promotional materials and association publications: that of the true professional and that of the ethical hero-warrior. As a result of the interplay between these typologies, security providers are required to be "not just warriors but also managers and peacekeepers, rational and tender all at the same time" (p. 499). One of the manifestations of peacekeeper masculinities in security work involves the discursive construction of security firms as similar to humanitarian nongovernmental organizations and missionary efforts engaged in the task of making the world a safer place. Accordingly, guarding work in the multinational technology sector is understood to require calmness, as described by Praneet:

> Most of the times the guards need to understand the presence of mind. Because though he might be well trained on how to handle a fire extinguisher or a hosepipe, at the end of the day what is going to make sense is how to react and what to do first. If he panics, then everything goes down the drain. If there's a fire, then he needs to

understand, okay, there's a fire, first he needs to check whether he can address the fire or not. If he can address the fire, how he is supposed to address the fire? After addressing the fire, he is to inform someone. If it is beyond his control, then he is to inform someone, "It is beyond our control; we cannot take care of it." . . . He has to be calm because he is the guard. If he panics, then who will look after the facility?

The increasing prominence of security provision for multinational technology firms has changed the conventional notions of militaristic masculinity that underlie much of India's security profession. Rather than strength or size, the industry has come to valorize neatness, order, deference, and the capacity for calm action. In this sense, as Joachim and Schneiker (2012) note, "feminine attributes formerly conceived of as being of lesser value are increasingly used to construct acceptable and superior forms of masculinity" (p. 498). Praneet described the shifting nature of guarding work in multinational companies by noting that guards must "know how to interact with people—how to be polite. Earlier they used to be stationed in one place; he used to look into it if emergency used to be mentioned, but now client is replacing full-time receptionist with a guard, so the guard has to do both the duties. They need to acquire both the skills. They need communication these days as well as perform their duties." In fact, women's assumed natural ability to be calm was cited by some contractors as a reason for their hiring. Vidhu, a contractor, explained, "Even if the girl is lean and thin, as long as she understands English, we put her there, whereas in manufacturing we need sturdy boys because they are operating in difficult conditions." He went on to describe the training his company provided: "We give first aid [training] to the boys. And then a bit of yoga to make his mind calm."

These attempts to counterbalance the traits associated with hegemonic masculinity are necessary not only because of the requirements of service jobs, but also because of men's assumed promiscuity. Indeed, the notion of the ideal worker as a desexualized man is most clearly illustrated in the conversations we had about workers in the transportation sector. Many multinational technology companies offer transportation services to their software programmers and call center workers. Unlike workers in the housekeeping and security sectors, drivers are uniformly men, and their work involves following a strict schedule to pick up and drop off employees at designated times and places. While being male is seen as essential for driving work, men are also continuously under suspicion because of their assumed promiscuity. Drivers' working conditions as well as their daily encounters with company employees who live extravagant lives are assumed to foster high levels of repressed sexuality and anger among drivers that have the potential to lead to brutally violent attacks against female passengers. GPS systems and security escorts are thus integrated into drivers' jobs as ways of mitigating the promiscuity and violence assumed to be associated with male workers. As discussed in chapter 3, the construction of male drivers as violent security threats has occurred largely as a result of several highly publicized rape cases in which the perpetrators were drivers for multinational call centers. In light of these incidents, ideal drivers (as well as ideal guards and house-keepers) are seen to be those men who display traits that signify that their sexuality cannot be "provoked." Such provocations are assumed to come from the young female employees who are part of the software and customer service firms' workforce. Vidhu explained that his company tried to hire older men for service work in the multinational technology industry because of the presence of young women among company employees. He stated, "If I put a 20-year-old boy or a 22-year-old boy, he won't understand [how to] handle a lady or interact with a lady, educated lady, that too. Therefore, we normally put a boy who is married, got his family, so that he behaves accordingly with the lady."

This perception that men are automatically promiscuous can also be traced to a particular rhetoric around poor, lower-caste men, who are often "accused of desiring upper caste women" (Rao, 2009, p. 235). Almost half (48 percent) of the drivers in our sample belonged to the lower classes and castes. Rao argues that the threat of violation of upper-caste women by lower-caste men has served to discipline men and entrench caste hierarchies (2009, p. 236). Consequently, the forms of masculinity that drivers in multinational technology services are assumed to embody are different from the hegemonic masculinities embodied by middle-class, upper-caste software professionals and managers.

Overall, there is a preference within the service sectors of the multi-national technology industry for workers who are quiet and deferential and for male workers. As a result, managers construct the ideal worker as a male who is feminized in terms of his work options, approach to his job, working conditions, and pay. These practices give rise to jobs that are poorly paid, have few protections, and operate on schedules dictated by organizational needs with little regard for household responsibilities. In these ways, service work in multinational technology firms has re-created gender norms around new kinds of feminized masculinity.

Gendered Enactments in Household Settings

Women's access to and involvement in waged work and self-employment have been heralded as key strategies through which patriarchal norms and gender relations can be reworked in India. Gonguly-Scarse (2003) notes that despite the fact that women have been negatively impacted by the structural adjustment policies that accompanied trade liberalization in India and women continue to experience inequality within the household, most lower-middle-class women in West Bengal see themselves as more empowered than earlier generations of women. Gonguly-Scarse attributes this perception in part to state rhetoric that promoted the employment of women in international factories established in the early phases of trade liberalization by forging a link between paid employment and empowerment. The existence of numerous "income generation" schemes directed specifically toward women attest to the widespread prevalence of this connection. Historically, Bengal has had a less restrictive gender regime governing the social and economic life of women than other parts of the country, such as Haryana or Delhi in North India. Gonguly-Scarse notes that the lower-middle-class Bengali women who she studied did not report being held back from engaging in education because of brothers or being asked to drop out of school to support their families. Instead, while they did not report experiencing concrete benefits from the economic liberalization of the past two decades, they did express aspirations for better futures for themselves and their children. Other studies of the links between employment and empowerment are less optimistic. Eisenstein (1998), for example, in a study exploring the relationship between feminism and global capitalism, notes that employers often use feminist demands for women's economic independence to create jobs for poor women. These jobs are celebrated as excellent opportunities yet bolster informality and poor working conditions. They also perpetuate class-based differences among women by encouraging professional women in waged work to offload the burden of social reproduction onto poorer women, who often work as domestics and caregivers.

While debates on whether women's participation in the workforce leads to their empowerment continue (Bachi, 1999; Banerjee, 1999; Kabeer, 1999; Kantor, 2009; Raju & Bagchi, 1993; Subaiya & Vanneman, 2016), it is clear that the relationships among gendered subjects, households, and spheres of capital have shifted in recent years. Salzinger (2016) argues that the breadwinner, as someone who provides for a family, was a central figure in Fordism, even though the role was accessible only to certain men. With growing precarity in the labor market, the possibility for nonelite men to exercise breadwinner masculinity has become more elusive (Cross, 2010). Both female and male workers are defined in contemporary neoliberalism not in terms of their roles vis-à-vis their families but in terms of their roles vis-à -vis capitalism. Indeed, it is in the domain of wages that service work within Indian multinational technology firms is most acutely feminized, in that the wages earned by workers are clearly completely insufficient to sustain families. Alongside the industry's stated preference for male workers, many jobs involve long hours and rotating shifts. It is assumed that all workers, whether female or male, have others managing their household and childcare responsibilities. Working times and fluctuations in schedules are also not supportive of dual-earner families.

As noted earlier, of the 92 housekeepers, security guards, and drivers we interviewed, 16 were women, and the remainder were men. Forty-six of the men in our sample were married, and only four had spouses who were employed. Many of the men in the sample expressed a strong desire to enact breadwinner masculinity and voiced patriarchal assumptions about women's "proper" place in the home, despite the fact that they did not earn wages approximating a family wage. Siddharth, a 23-year-old driver with no children who regularly completed his daily shift at midnight and was then served a meal at home by his wife, said emphatically that his wife "is not going to do any job. I am not going to send her for any job."

Such patriarchal assumptions about the proper role of wives are often accompanied by irregular and long workdays that leave working men unable to contribute to domestic and childcare responsibilities in any meaningful way (except financially). Kumar, a 24-year-old driver with one child who earned INR 8,000 per month, noted that even with his very long hours, it was difficult to make ends meet: "I have no choice but work for that amount. . . . INR 4,000 goes towards the payment of the rent. Then there are medical expenses when my child or wife falls ill. It's hard to manage within INR 4,000. . . . It's hard. One has to struggle a lot." House-keeping, security, and driving jobs are thus often depicted as particularly suitable for "bachelors" or for men in joint families, as Prabhu explained: "At some places they are working in three shifts, and at some places there are two shifts. Two shifts are designed especially for bachelors. What will they do after working for eight hours? They want to earn more so that after four, five months they can to go back to their native places, and after three, four months they will again come back." Such a perspective clearly reflects underlying patriarchal gender norms, as it assumes that married and single men do not have any responsibilities beyond those of the workplace. In effect, however, these men are "temporary breadwinners" (Leonard, 2016) who see their household role as the financial provider but because of the precarious nature of their work have neither the high salary nor the stability to allow them to properly fulfill this role.

Men's employment in precarious jobs has a direct impact on women's household as well as paid work patterns. Out of the 16 women we interviewed, 10 were married, 4 were widowed, and 2 were single. About two-thirds were housekeepers, and the rest were security guards. The range of their experiences provides a vivid illustration of the diverse impacts that the growth of service jobs within multinational firms have had on lower-class women's social and economic positions in India. For some of the married women, the combination of their own waged employment and the poor employment prospects of their spouse led to a clear shift in household power. This was clearly evident when we met Neeta at the cafeteria of her company. Aged 30 at the time of the interview, Neeta had been married at 14, but prior to that had been enrolled in an English-medium school, a background that made her an attractive candidate for her housekeeping job when she had applied for it a year and a half earlier. Neeta worked 12-hour shifts and earned INR 5,800 monthly, which was more than the earnings of her husband, who was a painter. We were struck by her assertive and confident manner as she told us that while others might feel shame at doing cleaning work, she preferred to work rather than to stay at home and was proud to be contributing to the financial well-being of her four children. Although her husband did not want their three daughters to be educated, Neeta expressed a strong determination to support their studies and told us:

> I want them to study hard and stand on their own feet. I won't marry them off in a hurry. I got married at a young age, when I was 14. . . . I won't let that happen to them. My only wish is that they should study. . . . I will educate them on my own. [My husband] does not support me. He doesn't speak about education. He has no desire to [educate the children]. I paint dreams of education for my children. "I work hard for 12 hours for you," I tell them.

While she did not share her husband's views on their children's education, Neeta was also sympathetic to his plight. She said that he often drank, an expense the family could not afford, but that this was necessary because of the poor quality of his job. She also said that her husband recognized that she needed to be employed for the family to meet their basic needs and reported with some pride that he even helped out at home by dropping the younger children off at school and cooking. Neeta described her determination to provide an education for her children as a constant battle, but one that she was clearly winning. She told us that the family had recently moved from a one-room to a two-room home because it had been difficult for the children to do their homework in the smaller space. She had rejected her father's offer to financially help marry off her 13-year-old daughter, whom she characterized as a bright girl who wanted to become a police officer. Her other children wanted to be doctors, engineers, and nurses. Neeta declared, "I must manage my family life. I must stand on my own feet. I work for my children, my home."

While Neeta's spouse contributed to the household income, many of the married women in our sample were sole breadwinners, and several reported spouses who were abusive or habitual alcoholics. For the women in these situations, paid employment allowed them to provide for their families as well as exert control over their children's educations. Sapana was such a sole earner and lived in a *chawl* with her husband and daughters. One of her daughters was married, one worked as a call center agent, and the third was in school. All had attended English-medium schools and helped their mother with household work. Sapana explained that her husband "has a problem with the fact that I work outside [the home]. And he drinks a lot, abuses me and my work. But I don't bother. I have to sustain the family. I am happy with my job." Because he had no employment, Sapana said that her husband sold scraps or did short-term labor to buy alcohol, as she refused to give him any money. Sapana told us that her husband was often verbally abusive, but she was largely dismissive of him. Instead, she spoke with pride and conviction about her daughters' prospects for better lives than her own.

Nabanita's experience was similar. She had started working because her husband was often unwell and was thus unemployed. She reported:

> Whatever it is, I am earning on my own. It is enough for me, and I do not need beg from others. It is enough for my daughter's expenditure. She studies in an English-medium school. I can pay for her education. That's why I have only one daughter. My husband is also often ill. . . . My mother-in-law used to tell me to enroll my daughter in a Marathi-medium school. I said no. I have studied in Marathi

medium. If we know some English, then things change in life. I do not want the same work for my daughter in future.

Despite married women's financial contributions to their households, very few received unequivocal support from their spouses or extended families. One exception was Narine, a 32-year-old security guard who told us that her husband faced discrimination in his job because of his rural background. The family had been on the verge of leaving Pune when she and her husband had decided that instead she would enter the labor market. She stated, "My husband and daughter helped a lot. My husband was home then. He felt uneasy and tense because I was working and he was at home." After her husband got a job, Narine continued to work, a decision that she said her husband often had to defend. She reported, "My mother-in-law was opposed to the idea of my working. She felt we should manage on my husband's salary. But when my husband told her that it is difficult to manage on one salary, and there is loan to be repaid, we have to spend on our children's education, how will I manage alone, she kept quiet." Aside from her paid employment, Narine also, as she informed us with considerable pride, managed the household finances: "My husband gives me all his salary, and I manage the expenses and keep some aside. He works 12 hours, so he cannot look after all these things."

Despite the hope and sense of promise workers attached to their children's educations, not all women were successful in shifting patriarchal expectations or motivating their children to do well academically. Many noted that high fees made it difficult to cover the cost of English-medium schools. Devika explained that her 15-year-old daughter had recently finished tenth grade and was awaiting an appropriate marriage proposal because her husband and father-in-law did not approve of her continuing her education. Her son had decided to become a car mechanic, and the family was saving money for him to set up his business. She reported waking up at 5 a.m. every day and doing some housework before leaving for her 12-hour shift as a housekeeper. Her daughter was responsible for the bulk of the remaining housework. Shital similarly told us that her 18-year-old son was not good at English and did not want to study any further. Disappointed in his decision, Shital said that her son wanted to be a driver but that she was determined to continue to work so that she could at least give him some capital to start a transportation business and not have to take a low-wage service job as she had.

For most women, the combination of low wages and patriarchal marital relations limited the extent to which they were able to use their jobs to achieve social and economic mobility. This was especially true for single and widowed women, who spoke about their access to paid employment as transformative but also reported difficulties in making ends meet given the low wages they received. Manjhu, a 31-year-old single woman with diabetes, lived with two of her sisters, one of whom was also unmarried and the other widowed. She told us that she did not want to marry, and that the three sisters could share their expenses. When we asked how they spent their Sundays, most of the women we interviewed said they did housework, but Manjhu noted that sometimes her elder sister, who was officer in the military, hired a car so they could visit faraway temples, and sometimes they listened to songs or watched serials on TV. She said, "There is no one in the house who will scold us." Despite waking up at 4 a.m. because of her long commute, and working from 7 a.m.-4 p.m. every day 4 a.m. Manjhu noted that she did not earn enough to cover her living expenses. She said, "You know everything is very expensive. Food, medicines, and travel expenses – it is very expensive. Our elder sister financially helps us".

Widows too said their jobs allowed them to exercise a certain degree of independence. Sangeeta characterized her marriage as a bad alliance and reported that she had moved back to her maternal home with her three young children after the death of her husband. She did domestic work in the mornings and her housekeeping job in the afternoons and evenings. Her income allowed her to pay for her children's school fees and groceries. Both her parents were employed in low-wage jobs and also supported Sangeeta's younger siblings. Priyanka too had been widowed after facing harassment and abuse from her alcoholic husband, who had not had a steady income and had not allowed her to work outside the home. After his death, however, she was allowed to work by her extended family because they were unable to support her. Shital, who had also been widowed after the death of her alcoholic husband, emphasized, "I feel proud because I raised my children on this job. When my husband died, I had nothing. I was totally dependent on my mother and brother. I didn't know the outside world. Now I have become independent."

In pointing to their financial independence and their ability to provide for their children, many women position themselves as breadwinners—a role typically associated with men. This kind of independence, however, is not without costs. Except for occasional or partial help from family members, most women continue to assume all domestic responsibilities, and, unlike middle-class technology workers, none of the female workers interviewed in this study reported being able to hire anyone to help them with their family responsibilities. Shital told us that she woke up at 4 a.m. every day to complete her domestic work before she left for her job. Her sons did not help her. She complained of back pain and other health effects related to her rotating shifts. Vijaya, who worked as a housekeeper, described her mornings as follows: "I get up at four o'clock. After bathing I make tea and give girls tea . . . then I prepare breakfast for them, pack their tiffins. . . . After that I do the cooking for all of us, and then I clean the utensils and wash clothes. Before going to the office, I finish all my household chores." Kavita similarly explained that on workdays she woke up at 4:45 a.m., in order to complete her domestic work and prepare meals for her husband and children. She got home at 9 p.m., finished her cooking and other domestic chores, and went to bed at 11:30 p.m. Her daughter helped her with washing clothes, cleaning utensils, and basic food preparation. Such long days of domestic and paid work leave limited time for women to engage in leisure activities, as Kavita lamented: "I don't find time to make friends. . . . Our nature of job is such that we can't take time for ourselves. Whatever time we have goes in doing household chores or with children and job." Such a time crunch also leaves little time for women to engage with their children. Sangeeta informed us that her job as a housekeeper did not even provide her an opportunity to talk to her youngest daughter on working days, because she was asleep when Sangeeta left and returned. Similar sentiments were shared by Priyanka, who explained that when she had first been widowed, she had sent her teenage son to live with his aunt and he was now deeply resentful of her, making their family situation very tense. She regretted that her long hours of employment and the fact that she had sole financial responsibility for the upbringing and education of her children had resulted in her son's hostility. However, with household expenses, which included the need to repay the loan she had taken out for her daughter's marriage (equivalent to a year and a half's income), Priyanka continued to need to work long hours.

These accounts of the household lives of low-wage service workers resonate with analyses that characterize poor and working-class men as "failed patriarchs" because of their inability to access jobs that pay breadwinner wages. The analysis in this chapter shows that while there may be some women employed as service workers in transnational firms, there continues to be a stated preference for male workers who can be hired at a low wage. These men, uniformed and employed in glossy glass and steel buildings associated with modernity and progress, struggle to provide for their families. The women who do manage to get jobs as low-wage service workers have similar experiences of being both proud to be providers and frustrated by the difficulty of doing so properly. As Radhakrishnan and Solari (2015) note, women's increased access to waged work has led to some economic gains for women, but these gains do not always result in greater power in household settings. Some of the women we interviewed clearly experienced greater decision-making power. However, these women were expected to engage in paid work while continuing to meet all of their existing family responsibilities (Radhakrishnan, 2014), which they did not have the resources to outsource.

Overall, the analysis in this chapter suggests that aspirations for greater social mobility attract women to jobs as housekeepers or security guards in the multinational technology industry. Vijayakumar (2013) argues that aspiration is a "mediating force" that links lower-middle-class workers to elite professionals and produces a longing for social mobility that differently affects women and men. She explains that "the act of aspiring itself can help produce gendered class distinction" (p. 779). Female and male low-wage, low-caste workers employed in India's multinational technology firms hold jobs in which they draw a relatively regular wage and are able to imagine future mobility by investing in savings, entrepreneurship, and their children's education. Some female workers also experience shifts in household power and decision-making authority.

Yet within the professed modern and progressive spaces of multinational technology firms, static and archaic divisions between appropriate work for women and men continue to uphold a rigid division of labor. Despite the flat organizational structures of these companies and the presence of large numbers of middle-class professional women within them, women who are housekeepers and security guards learn that the gender equity promoted for software programmers or call center workers does not extend to them. Their work is structured by gender relations are governed by both "traditional" patriarchal gender regimes (e.g., prohibitions on women working in public spaces, taboos against cross-gender contact, caste stigma around male promiscuity) and a new rhetoric of training (that emphasizes "grooming" and soft skills) and professionalization that under the guise of modernity continues to feminize service work and workers as unskilled and cheap. Discourses of cross-gender and cross-caste contact as taboo, of the dangers of night work for women, and of the linkages between professionalization, risk taking, and technology all result in the construction of men as the service sector's ideal workers. However, these men, many of whom are migrants from nearby villages and lower-caste communities, are also perceived as potential threats in the form of sexual offenders and rapists. They are expected never to draw attention to their masculine sexuality and to embody feminized ways of working. Collectively, these gendered practices serve to maintain lower labor costs through "culturally appropriate" discourses of occupational gender segregation among low-wage service workers that are rooted in local gender-, class-, and caste-based hierarchies.

Endnotes

1. There are, however, exceptions. Within India, for example, scholars have noted that men of color as well as poor and lower-caste men have historically worked as janitors, houseboys, and domestic workers (Banerjee, 2004; Bujra, 2000; Lowrie, 2008; Ray, 2000; Sarti & Scrinzi, 2010; Soni-Sinha & Yates, 2013; Qayum & Ray, 2010). The trends of increases in men and decreases in women are also occurring in other historically female-dominated occupations such as waste pickers, home-based workers, and street vendors (Chen & Raveendran, 2012).

2. As described in chapter 2, "mechanized cleaning" with particular kinds of chemicals, the ability to read labels, and familiarity with ingredients are constructed as skills linked to masculinity. This association between masculinity and technology is not new. Feminist scholars have long demonstrated the links between hegemonic masculinity and rationality, logic, and technical prowess that have effectively kept women out of some professions or led to their encountering glass ceilings within them (Cockburn & Ormrod, 1993; Massey, 1996; Wajcman, 1991).

CHAPTER 6

Left Out

Service Workers in India's Multinational Technology Sector

In a report on the changing nature of cleaning jobs, Irwin (2017) observes that large corporations have "flocked to a new management theory: Focus on core competence and outsource the rest. The approach has made companies more nimble and more productive, and delivered huge profits for shareholders. It has also fueled inequality." Nowadays, those who clean for highly profitable companies work through contractors, have low wages, and receive few benefits. Most significantly, however, these workers have few learning and career growth opportunities. Even as they witness the economic progress of their company and its direct employees, these workers "find themselves excluded from that select group. Rather than being treated as assets that companies seek to invest in, they have become costs to be minimized" (Irwin, 2017). The experiences of service workers in India's multinational technology sector reveal the impact of the globalized trend of companies moving toward subcontracting to fulfill their labor needs. The analysis in this book shows that while globalization may bring with it both challenges and opportunities for working people around the world, the combination of global capital flows and local subcontracting systems prevents those workers who perform significant organizational labor outside the boundaries of work labeled as "core" from having fulfilling jobs or experiencing economic mobility. As a result, work is "atomized" (Flemming, 2017, p. 693), and individual workers within subcontracting chains hold little collective power and work under conditions of vulnerability and invisibility. As Adkins (2016) summarizes, subcontracting allows capital to offload the costs and risks of employment to labor and facilitates the decollectivization of labor. It gives rise to a new provisional and contingent social contract in which "nothing is guaranteed for the worker or would-be worker other than the hope or possibility of work but not necessarily a sustaining wage or a life that can be planned into the future" (p. 1).

Even so, in contrast to universalizing discourses that paint the cheap laborers of the global South as predominantly victims of global capital, the everyday lives of working people reveal much more contradictory experiences. The drivers, security guards, and housekeepers who service India's multinational technology companies occupy an ambiguous position in the urban labor markets of neoliberal India. While these workers are outsiders in the high-tech spaces within which they perform their jobs and remain mostly unmentioned in celebratory narratives of globalization, their labor is crucial to the very project of development and economic progress linked to the IT boom, the most popular marker of India's neoliberal success story. These low-wage service workers are neither part of the "new middle class" professional workforce who have been the main beneficiaries of neoliberal policies nor members of the lowest strata of the urban poor who work as sweepers, peddlers, street vendors, and daily wage workers. Indeed, based on the criteria traditionally used to demarcate the boundaries between formal and informal employment, such as the type or nature of a job contract, methods of payment of wages, the provision of social security, and eligibility for paid leave, these workers occupy a distinctly liminal space. Their daily lives are enmeshed within the formal spaces of multinational technology firms, and their wages for the most part are fixed, albeit sometimes paid in cash like the wages of casual laborers. Yet all of them work within complex networks of subcontracting relationships with few written formal contracts and limited provision of social security. Many of these drivers, security guards, and housekeepers have attained levels of education that are higher than the Indian average but not high enough to allow them to access professional or managerial-level jobs. A number of workers who are migrants from neighboring villages own land, thus wielding some power in their place of birth. Overall, while they are not the most marginal of Indian workers, their experiences demonstrate the rampant informality that is characteristic of formal multinational organizations in India and that severely curtails their access to the social and economic benefits of development frequently associated with this sector.

Numerically, these workers account for only a small section of India's urban economy. Despite their limited numerical strength, they play an important material as well as ideological role in India's economy. Materially, their importance derives from the fact that these workers provide valuable services to the multinational technology industry without which it would not be able to function. Ideologically, as "indirect" workers, this group is assumed to be at the "frontlines" of trickle-down development resulting from transnational economic flows, and thus justifies neoliberal policy prescriptions. The IT-ITES sector is constructed as a large employment generator of both direct employment and jobs in ancillary industries such as transportation, real estate and catering, security and housekeeping. The indirect employment attributed by the sector is estimated at about 10 million (Mishra, 2016). Despite their prominence in such narratives, the lives of these "10 million" workers have largely been rendered invisible within popular accounts of neoliberal globalization. The accounts of the workers central to this book suggest that the discourses of futurity that are characteristic of the IT industry in India (Gupta & Mankekar, 2017) pervade service workers' environments, but that their employment does not guarantee them access to improved social and economic futures. Aside from the isolated celebratory rags-to-riches stories that pepper popular media, there have been few attempts to capture exactly how benefits can be secured for workers in low-wage jobs servicing multinational corporations.

While neoliberal globalization has not led to the clear-cut trickling down of economic benefits, several practices tied to globalization are clearly trickling down. First, the influx of multinational firms in India has given rise to the development of a new sense of self among workers through corporate practices of grooming and entrepreneurial aspirations, impacting not only middle-class professionals but also low-wage workers within the sector. It is the self-directed, professional, aspirational worker who is idealized within neoliberalism. Second, employment relations based on subcontracting that have become widespread in Western economies in the last half century have become the "new" model for business operations among multinationals in India as a result of discourses of "core competencies" (Weil, 2014). For workers, the combination of new aspirations and subcontracting relations has created contradictions, frustrations, fragmentation, and deep resentment. Workers have limited access to the benefits of the development miracle embodied by the firms they service because of the "fissured" nature of their workplaces (Weil, 2014). Workers' identities, too, become fissured as their bodies, uniforms, and demeanors are transformed into emblems of economic progress even as their economic assets remain severely limited. They are simultaneously part of the physical architecture of the multinational technology firms that are distinguished by their high levels of security, clean premises, and organized transportation and the cheap labor that performs the "noncore" activities that make this wealth possible. Such fissured identities are integral to the contradictory subjectivities they are expected to embody. Housekeepers are supposed to keep these companies' premises clean but are themselves perceived to be unclean because of their caste and class positions and hence must be trained on how to *be clean* through bodily practices of comportment, speech, hygiene, and grooming. Drivers are supposed to minimize risk during travel but often bear significant financial risk as potential entrepreneurs and are constantly under suspicion of being sexual offenders. Security guards are responsible for ensuring companies' safety and security but also face suspicion for thefts and must daily negotiate the dual pressures of subservience and surveillance as they monitor the entrance and exits of firms' premises.

Hidden Informality in Formal Firms

Neoliberalism has had deeply diverse effects on different groups of workers-effects that both are mediated through existing class-, caste-, and gender-based hierarchies and are responsible for creating and reconfiguring these hierarchies in new ways. The new discourses of compliance, entrepreneurialism, and professionalism have accompanied the transformation of the occupations of housekeepers, drivers, and security guards servicing the multinational technology sector. These discourses serve to mask the informal nature of employment relations within firms that through their formidable architectures and promotional branding have come to signify the benefits of formal employment. We refer to this informality as hidden for several reasons. First, rather than occurring in a separate sector or space, informal jobs exist within large transnational organizations that are symbols of modernity and progress. These spaces exude architectural and infrastructural wealth not typically associated with informality, which is associated with work that occurs in homes or on streets. Second, informality is masked because these workers are both materially and ideologically highly visible—uniformed in distinctive and smart attire, with name badges signifying organizational belonging, and working within lavish organizational campuses constructed as emblems of India's progress. Third, informality is hidden by the discourses of compliance liberally used by managers at technology firms and contractors in reference to these service workers. Multinational technology firms are visual reminders of the fact that even in a country with widespread abject poverty, extreme wealth is possible. Water and electricity shortages do not prevent the existence of manicured lawns and heavily air-conditioned offices. Managers and contractors refer frequently to their compliance with labor laws, especially those related to minimum wage, overtime pay, medical benefits, and pensions, constructing a veneer of professionalism. Significant attention is devoted to the creation of documentary evidence demonstrating compliance with state-established minimum wage standards.

While such forms of hidden informality erode workers' wages and prospects for mobility, we are not arguing that the formalization of service jobs will automatically enhance workers' lives. Indeed, in the context of India, even if the workers we interviewed had full access to minimum wages and benefits, they would be only marginally better off. Indeed, informality is hidden because of the very use of the benchmark of the "minimum wage" by multinationals, a focus that completely sidesteps the near-complete consensus within local settings that this measure is totally insufficient to allow full-time workers to transcend poverty. The fact that these workers do not even receive wages and benefits that meet this extremely low threshold is a sign of their broader marginalization. Challenging this marginalization involves developing robust structures in which greater collective voices can be heard and changing these workers' construction as disposable, highly individualized actors. Most importantly, it requires the payment of wages that allow individuals to improve their lifestyles as well as plan for better futures. As Surie and Koduganti (2016) show, even Uber drivers, whose employment is extremely unstable and risky, express satisfaction with their work when they are able to earn INR 120,000 per month (i.e., 10 times more than the drivers in our sample). In the context of India, where a majority of the working population is informally employed, there are vast differences within the informal economy (see Raju & Bose, 2016, for a review). However, transnational firms and their representatives use discourses of compliance to make the claim that they pay fair wages. Not only do they not do so, but the discourse of compliance also masks the broader marginalization of workers who, even if formally employed, would not have access to the welfare safety nets and enforcement regimes that some formally employed workers in the global North enjoy.

Even the basic minimum wage established by the state, however, is often not paid to workers. As is typical of subcontracting arrangements, multinational firms offload the burden of compliance with wage standards to smaller vendors and subcontractors. Many of these individuals, in order to maintain their profit margins, bid competitively on contracts while skirting these responsibilities. Ironically, right in the midst of the highly regulated and controlled spaces of multinational technology firms, labor informality is rampant. Often, subcontractors themselves fall into the category of "self-employed," with diverse scales of operation. Many workers do not receive the benefits they have been promised. Nor are their jobs accompanied by long-term security or higher pay. Finally, their work provides limited scope for upward social mobility and lacks a sense of dignity for many workers.

Despite their poverty-level wages, service workers in the multinational technology industry are seen as ideal neoliberal subjects, being both flexible and "professional." In this context, informality takes different forms and is often riddled with contradictions. For example, we found that among housekeepers, discourses of professionalization served to cut cleaning work's historical ties to caste-based hierarchies. The notion of cleaning as "dirty work" performed by the "contaminated and backward castes" has been sanitized through the practice of wearing gloves, using environmentally friendly cleaning products, utilizing modern cleaning tools, and adopting Western corporate standards of cleanliness. The professionalization of cleaners has been achieved through the use of terms such as "mechanized housekeepers," as well as aesthetic requirements like proper "grooming" and cleanliness that cleaners are expected to embody. Such aesthetic practices are taught to housekeepers through different training initiatives linking clean workers with moral virtues such as honesty, discipline, self-control, and good manners. Yet despite this veneer of professionalization, housekeepers continue to experience social stigma associated with cleaning work and do not earn salaries that allow them to challenge caste-and gender-based stereotypes linked to cleaning jobs in India. Although they are responsible for keeping the premises of India's multinational technology firms clean, their wages are insufficient to allow them to upgrade their own homes. Many of the migrant men who fill such jobs live in cramped quarters, sharing their living spaces with other fellow workers in the city. Even though workers both maintain and embody hegemonic symbols of Western modernity associated with the multinational technology sector, they can access this modernity only through the exploitative employment relationships within which they are situated.

Drivers face a similar predicament. They are constructed as ideal neoliberal subjects who play an important role in mediating the orderly, clean, and safe environment of the multinational organization and the seemingly chaotic, unclean, and potentially unsafe city outside its gates. They are also central to discourses of entrepreneurialism because of their self-employment and their potential to become owners of the cars they drive. However, such constructions are contradicted by the fact that micro-level entrepreneurship is very risky, as drivers have to endure very long hours, are not protected by labor laws, and often have to bear the costs of any accidents. Many of the vendors in this sector who we interviewed described their personal rags-to-riches stories of rising from poverty to achieve their dreams of economic and social stability. Yet the transformation from driver to owner brings with it specific challenges, including long, grueling hours and significant financial risk. Nevertheless, the lure of entrepreneurship is one of the main motivators for drivers to struggle through the hardships they face in this industry. Entrepreneurialism is not merely a matter of economic empowerment but also affects the more subtle ways in which individuals construct their sense of self, of being and feeling, a process that obfuscates the boundaries separating public and private spaces (Freeman, 2014). This kind of entrepreneurialism is always an ongoing process and often registers in the emotional and affective realms that are most often ignored. For drivers, entrepreneurship is reflected not only in their faith in an industry that will allow them opportunities for self-employment but also in their emotional ties to other fellow drivers, whom they often support and mentor, especially if they originate from their own villages or communities, and their sense of endurance despite their occupation's long working hours, verbal abuse, and heightened suspicions of criminalization in recent years. Many drivers note their comfort with GPS monitoring of their cars by emphasizing that it is proof of their honesty and integrity (Nayar, 2015). This kind of entrepreneurialism is also linked to the aspirations, dreams, and hopes tied to service jobs within multinational technology firms in general. All the workers we interviewed to some degree described their hopes for their children, and especially their desire that they be enrolled in English-medium schools so that they did not end up doing similar work. These notions of neoliberal entrepreneurialism are by no means new or only found among low-income workers. In fact, English education as a means to upward social mobility has been one of the key dynamics of "middle-classness" in India since colonial times. The difference between that paradigm and the new one, however, is that for the majority of workers today, these dreams of entrepreneurialism remain laden with significant risk and largely out of reach. The intricate web of subcontracting in which workers find themselves, accompanied by high levels of job insecurity, poor wages, dismal social security provisions, and a lack of dignity, prevent these workers as a group from becoming "entrepreneurs."

Driver-entrepreneurs are at the forefront of the "radical responsibilization of employment" in what Flemming refers to as "the era of Uberization" (2017, p. 693). This transformation occurs when both the risks and the benefits of being employed are borne entirely by individuals, resulting in a proliferation of job insecurity. This "atomization of the employee" (Flemming, 2017, p. 693) is clear in the recent emergence of private Uber and Ola cabs in India. Despite the positioning of these services as innovative organizational systems that challenge cumbersome state regulations to benefit workers and customers alike, "for all the innovation that Uber and Ola keep talking about, they seem to have reproduced, and in some cases, reinforced the exploitative structures of the previously existing taxi services" (Mazumdar, 2017). Like Uber and Ola drivers, those who drive transnational corporate executives for a living face extremely long work hours, few benefits, and little insurance against the risk of accidents on the road.

Security guards are also crucial to the maintenance of a safe environment and the protection of the company site, property, and employees from any outside threat. Their professionalism is constructed through scripted codes of conduct like wearing clean and ironed uniforms, having a disciplined attitude, and possessing the ability to interact with employees in a proper and civil manner without displaying any overt characteristic of servitude like saluting (popular within traditional bureaucratic spaces in India). Guards are required to have functional knowledge of English so that they can interact with employees during frisking or other security-related checks. Knowledge of computer skills is sometimes also required, especially since some security guards have to handle digital screening devices at entry and exit points. However, such constructions of the ideal security guard are imbued with problematic discourses of embodiment that are often rooted in a military-like disciplinary regime that centers on long-term endurance and loyalty as key values. Additionally, guards also have to maintain a tricky balance between civility and their duty as gatekeepers, a task that gives rise to subtle power struggles with the more entitled software and call center employees they are supposed to monitor but not offend. Despite being constructed as key figures in a firm who may wield some power in determining who is allowed entry to the company premises, they also risk being fired if they are unable to manage the complex emotional requirements of their job. Finally, guards, who are frequently migrant workers, are often themselves perceived as threats and hence face constant surveillance themselves.

Feminized Masculinities

Despite substantial advances in women's access to education, studies reveal that India has among the lowest rates of formal female labor force participation in the world (Bhandare, 2017a). Andres and colleagues (2017) note that there was in fact a substantial drop in women's labor force participation in India between 1993 and 2012, which coincided with the period that saw an influx of foreign capital and high levels of economic growth. Significantly, the lowest level of female labor force participation in India's urban areas is among those who have secondary levels of education (compared to those who have much less education or those who have college degrees). These are precisely the women who hold housekeeping and security jobs with multinational technology companies. Explanations for the surprisingly low female labor force participation rates in India include women's exceptionally high levels of responsibility for household work compared to men (Bhandare, 2017b). In addition, patriarchal social norms are shown to limit women's ability to participate in paid work (Andres et al., 2017). The analysis in this book reveals, however, that women are also excluded from paid jobs because of organizational constructions of men as ideal workers, even in typically feminized occupations such as housekeeping.

Alongside the feminization and masculinization of jobs, which operate in conjunction with assumptions about caste and class, the accounts of low-wage service workers provide a stark reminder that gender-based exclusion also operates through overt forms of discrimination that define women as unable to perform or inappropriate for particular kinds of work. These practices are evident among many multinational corporations operating in India, which dictate service needs for contractors to fulfill and specify a preference for male workers. Often, such preferences are justified through patronizing discourses of cultural sensitivity or the protection of women that are rooted in perceived notions of local patriarchal gender and caste regimes. Hiring and work practices within these firms reproduce rather than simply support regressive gender norms perpetuating inequalities. Our analysis supports Raju and Bose's (2016) observation that "global capitalism, while providing new job prospects for women, not only exploits the prevailing gendered stereotypes, but also rearticulates them (p. 37). Gender norms are both created and sustained within cleaning, guarding, and driving jobs and impact who is hired, for what kinds of jobs, and how the work is imbued with certain kinds of masculine and feminine attributes. Within the housekeeping sector, women are seen as inappropriate for work that is defined as physically strenuous or requires night shifts and, while not uniformly so, are sometimes paid lower salaries than men. Guarding work is organized in terms of assumptions of taboos around cross-gender contact. Finally, driving jobs are structured on the basis of the assumed promiscuity of men and women's need for protection.

In fact, despite discourses of gender neutrality in the so-called modern multinational companies, gender norms are being continually created anew. Service jobs within multinational technology firms are poorly paid and unstable, but they do provide access to full-time employment. These jobs are gendered in unique ways, because on the one hand, they require both male and female workers to cultivate feminine and feminized characteristics like modesty, obedience, loyalty, deference, and patience, but on the other hand, archaic patriarchal and caste-based ideologies construct women as liabilities and such work as a threat to women's safety as a result of cross-gender, cross-caste contact and masculine promiscuity. As a result, work is feminized and women are simultaneously constructed as less ideal than men for these jobs. The preference for men is justified because of the service sector's predominance of night work, women's assumed lack of physical strength, and the assumption that men are more appropriate for technologically infused "mechanized cleaning." These strategies provide a vivid illustration of the malleable ways in which gender norms are defined and manipulated to serve the economic needs of global capital. They reveal that at least part of the reason for women's shockingly low participation in the Indian labor market is due to the fact that organizational practices, including those originating in seemingly progressive, Westernized firms, buttress rather than challenge patriarchal social norms. Most insidious is that these practices also do not provide either men or women with a living wage, and families as a result feel trapped in never-ending cycles of poverty.

In the so-called "traditional" spaces of workers' homes, some women are able to challenge some gender norms as a result of their employment in the multinational technology sector. Many of the women we interviewed expressed a sense of pride or elevated status among their family and community members because they earned wages, wore uniforms, and were associated with fancy new high-tech companies in Pune. They often became significant contributors to their household income, and some were their family's sole breadwinner. Earning money also gave many women more power in household decision-making, especially that related to their children's education and futures. Some women and men were able to escape feudal relationships by working in the city, where their extended families had more limited control over their lives.

Despite many women's enhanced economic standing arising out of their paid employment, the domestic division of labor is generally not overturned, and female workers continue to bear the major responsibility of domestic care work. Unlike middle-class women, female service workers do not have the resources to hire others to help them. Men's feminized and poorly paid labor does not, for many men, lead to a shift in patriarchal assumptions about women's natural role as caregivers and domestic workers. Instead, organizational routines and time demands lead to an intensification in domestic divisions of labor, with jobs being structured in such a way that many men, particularly drivers, have little or no time to participate in domestic routines. Neither earning sufficient wages to sustain a family nor doing a portion of unpaid domestic work or childcare, such men are part of a group that has been referred to as "failed patriarchs" who "experience a painful dissonance between breadwinner expectations and economic opportunities" (Radhakrishnan, 2015, p. 785). Although they share their workplaces with elite men and are uniformed to suggest that they have opportunities to become part of the domestic elite, hegemonic masculinities based on economic power and control are elusive for these workers. Instead, like the women in our sample, they are required to be deferential to the domestic elite they serve.

While global subcontracting chains are assumed to be characterized by weak employment relationships, this characterization can be misleading, since employees are on the payrolls of contractors rather than paid directly by the organizations in whose facilities they work. In fact, organizations exert great control over workers, whether they directly employ them or not. Such forms of indirect control include the inculcation of practices of inequity on the basis of gender, caste, regional background, and bodily characteristics. Large multinational firms are not held accountable for the central role they play in promoting such practices of inequity. Global labor regulatory bodies have failed to provide oversight of or incentives for multinational firms to follow the ideals espoused by their brand images in their interactions with their large service workforces. These trends are not limited to India. Guynn's (2014) study of cleaners, caterers, guards, and drivers working for Silicon Valley's high-tech companies reveals that because these workers are employed through contractors, "the bounty from the technology boom is not trickling down to them." One shuttle operator is quoted as saying, "They say you are a professional driver, but you are not getting professional pay."

Ways Forward

The normalization of poorly paid precarious employment is a phenomenon that poses one of the greatest challenges for working people around the world. As an article in the *New York Times* aptly captures, it is the "wage problem" rather than the unemployment problem that plagues many people in American cities, who have full-time jobs but are still unable to pay for their basic shelter and food needs (Fausset, 2016). But this problem is not unique to the global North. Many of the workers we interviewed in India faced the same situation, in which, despite their engagement in paid work for between 40 and 80 hours per week in large, formal high-tech firms, they reported little optimism about their capacity to improve their social and economic positions.

Under such circumstances, what are the wider implications for economic development among the communities and cities of the global South? Clearly, the workers profiled in this book contest the accounts of optimistic development advocates who assume that the wealth generated by foreign and multinational investors will automatically be diffused throughout local communities. Yet their stories also do not fully support the views of antiglobalization advocates who equate colonialism and contemporary special economic zones. Many of the migrant men we interviewed did not romanticize agrarian lifestyles, and many of the women were critical of patriarchal practices that limited both their own lives and their daughters' prospects in mainstream and more "traditional" sectors. Many workers welcomed opportunities to participate in jobs that were constructed as "professional," although some lamented the superficiality of the entrepreneurialism they were allowed to exercise in their jobs. All, however, noted the exploitative nature of contracting relationships, and their life experiences provide a vivid illustration of the failures of such relationships to foster stability and development.

In this context, more could be done to better protect workers and provide sustainable livelihoods. Worker associations, enforcement agencies, and stronger legislation would provide the necessary infrastructure through which wealth, now primarily enjoyed by a small elite and embodied in infrastructure, could benefit service workers. Rather than working through subcontractors, organizations with constant cleaning, security, and transportation needs could hire permanent and direct employees to carry out these tasks and pay them living wages. Yet such strategies would also lead to higher costs for multinational corporations, who could then seek cheaper labor forces elsewhere and thus perpetuate the global "race to the bottom" (Stiglitz, 2002). Such an analysis suggests that local endeavors and efforts to ensure better worker protections are likely to be short-lived unless they are situated within the context of global efforts. McCallum (2013) has explored several very interesting transnational mobilizations of security guards who work for the global security corporation G4S. Emphasizing many of the local dimensions of collective organizing, McCallum argues that workers around the world may be able to unite if they focus their efforts not on common oppressions, but on common employers. This approach may open up exciting opportunities to address the collective concerns of service workers transnationally, especially since capital and labor operate across borders, albeit to different degrees. Zlolniski (2006) similarly recounts the organizing efforts of janitors in Silicon Valley who set up highly visible protests of their poor wages in an effort to spread public awareness of their plight. Given organizations' significant investments in branding themselves as modern and progressive, these protests were successful because company officials did not want negative global publicity to damage their brands. Such strategies may also be successful in India, particularly when solidarities cut across class interests and focus on the need for more responsible employment relationships (Flemming, 2017). For example, the National Confederation of Union for IT Enabled Services, a trade union that advocates for the rights of IT professionals, and especially better health and safety protections, was created in 2014 in India amid much publicity. The first organization of its kind, it addresses challenges faced by information and communication technology workers (Sridhar, 2014). Such collectives could extend to service workers like housekeepers, drivers, and security guards, who provide the crucial infrastructure for the proper functioning of this industry.

While this book has sought to problematize the universalizing discourses of workers from the global South as perpetual victims, it is clear that discourses of Western modernity encapsulated within neoliberalism continue to foster caste-, class-, and gender-based inequalities. Ironically, incorporation into the global economy may be the key impetus to solve the very problems that such incorporation engenders. Workers engaged in cleaning, guarding, and driving work for multinational technology firms in India stand out as visible, uniformed markers of the progress and wealth signified by these firms' glass and steel buildings. At the same time, they are left out of the prospects for future mobility signified by their places of work. They appear at these companies' gates, clean in their lobbies, and guard their boundaries but receive only a tiny, temporary trickle of the wealth generated through the global flow of capital.

REFERENCES
....

Abraham, A., Singh, D., & Pal, P. (2014). *Critical assessment of labour laws, policies and practices through a gender lens*. National Resource Center for Women. Retrieved from http://nmew.gov.in/WriteReadData/l892s/8261924589Final%20World%20Bank%20Report.pdf.

Abrahamsen, R., & Williams, M. C. (2011). Security privatization and global security assemblages. *Brown Journal of World Affairs, 18*(1), 171–180.

Acker, J. (1990). Hierarchies, jobs and bodies: Toward a theory of gendered organizations. *Gender & Society,* 4(2),139–158.

Adkins, L. (2001). Cultural feminization: Money, sex and power for women. *Signs, 26*(3), 669–680.

Adkins, L. (2016). Contingent labour and the rewriting of the sexual contract. In Dever, M., & Adkins, L. (Eds.), *The post-Fordist sexual contract: Working and living in contingency.* (pp. 1–28). Basingstoke, UK: Palgrave Macmillan.

Agarwala, R. (2007). Resistance and compliance in the age of globalization: Indian women and labor organizations. *Annals of the American Academy of Political and Social Science, 610*(1), 143–159.

Agarwala, R. (2008). Reshaping the social contract: Emerging relations between the state and informal labor in India. *Theory and Society, 37*(4), 375–408.

Agarwala, R. (2013). *Informal labor, formal politics, and dignified discontent in India.* New York: Cambridge University Press.

Aguiar, L. (2001). Doing cleaning work "scientifically": The reorganization of work in the contract building cleaning industry. *Economic and Industrial Democracy, 22*(2), 239–269.

Aguiar, L.L.M., & Ryan, S. (2009). The geographies of the justice for janitors. *Geoforum, 40*(6), 949–958.

Alexandra, A. (2012). Private military and security companies and the liberal conception of violence. *Criminal Justice Ethics, 31*(3), 158–174.

Ameeriar, L. (2017). *Downwardly global: Women, work, and citizenship in the Pakistani diaspora.* Durham, NC: Duke University Press.

Anand, G. & Kumar, H. (2016). Hoping jobs for India follow, Modi clears investors' path. *New York Times,* June 20. Retrieved from https://www.nytimes.com/2016/06/21/world/asia/india-needing-jobs-eases-rules-on-foreign-investment.html.

Ananthanarayanan, S. (2008). New mechanisms of imperialism in India: The special economic zones. *Socialism and Democracy, 22*(1), 35–60.

Andreopoulos, G., & Brandle, S. (2012). Revisiting the role of private military and security companies. *Criminal Justice Ethics, 31*(3), 138–157.

Andres, L. A., Dasgupta, B., Joseph, G., Abraham, V., & Correia, M. (2017). Precarious drop: Re-assessing patterns of female labor force participation in India. Policy Research Working Paper No. WPS 8024. Washington, DC: World Bank Group. Retrieved from http://documents.worldbank.org/curated/en/559511491319990632/pdf/WPS8024.pdf.

Anjaria, J. S., & Anjaria, U. (2013). The fractured spaces of entrepreneurialism in post-liberalization India. In N. Gooptu (Ed.), *Enterprise culture in neoliberal India* (pp. 190–205). New York: Routledge.

Anker, R. (2011). *Estimating a living wage: A methodological review.* Conditions of Work and Employment Series No. 29. Geneva: International Labour Organization. Retrieved from http://www.ilo.int/wcmsp5/groups/public/—ed_protect/—protrav/—travail/documents/publication/wcms_162117.pdf.

Bair, J. (2010). On difference and capital: Gender and the globalization of production. *Signs, 36*(1), 203–226.

Ball, K. (2005). Organization, surveillance and the body: Towards a politics of resistance. *Organization, 12*(1), 89–108.

Banerjee, N. (1999). Can markets alter gender relations? *Gender, Technology and Development, 3*(1), 103–122.

Banerjee, S. M. (2004). *Men, women, and domestics: Articulating middle-class identity in colonial Bengal.* New York: Oxford University Press.

Barrientos, S. W. (2013). "Labour chains": Analysing the role of labour contractors in global production networks. *Journal of Development Studies, 49*(8), 1058–1071.

Barnes, T. (2013). The IT industry and economic development in India: a critical study. *Journal of South Asian Development* 8(1): 61–84.

Barnes, T. (2015). The IT industry, employment and informality in India: Challenging the conventional narrative. The Economic and Labour Relations Review. 2015, Vol. 26(1) 82–99.

Baviskar, A., & Ray, R. (2011). *Elite and everyman: The cultural politics of the Indian middle classes.* New Delhi: Routledge.

Beale, D. (2017). India at the Crossroads? Economic Restructuring, Deregulation and the Instability of Labour Relations. Pp. 241-263. In P. D'Cruz & E. Noronha (Eds.), *Critical Perspectives on Work and Employment in Globalizing India.* (pp. 241–263) Singapore: Springer.

Belser, P., & Rani, U. (2011). *Extending the coverage of minimum wages in India: Simulations from household data.* Conditions of Work and Employment Series 26. Geneva: International Labour Organziation. Retrieved from http://www.wiego.org/sites/default/files/publications/files/Amara_Minimum_Wages.pdf.

Benjamin, O., Bernstein, D., & Motzafi-Haller, P. (2011). Emotional politics in cleaning work: The case of Israel. *Human Relations, 64*(3), 337–357.

Berndtsson, J. (2012). Security professionals for hire: Exploring the many faces of private security expertise. *Millennium—Journal of International Studies, 40*(2), 303–320.

Berrong, S. (2009). India's growing security industry. *Security Management, 53*(6). Retrieved from https://sm.asisonline.org/Pages/Indias-Growing-Security-Industry.aspx.

Bezuidenhout, A., & Fakier, K. (2006). Maria's burden: Contract cleaning and the crisis of social reproduction in post-apartheid South Africa. *Antipode, 38*(3), 462–485.

Bhandare, N. (2017a). Why Indian workplaces are losing women: Our nationwide investigation begins. *Indiaspend*, August 5. Retrieved from http://www.indiaspend.com/cover-story/why-indian-workplaces-are-losing-women-our-nationwide-investigation-begins-53927.

Bhandare, N. (2017b). Domestic chores keep women in India tied to homes but some are changing that trend. *Hindustani Times*, August 23. Retrieved from http://www.hindustantimes.com/india-news/domestic-chores-keep-women-in-india-tied-to-homes-but-some-are-changing-that-trend/story-MaFMf2GJRoN6kUxbX7emYL.html.

Bhatt, A., Murty, M., & Ramamurthy, P. (2010). Hegemonic developments: The new Indian middle class, gendered subalterns, and diasporic returnees in the event of neoliberalism. *Signs, 36*(1), 127–152.

Bhatt, E. R. (2006). *We are poor but so many: The story of self-employed women in India.* New York: Oxford University Press.

Bhowmik, S. (2004). Work in a globalizing economy: Reflections on outsourcing in India. *Labour, Capital & Society, 37*(1), 76–96.

Bhowmik, S. K., & Saha, D. (2012). *Street vending in ten cities in India: A report for the National Association of Street Vendors of India, Delhi.* Mumbai: School of Management and Labour Studies, Tata Institute of Social Sciences. Retrieved from http://www.streetnet.org.za/docs/research/2012/en/NASVIReport-Survey.pdf.

Biswas, P. S. (2017). In Pune, cab aggregators leading vehicle growth. *Indian Express*, March 21. Retrieved from http://indianexpress.com/article/cities/pune/in-pune-cab-aggregators-leading-vehicle-growth-4578382/.

Bourdieu, P. (1984). *Distinction: A social critique of the judgement of taste.* Cambridge, MA: Harvard University Press.

Breman, J. (2010). *Outcast labour in Asia: Circulation and informalization of the workforce at the bottom of the economy.* New Delhi: Oxford University Press.

Breman, J. (2013a). A bogus concept. *New Left Review, 84*(130), 138.

Breman, J. (2013b). *At work in the informal economy of India: A perspective from the bottom up.* New Delhi: Oxford University Press.

Brignall, M. (2015). Fraud threat to millions of Talk customers. *Guardian*, February 27. Retrieved from https://www.theguardian.com/money/2015/feb/27/threat-to-millions-of-talktalk-customers.

Briken, K. (2012). Suffering in public? Doing security in times of crisis. *Social Justice*, *38*(1/2), 128–145.

Brody, A. (2006). The cleaners you aren't meant to see: Order, hygiene and everyday politics in a Bangkok shopping mall. *Antipode*, *38*(3), 534–556.

Bujra, J. (2000). *Serving class: Masculinity and the feminisation of domestic service in Tanzania*. Edinburgh: Edinburgh University Press for the International African Institute.

Campbell, I., & Peeters, M. (2008). Low pay, compressed schedules and high work intensity: A study of contract cleaners in Australia. *Australian Journal of Labour Economics*, *11*(1), 27–46.

Carrillo Rowe, A., Malhotra, S. and Perez, K. (2013), *Answer the call: Virtual migration in Indian call centers*. Minneapolis: University of Minnesota Press.

Chakrabarty, D. (2002). *Habitations of modernity: Essays in the wake of subaltern studies*. Chicago: University of Chicago Press.

Chakraborty, (2016). India's service sector grew 10% a year in 2015–16: CIT report. *Business Standard*, April 21. Retrieved from http://www.business-standard.com/article/economy-policy/india-s-services-sector-grew-10-a-year-in-2015-16-cii-report-116042001082_1.html.

Chandrashekhar, C. P. (2014). India's informal economy. *Hindu*, September 3. Retrieved from http://www.thehindu.com/opinion/columns/Chandrasekhar/indias-informal-economy/article6375902.ece.

Chatterjee, R. (2014). Margins within margins: A case study of street cleaners in Mumbai. In Britwum, A., & Ledwith, S. (Eds.), *Visibility and voice for union women: Country case studies from global labour university researchers* (pp. 33–53). Munich and Mering: Hampp.

Chen, M., & Raveendran, G. (2012). Urban employment in India: Recent trends and patterns. *Margin: The Journal of Applied Economic Research*, *6*(2), 159–179.

Chowdhry, P. (2013). Militarized masculinities: Shaped and reshaped in colonial south-east Punjab. *Modern Asian Studies*, *47*(3), 713–750.

Cockburn, C., & Ormrod, S. (1993). *Gender and technology in the making*. London: SAGE.

Craig, D., & Porter, D (2006). *Development beyond neoliberalism? Governance, poverty reduction and political economy*. London and New York: Routledge.

Cross, J. (2009). From dreams to discontent. *Contributions to Indian Sociology*, *43*(3), 351–379.

Cross, J. (2010). Neoliberalism as unexceptional: Economic zones and the everyday precariousness of working life in south India. *Critique of Anthropology*, *30*(4), 355–373.

Cross, J. (2014). Dream zones: Anticipating capitalism and development in India. London: Pluto Press.

Das, S. (2010). *Managing people at work: Employment relations in globalizing India*. Thousand Oaks, CA: SAGE.

Dastane, S. (2010). RTO makes uniforms compulsory for cab drivers *Times of India*, September 6. Retrieved from http://timesofindia.indiatimes.com/city/pune/RTO-makes-uniform-compulsory-for-cab-drivers/articleshow/6502690.cms.

Desai, M., & Rinaldo, R. (2016). Reorienting gender and globalization: Introduction to the special issue. *Qualitative Sociology, 39*, 337–351.

Deshpande, P. (2007). *Creative pasts: Historical memory and identity in western India, 1700–1960*. New York: Columbia University Press.

Doane, D. (2014). Social enterprise: Can it succeed where traditional development has failed? *Guardian*, February 25. Retrieved from https://www.theguardian.com/global-development/poverty-matters/2014/feb/25/social-enterprise-succeed-traditional-development-failed.

Dossani, R., & Kenney, M. (2004). The next wave of globalization? Exploring the relocation of service provision to India. Retrieved from https://www.researchgate.net/publication/228397461_The_Next_Wave_of_Globalization_Exploring_the_Relocation_of_Service_Provision_to_India.

Drèze, J., & Sen, A. (2013). *An uncertain glory: India and its contradictions*. Princeton, NJ: Princeton University Press.

Dube, A., & Kaplan, E. (2010). Does outsourcing reduce wages in the low-wage service occupations? *Industrial & Labor Relations Review, 63*(2), 287–306.

Dutta, M. (2016). Place of life stories in labour geography: Why does it matter? *Geoforum, 77*, 1–4.

Eichengreen, B., & Gupta, P. (2011). The service sector as India's road to economic growth. *India Policy Forum*, 1–42. Retrieved from http://testnew.ncaer.org/image/userfiles/file/IPF-Volumes/Volume%207/1_Barry%20Eichengreen%20and%20Poonam%20Gupta.pdf.

Eisenstein, Z (1998). *Global obscenities: Patriarchy, capitalism and the lure of cyberfantasy*. New York: New York University Press.

Entwistle, J., & Wissinger, E. (2006). Keeping up appearances: Aesthetic labour in the fashion modelling industries of London and New York. *Sociological Review, 54*(4), 774–794.

Express News Service. (2012). Security guard inspector arrested for taking bribe. *Indian Express*, February 8. Retrieved from http://indianexpress.com/article/cities/mumbai/security-guard-board-inspector-arrested-for-taking-bribe/.

Faussett, R. (2016). Feeling let-down and left behind with little hope for better. *New York Times*, May 25. Retrieved from http://www.nytimes.com/2016/05/26/us/feeling-let-down-and-left-behind-with-little-hope-for-better.html.

Federation of Indian Chambers of Commerce and Industry (FICCI). (n.d.). Private security industry in India. Retrieved from http://www.ficci.com/sector/91/Project_docs/PSi-profile.pdf.

Feldman, G. (2011). If ethnography is more than participant-observation, then relations are more than connections: The case for nonlocal ethnography in a world of apparatuses. *Anthropological Theory, 11*(4): 375–395.

Fernandes, L. (2006). *India's new middle class: Democratic politics in an era of economic reform*. Minneapolis: University of Minnesota Press.

Fernandes, L., & Heller, P. (2006). Hegemonic aspirations. *Critical Asian Studies*, *38*(4), 495–522.

Fernandez, L. (2004). The politics of forgetting: Class politics, state power and the restructuring of urban space in India. *Urban Studies*, *41*(12), 2415–2430.

Ferus Comelo, A. (2014). Migration and precariousness: Two sides of the contract labour coin. *Economic & Political Weekly*, *49*(36). Retrieved from http://www.epw.in/author/anibel-ferus-comelo.

Flemming, P. (2017). The human capital hoax: Work, debt and insecurity in the era of Uberization. *Organization Studies*, *38*(5), 691–709.

Freeman, C. (2001) Is local:global as feminine:masculine? Rethinking the gender of globalization. *Signs*, *26*(4), 1007–1037.

Freeman, C. (2013). Review essay: Outsourcing service and affective labor. *Anthropology of Work Review*, 35(2), 94–99.

Freeman, C. (2014). *Entrepreneurial selves: Neoliberal respectability and the making of a Caribbean middle class*. Durham, NC: Duke University Press.

Gándara, P. C. (1995). *Over the ivy wall: The educational mobility of low-income Chicanos*. Albany: State University of New York Press.

Gandhi, A. (2011). Informal moral economies and urban governance in India. In McFarlane, C., & Waibel, M. (Eds.), *Urban informalities: Reflections on the formal and informal* (pp. 51–57). Burlington, VT: Ashgate.

Ganguly-Scrase, R. (2003). Paradoxes of globalization, liberalization, and gender equality: The worldviews of the lower middle class in West Bengal India. *Gender & Society*, *17*(4), 544–566.

Ganti, T. (2014). Neoliberalism. *Annual Review of Anthropology*, *43*, 89–104.

Ghosh, J. (2015). Growth, industrialization and inequality in India. *Journal of the Asia Pacific Economy*, *20*(1), 42–56.

Gonguly-Scarse, R (2003). Paradoxes of Globalization, Liberalization, and Gender Equality: The Worldviews of the Lower Middle Class in West Bengal, India. Gender and Society Vol. 17, No. 4 (Aug., 2003), pp. 544–566.

Goold, B., Loader, I., & Thumala, A. (2010). Consuming security? *Theoretical Criminology*, *14*(1), 3–30.

Gooptu, N. (2009). Neoliberal subjectivity, enterprise culture and new workplaces: Organised retail and shopping malls in India. *Economic and Political Weekly*, *44*(22), 45–54.

Gooptu, N. (Ed.). (2013a). *Enterprise culture in neoliberal India: Studies in youth, class, work and media*. New York: Routledge.

Gooptu, N. (2013b). Servile sentinels of the city: Private security guards, organized informality, and labour in interactive services in globalized India. *International Review of Social History*, *58*(1), 9–38.

Gopal, M. (2013). Ruptures and reproduction in caste/gender/labour. *Economic & Political Weekly*, *48*(18), 91–97.

Graham, S., & Kaker, S. A. (2014). Living the security city: Karachi's archipelago of enclaves. *Harvard Design Magazine*, 37, 12–17.

Gupta, A. (2012). *Red tape: Bureaucracy, structural violence, and poverty in India*. Durham, NC: Duke University Press.

Gupta, A., & Sivaramakrishnan, K. (Eds.) (2011). *The state in India after liberalization: Interdisciplinary perspectives*. London and New York: Routledge.

Gupta, K., & Mankekar, P. (2017). Disjunctive temporalities, discrepant futures: Affective labor and informatics in a global industry. Lecture given October 18 at University of Rochester, New York.

Guynn, J. (2014). High-tech's service workers are a growing underclass. *USA Today*, August 15. https://www.usatoday.com/story/tech/2014/08/13/tech-service-workers-amazon-apple-facebook-google/13461027/

Hall, A., Hockey, J., & Robinson, V. (2007). Occupational cultures and the embodiment of masculinity: Hairdressing, estate agency and firefighting. *Gender, Work and Organization*, 14(6), 534–551.

Hegde, R. (2011). Spaces of exception: Violence, technology, and the transgressive gendered body in India's global call centers. In Hegde, R. S. (Ed.), *Circuits of visibility* (pp. 178–195). New York: New York University Press.

Heiman, R., Freeman, C., & Liechty, M. (Eds.). (2012). *The global middle classes: Theorizing through ethnography*. Santa Fe, NM: SAR Press.

Herod, A., & Aguiar, L.L.M. (2006). Introduction: Cleaners and the dirty work of neoliberalism. *Antipode*, 38(3), 425–434.

Higate, P. (2012a). "Cowboys and professionals": The politics of identity work in the private and military security company. *Millennium—Journal of International Studies*, 40(2), 321–341.

Higate, P. (2012b). The private militarized and security contractor as geocorporeal actor. *International Political Sociology*, 6(4), 355–372.

Ians [Indo Asian News Service] (2013). Once land owners, they now work as security guards. *Factiva*, May 14 https://www.business-standard.com/article/current-affairs/once-landowners-they-now-work-as-security-guards-113051400605_1.html

Ians [Indo Asian News Service] (2012). Skilled youth needed for private sector agencies. Dec 15th. http://www.sify.com/finance/skilled-youth-needed-for-private-security-agencies-news-national-mmptujaabfisi.html

Iedema, R., & Rhodes, C. (2010). The undecided space of ethics in organizational surveillance. *Organization Studies*, 31(2), 199–217.

Indian Ministry of Labor and Employment. (2012). *Report on the Working of the Minimum Wages Act 1948 For the Year 2010*.

International Labour Organization. (2012). Statistical update on employment in the informal economy. June. Retrieved from http://laborsta.ilo.org/applv8/data/INFORMAL_ECONOMY/2012-06-Statistical%20update%20-%20v2.pdf.

International Labour Organization. (2013). *Women and men in the informal economy: A statistical picture*. Geneva: International Labour Organization.

Inglis, P. (2013). It will become: Modern India and the labor of aspiration. Ph.D. dissertation, City University of New York.

Irwin, N. (2017). To understand rising inequality, consider the janitors at two top companies, then and now. *New York Times*, September 3. Retrieved from https://www.nytimes.com/2017/09/03/upshot/to-understand-rising-inequality-consider-the-janitors-at-two-top-companies-then-and-now.html.

Jhabvala, R. (1998). Minimum wages based on workers' needs. *Economic and Political Weekly*, *33*(10), 500–502.

Jhabvala, R., & Standing, G. (2010). Targeting to the "poor": Clogged pipes and bureaucratic blinkers. *Economic and Political Weekly*, *45*(26), 239–246.

Joachim, J., & Schneiker, A. (2012a). Masculinizing security? Gender and private military and security companies. In Ahall, L., & Shepherd, L. J. (Eds.), *Gender, agency and political violence* (pp. 39–55). London: Palgrave.

Joachim, J., & Schneiker, A. (2012b). Of "true professionals" and "ethical hero warriors": A gender-discourse analysis of private military and security companies. *Security Dialogue*, *43*(6), 495–512.

Kabeer, N. (1999). Resources, Agency, Achievements: Reflections on the Measurement of Women's Empowerment. *Development and Change* 30: 435–464.

Kantor, P. (2009). Women's exclusion and unfavorable inclusion in informal employment in Lucknow, India: Barriers to voice and livelihood security. *World Development*, *37*(1), 194–207.

Kasali, M. A. (2011). Analyzing the evolution of private security guards and their limitations to security management in Nigeria. *African Journal of Criminology & Justice Studies*, *5*(1), 32–48.

Korde, K. (2017). Permits for Ola, Uber taxis in Maharashtra now available online. *Hindustan Times*, March 21. Retrieved from http://www.hindustantimes.com/mumbai-news/permits-for-ola-uber-taxis-in-maharashtra-now-available-online/story-Gs8tTD7iWpV6ioQVBnTkKJ.html.

Krahmann, E. (2008). Security: Collective good or commodity? *European Journal of International Relations*, *14*(3), 379–404.

Kukreja, R. (2017). Dispossession of matrimonial choice in contemporary India: Examining the link between cross-region marriages, neoliberal capitalism, and new forms of gender subordination. Ph.D. dissertation, Queens University, Kingston, Ontario.

Kumar, M. (2017). India scraps foreign investment board in push for more FDI. Reuters, May 24. Retrieved from https://www.reuters.com/article/us-india-investments-fipb/india-scraps-foreign-investment-board-in-push-for-more-fdi-idUSKBN18K28G.

Kumar, R., & Beerepoot, N. (2017) Altering the social fabric of the working poor? Work and employment issues of support workers catering to international ICT-ITES firms in Mumbai. Pp. 133-152 In P. D'Cruz & E. Noronha (Eds.), *Critical Perspectives on Work and Employment in Globalizing India*. Singapore: Springer.

Kumar, R. (2016) *Globalisation of Services Production: Economic and Social Upgrading in Support-Service Industry Catering to International*

ICT-ITES firms in Mumbai, Amsterdam: University of Amsterdam (ISBN: 978-90-78862-28-4)

Kumar, R. (2010). Social security of contractual workers. In Verma, N.M.P., Awasthi, I. C., & Babasaheb Bhimrao Ambedkar University (Eds.), *Contractual employment in Indian labour market: Emergence and expansion* (pp. 145–157). New Delhi: Concept.

Lakha, S. (1999). The state, globalisation and Indian middle-class identity. In M. Pinches (Ed.), *Culture and privilege in capitalist Asia* (pp. 251–274). London & New York: Routledge.

Leonard, L. (2016). Pharmaceutically-made men: Masculinities in Chad's emergent oil economy. *Qualitative Sociology, 39*(4), 421–437.

Lerche, J., Guérin, I., & Srivastava, R. (2012). Special issue on labour standards in India. *Global Labour Journal, 3*(1).

Levien, M. (2018). *Dispossession without development: Land grabs in neoliberal India*. New York: Oxford University Press.

Loader, I. (1999). Consumer culture and the commodification of policing and security. *Sociology, 33*(2), 373–392.

Löfstrand, H. C. (2015). Private security policing by "ethnic matching" in Swedish suburbs: Avoiding and managing accusations of ethnic discrimination. *Policing and Society, 25*(2), 150–169.

Lowrie, C. (2008). In service of empire: British colonialism and male domestic servants in Darwin and Singapore, 1890s–1920s. Journal of the Oriental Society of Australia 39-40: 2 (2008): 334–356.

Mann, C. (2007). Globalization of services: Friend or foe? In Paus, E. (Ed.), *Global capitalism unbound: Winners and losers from offshore outsourcing.* (pp. 63–76). New York: Palgrave Macmillan.

Massey, D. (1996). Masculinity, dualisms and high technology. In N. Duncan (Ed.), *BodySpace: Destabilizing geographies of gender and sexuality* (pp. 109–126). New York: Routledge.

Maynes, M. J, Pierce, J. L., & Laslett, B. (2008). *Telling stories: The use of personal narratives in the social sciences and history.* Ithaca, NY: Cornell University Press.

Mazumdar, A. (2017). Why the problems of Uber, Ola drivers are far from over. *Wire*, May 3. Retrieved from https://thewire.in/113979/ola-uber-driver-problem-far/.

McCallum, J. K. (2013). *Global unions, local power: The new spirit of transnational labor organizing.* London: ILR Press.

McDougall, D. (2007). Waste not, want not in the £700m slum. *Guardian*, March 4. Retrieved from https://www.theguardian.com/environment/2007/mar/04/india.recycling.

McDowell, L. (1997). *Capital culture: Gender at work in the city.* Malden, MA: Blackwell.

Mirchandani, K. (2012). *Phone clones: Authenticity work in the transnational service economy.* Ithaca, NY: ILR Press/Cornell University Press.

Mirchandani, K., Mukherjee, S., Tambe, S. (2018). Researching the ambiguous global elite: methodological reflections on the invisible realities and contradictory politics of neoliberal globalization. In K. Gallagher ed.

The Methodological Dilemma Revisited: Creative, Critical and Collaborative Approaches to Qualitative Research for a New Era (pp. 153–171). New York: Routledge.

Mishra, N. (2016). Making diversity work: Key trends and practices in the Indian IT-BPM industry. Delhi: PWC. https://community.nasscom.in/servlet/ JiveServlet/downloadBody/1145-102-1-1145/PwC-NASSCOM-Making%20 Diversity%20Work-IT-BPM%20industry%20-%20Mar%2014,%202016%20 %28Print%20Ready%20v1%29%20%281%29.pdf

Modi, N. (2014). PM launches Swachh Bharat Abhiyaan. October 2. Retrieved from https://www.narendramodi.in/pm-launches-swachh-bharat-abhiyaan-6697.

Mohanty, C. T. (2003). *Feminism without borders: Decolonizing theory, practicing solidarity*. New Delhi: Zubaan.

Mukherjee, S. (2008a). Producing the IT miracle: The neoliberalizing state and changing gender and class regimes in India. Ph.D. diss., Syracuse University, Syracuse, NY. Retrieved from http://surface.syr.edu/geo_etd/3.

Mukherjee, S. (2008b). Producing the knowledge professional: Gendered geographies of alienation in India's high-tech workplace. In Vasavi, A. R., & Upadhya, C. (Eds.), *In an outpost of the global economy: Work and workers in India's information technology industry* (pp. 50–75). New York: Routledge.

Mukherjee, S. (2014). Globalizing Bangalore: Urban transformation in the high-tech city. In Wadley, S. S. (Ed.), *South Asia in the world: An introduction* (pp. 91–275). Foundations in Global Studies: The Regional Landscape. New York: M. E. Sharpe.

Mullings, B. (2005). Women rule? Globalization and the feminization of managerial and professional workspaces in the Caribbean. *Gender, Place & Culture, 12*(1), 1–27.

Nadeem, S. (2011). *Dead ringers: How outsourcing is changing the way Indians understand themselves*. Princeton, NJ: Princeton University Press.

Nagar, R., Lawson, V., McDowell, L., & Hanson, S. (2002). Locating globalization: Feminist (re)readings of the subjects and spaces of globalization. *Economic Geography, 78*(3), 257–284.

Nagaraj, V. (2012). Mapping the political economy of India's private security industry. *Economic & Political Weekly, 47*(43), 10–14.

Nalla, M. K. (1998). Opportunities in an emerging market. *Security Journal, 10*(1), 15–21.

Narayanamoorthy, A. (2013). Diagnosing Maharashtra's water crisis. *Economic and Political Weekly, 48*(41): 23–25

Nash, J. C., & Fernández-Kelly, M. P. (Eds.). (1983). *Women, men, and the international division of labor*. Albany: State University of New York Press.

National Association of Software and Services Companies (NASSCOM). (2014). *Indian IT—BPM revenue*. Retrieved from http://www.nasscom.in/ indian-itbpo-industry.

National Sample Survey Office. (2014). *Informal sector and conditions of employment in India*. NSS 68th Round. Delhi: Government of India.

Nayar, P. K. (2015). *Citizenship and identity in the age of surveillance*. Cambridge: Cambridge University Press.

Nayyar, G. (2012a). The quality of employment in India's services sector: Exploring the heterogeneity. *Applied Economics*, 44(36), 4701–4719.

Nayyar, G. (2012b). *The service sector in India's development*. New York: Cambridge University Press.

Nigam, A. (1997). Rethinking the unorganised sector. *Social Action*, 47(1), 125–134.

Noronha, E. and D'Cruz, P. Eds. (2017). *Critical Perspectives on Work and Employment in Globalizing India*. Singapore: Springer.

Noronha, E. and D'Cruz, P (2009). Employee Identity in Indian Call Centres: The Notion of Professionalism, New Delhi: Response Books.

Omvedt, G. (1994). *Dalits and the democratic revolution: Dr. Ambedkar and the Dalit movement in colonial India*. New Delhi: Sage Publications.

Ong, A. (2006). *Neoliberalism as exception: Mutations in citizenship and sovereignty*. Durham, NC: Duke University Press.

Otis, E. M. (2012). *Markets and bodies: Women, service work, and the making of inequality in China*. Stanford, CA: Stanford University Press.

Patel, R. (2010). *Working the night shift: Women in India's call center industry*. Stanford, CA: Stanford University Press.

Patel, S. (2016). De-colonial lens on cities and urbanisms: Reflections on the system of petty production in India. Singapore: Asian Research Institute (ARI) Working Paper No. 245 (January). http://www.ari.nus.edu.sg/wps/wps16_245.pdf

Pearson, R. (1998). 'Nimble fingers' revisited. Reflections on women and Third World industrialisation in the late twentieth century. In Jackson, C. and Pearson, R. (Eds.) *Feminist Visions of Development: Gender Analysis and Policy* (pp. 171–188). London: Routledge.

Peck, J., & Tickell, A (2002). Neoliberalizing space. *Antipode*, 34, 380–404.

Poster, W. R. (2007). Who's on the line? Indian call center agents pose as Americans for U.S.- outsourced firms. *Industrial Relations: A Journal of Economy and Society*, 46(2), 271–304.

Pow, C. (2013). Consuming private security: Consumer citizenship and defensive urbanism in Singapore. *Theoretical Criminology*, 17(2), 179–196.

Prenzler, T., Earle, K., & Sarre, R. (2009). Private security in Australia: Trends and key characteristics. *Trends and Issues in Crime and Criminal Justice*, 374: 1–6. https://aic.gov.au/publications/tandi/tandi374

DNA Correspondent. (2012). Pune IT BPO staffers now have safety cover. DNA India. March 18th 2012. Retrieved from https://www.dnaindia.com/mumbai/report-pune-it-bpo-staffers-now-have-safety-cover-1663925

Purandara, P. (2013). Water governance and droughts in Marathwada. *Economic and Political Weekly*, 48(25): 18–21.

Pyle, J., & Ward, K. (2003). Recasting our understanding of gender and work during global restructuring. *International Sociology*, 18(3), 461–489.

PTI 2018 instead in the text. PTI (2018). 17 security guard agencies to train over 3 lakh guards under the government scheme. The Times of India. Aug 5 2018 http://timesofindia.indiatimes.com/articleshow/65281663.cms?utm_source=contentofinterest&utm_medium=text&utm_campaign=cppst https://timesofindia.indiatimes.com/business/india-business/

17-security-guard-agencies-to-train-over-3-lakh-guards-under-the-govt-scheme/articleshow/65281663.cms

Qayum, S., & Ray, R. (2010). Male servants and the failure of patriarchy in Kolkata (Calcutta). *Men and Masculinities*, *13*(1), 111–125.

Radhakrishnan, S. (2011). *Appropriately Indian: Gender and culture in a new transnational class*. Durham, NC, & London: Duke University Press.

Radhakrishnan, S. (2014). Gendered opportunity and constraint in India's IT industry: The problem of too much "headweight." *In Handbook on Gender and South Asia*. Leela Fernandes, ed. Routledge. 234–246. London: Routledge.

Radhakrishnan, S. (2015). "Low profile" or entrepreneurial? Gender, class, and cultural adaptation in the global microfinance industry. *World Development*, *74*, 264–274.

Radhakrishnan, S., & Solari, C. (2015). Empowered women, failed patriarchs: Neoliberalism and global gender anxieties. *Sociology Compass*, *9*, 784–802.

Raju, S., & Bagchi, D. (Eds.). (1993). *Women and work in south Asia: Regional patterns and perspectives*. New York: Routledge.

Raju, S., & Bose, D. (2016). Women workers in urban India and the cities. In Raju, S., & Jatrana, S. (Eds.), *Women workers in urban India* (pp. 1–36). New Delhi: Cambridge University Press.

Raka, R. (2015). "The Precarious Middle Class: Gender and Mobility in the New Economy" Lecture at University of Toronto, Canada.

Ramamurthy. P. (2010). Why are men doing floral sex work? Gender, cultural reproduction, and the feminization of agriculture. *Signs: Journal of Women in Culture and Society*, *35*(2), 397–424.

Ramamurthy, P. (2011). Rearticulating caste: The global cottonseed commodity chain and the paradox of smallholder capitalism in South India. *Environment and Planning*, *A*(43), 1035–1056.

Ramesh, R. (2006). A tale of two Indias. *Guardian*, April 4. Retrieved https://www.theguardian.com/world/2006/apr/05/india.randeepramesh2.

Rao, A. (2009). *The caste question: Dalits and the politics of modern India*. Berkeley: University of California Press.

Ray, R. (2000). Masculinity, femininity, and servitude: Domestic workers in Calcutta in the late twentieth century. *Feminist Studies*, *26*(3), 691–718.

Ray, R., & Qayum, S. (2009). *Cultures of servitude: Modernity, domesticity, and class in India*. Stanford, CA: Stanford University Press.

Rogaski, R. (2004). *Hygienic modernity: Meanings of health and disease in treaty-port China*. Berkeley: University of California Press.

Routh, S. (2017). Locating worker power in a changing scenario. In Noronha, E., & D'Cruz, P. (Eds.), In P. D'Cruz & E. Noronha (Eds.), *Critical Perspectives on Work and Employment in Globalizing India* (pp. 221–240). Singapore: Springer.

Roy, A. (2003). *City requiem, Calcutta: Gender and the politics of poverty*. Minneapolis: University of Minnesota Press.

Roy, A. (2005). Urban informality: toward an epistemology of planning. *Journal of the American planning association*, *71*(2), 147–158.

Roy, A. (2011). Slumdog cities: Rethinking subaltern urbanism. *International Journal of Urban and Regional Research*, 35(2), 223–238.

Russell, B. (2009). *Smiling down the line: Info-service work in the global economy.* Toronto: University of Toronto Press.

Saini, D. S. (2010). The Contract Labour Act 1970: Issues and concerns. *Indian Journal of Industrial Relations*, 46, 1:32–44.

Salve, P. (2015). India's SEZ failures a cautionary tale for land acquisition bill. *Business Standard*, May 20. Retrieved from http://www.business-standard. com/article/specials/india-s-sez-failures-a-cautionary-tale-for-land-acquisition-move-115052000399_1.html.

Salzinger, L. (2003). *Genders in production: Making workers in Mexico's global factories.* Berkeley: University of California Press.

Salzinger, L. (2016). Re-making men: Masculinity on a terrain of the neoliberal economy. *Critical Historical Studies*, 3(2), 1–25.

Sampath, G. (2016). Do we need a minimum wage law? *Hindu*, September 1. Retrieved from http://www.thehindu.com/opinion/op-ed/Do-we-need-a-minimum-wage-law/article14616002.ece.

Sarkar, S., & Mehta, B. S. (2010). Income inequality in India: Pre- and post-reform periods. *Economic and Political Weekly*, 45(37), 45–55.

Sarti, R., & Scrinzi, F. (2010). Introduction to the special issue: Men in a woman's job: Male domestic workers, international migration and the globalization of care. *Men and Masculinities*, 13(1), 4–15.

Sassen, S. (2002). *Cities in a world economy* (2nd ed.). Thousand Oaks, CA: Pine Forge Press.

Shepard, W. (2017). How India is surviving post-demonetization. *Forbes*, July 29. Retrieved from https://www.forbes.com/sites/wadeshepard/2017/07/29/how-india-is-surviving-post-demonetization/2/#16f5ef7e46b2.

Shankar, K., & Sahni, R. (2017). The inheritance of precarious labor: Three generations in waste picking in an Indian city. *Women's Studies Quarterly*, 45(3–4), 245–262.

Shlaes, E., & Mani, A. (2013). A case study of the auto-rickshaw section in Mumbai. EMBARQ India. Retrieved from http://wricitieshub.org/sites/default/files/Mumbai%20auto-rickshaw%20sector_Case%20study_EMBARQ%20India.pdf.

Shyam Sundar, K. R. (2010). *Labour reforms and decent work in India: A study of labour inspection in India.* New Delhi: Bookwell.

Simpson, R., Slutskaya, N., Lewis, P., & Höpfl, H. (Eds.). (2012). *Dirty work: Concepts and identities.* New York: Palgrave Macmillan.

Singh, L. S. (2010). Earning pattern of contractual employment in Indian labour market. In Verma, N.M.P., Awasthi, I. C., & Babasaheb Bhimrao Ambedkar University (Eds.), *Contractual employment in Indian labour market: Emergence and expansion* (pp. 97–111). New Delhi: Concept.

Skeggs, B. (2010). Class. In Wetherell, M., & Mohanty, C. (Eds). *The SAGE handbook of identities.* London: Sage.

Smith, D. E. (2005). *Institutional ethnography: A sociology for people*. Lanham, MD, & Toronto: AltaMira Press.

Søgaard, K., Blangsted, A. K., Herod, A., & Finsen, L. (2006). Work design and the labouring body: Examining the impacts of work organization on Danish cleaners' health. *Antipode, 38*(3), 579–602.

Soni-Sinha, U., & Yates, C.A.B. (2013). "Dirty work"? Gender, race and the union in industrial cleaning. *Gender, Work & Organization, 20*(6), 737–751.

Sridhar, G. N. (2014). National confederation of ITes employees' union launched. *Hindu Businessline*, November 30. Retrieved from http://www.thehindubusinessline.com/info-tech/national-confederation-of-ites-employees-unions-launched/article6648709.ece.

Srija, A. (2014). Implementation of the Minimum Wages Act, 1948: Case study of India. *Global Journal of Human-Social Science: F Political Science, 14* (7). Retrieved from http://niti.gov.in/writereaddata/files/document_publication/Publication%20in%20Global%20Journal.pdf.

Srivastava, M. (2013). G4S plans to target IT infrastructure and hospital sectors. *Factiva*, May 20. https://www.livemint.com/Companies/dhG2p6FScwD7GoZAzX36KN/G4S-plans-to-target-IT-infrastructure-and-hospitality-secto.html

Standing, G. (1989). Global feminization through flexible labor. *World Development, 17*(7), 1077–1095.

Standing, G. (1999). Global feminization through flexible labor: A theme revisited. *World Development, 27*(3), 583–602.

Stiglitz, J. (2002). *Globalization and its discontents*. New York: Norton Paperback.

Subaiya, L., & Vanneman, R. (2016). The multidimensionality of development and gender empowerment: Women's decision-making and mobility in India. India Human Development Survey. Retrieved from https://ihds.umd.edu/sites/ihds.umd.edu/files/Subaiya%20and%20Vanneman%20Sept%202016.pdf.

Sudarshan, R. (2009). *Gender statistics and development policy: Women's work in India*. Organisation for Economic Co-operation and Development. Retrieved from http://www.oecd.org/dataoecd/22/10/41746107.pps.

Surie, A., & Koduganti, J. (2016). The emerging nature of work in platform economy companies in Bengaluru, India: The case of Uber and Ola cab drivers. *E-journal of International & Comparative Labour Studies, 5*(3). http://ejcls.adapt.it/index.php/ejcls_adapt/article/view/224

Tambe, A., & Tambe, S. (2013). Sexual incitement, spectatorship and economic liberalization in contemporary India: Interventions. *International Journal of Postcolonial Studies, 15*(4), 494–510.

Tara, S., & Ilavarasan, V. P. (2012). Cabs, male drivers and midnight commuting: Manufacturing respectability of the unmarried women agents of call centers in India. *AI & Society, 27*(1):157–163.

Thorat, S., & Newman, K. S. (Eds.). (2010). *Blocked by caste: Economic discrimination in modern India*. New Delhi: Oxford University Press.

Thumala, A., Goold, B., & Loader, I. (2011). A tainted trade? Moral ambivalence and legitimation work in the private security industry. *British Journal of Sociology*, *62*(2), 283–303.

Tomic, P., Trumper, R., & Dattwyler, R. H. (2006). Manufacturing modernity: Cleaning, dirt, and neoliberalism in Chile. *Antipode*, *38*(3), 508–529.

Transit Cooperative Research Program. (2010). *Vehicle operator recruitment, retention, and performance in ADA complementary paratransit operations.* No. 142. Washington, DC: Transit Cooperative Research Program.

Trevaskes, S. (2007). The private/public security nexus in China. *Social Justice*, *34*(3/4), 38–55.

Upadhya, C. (2016). *Reengineering India: Work, capital, and class in an offshore economy.* New Delhi: Oxford University Press.

Upadhyay, S. (2011). Labour, employment and social security challenges faced by security personnel engaged by private agencies. *Indian Journal of Labour Economics*, *54*(2), 345–357.

Verma, R., & Karinje, P. (2014). A critical analysis of growth and performance of inter-sectoral service sector in India. *International Journal of Commerce, Business and Management*, *3*(1). Retrieved from http://www.iracst.org/ijcbm/papers/vol3no12014/9vol3no1.pdf.

Vijayakumar, G. (2013). "I'll be like water": Gender, class, and flexible aspirations at the edge of India's knowledge economy. *Gender & Society*, *27*(6), 777–798.

Wajcman, J. (1991). *Feminism confronts technology.* University Park, PA: Penn State University Press.

Walsh, C. (2006). New data theft scandal rocks subcontinent's call centres. *Guardian*, September 3. *https://www.theguardian.com/money/2006/sep/03/business.india*

Weil, D. (2014). *The fissured workplace: Why work became so bad for so many and what can be done to improve it.* Cambridge, MA: Harvard University Press.

Witz, A., Warhurst, C., & Nickson, D. (2003). The labour of aesthetics and the aesthetics of organization. *Organization*, *10*(1), 33–54.

Wright, M. W. (2006). *Disposable women and other myths of global capitalism.* New York and London: Routledge.

Yusuff, O. S. (2011). A theoretical analysis of the concept of informal economy and informality in developing economies. *European Journal of Social Science*, *20*(4): 624–636.

Zlolniski, C. (2006). *Janitors, street vendors, and activists: The lives of Mexican immigrants in Silicon Valley.* Berkeley: University of California Press.

INDEX

....

Note: Page references followed by an *f* indicate figure.